WAR OF WORDS

WAR OF WORDS

ABRAHAM LINCOLN AND THE CIVIL WAR PRESS

Harry J. Maihafer

BRASSEY'S, INC.
Washington, D.C.

Library of Congress Cataloging-in-Publication Data

Maihafer, Harry J. (Harry James), 1924–
    War of words : Abraham Lincoln and the Civil War press / Harry J.
Maihafer.—1st ed.
        p. cm.
    Includes bibliographical references (p.) and index.
    ISBN 1-57488-305-4
        1. Lincoln, Abraham, 1809–1865—Relations with journalists. 2. United
States—History—Civil War, 1861–1865—Journalists. 3. United States—
History—Civil War, 1861–1865—Press coverage. 4. United States—Politics
and government—1861–1865. 5. Press and politics—United States—
History—19th century. I. Title.

E457.2.M28 2001
973.7'092—dc21

2001037856

ISBN 1-57488-305-4   (alk. paper)

Printed in the United States of America on acid-free paper that meets the
American National Standards Institute Z39-48 Standard.

Brassey's, Inc.
22841 Quicksilver Drive
Dulles, Virginia 20166

First Edition

10 9 8 7 6 5 4 3 2 1

CONTENTS

PREFACE:
LINCOLN AND THE MEDIA

—◦—

This book stems from a lifelong fascination with Abraham Lincoln and the Civil War. Added to that is a more recent interest in Civil War journalism—if going back more than thirty years can be considered "recent." During the 1960s, someone at the Great Stone Paper Mill, aka the Pentagon, sent me to the University of Missouri to pursue a graduate degree in journalism. The Vietnam War was at its height, and military/media relationships were "adversarial," to say the least. Reporters acted toward Army press officers, if not with hostility, at least with profound skepticism. My assignment to Missouri probably resulted from someone believing an infantry officer with combat experience could relate to the press better than someone whose background was solely in public relations. Whether it worked out that way is hard to say; I suspect my later impact on press attitudes was marginal at best. On a personal level, however, J-School made me want to write. And as a happy by-product, my master's thesis, "Ulysses Grant and the Northern Press," introduced me to Civil War journalism.

In writing this book, I feel indebted to many people: my West Point classmate, Curt Anders, who suggested the topic; gifted historians such as

Carl Sandburg, Allan Nevins, and Bruce Catton, men I'd read but never met; helpful scholars I *did* meet along the way, such as John Simon and Bell Wiley; and faculty members at the University of Missouri School of Journalism, with a special nod to Professors John Merrill and Bill Taft. Let me also voice my appreciation to the librarians of Vanderbilt University and the Nashville Public Library, especially Kathy Roselli, Meg Sherill, and Claudia Schauman, three very gracious ladies. Lastly, a special vote of thanks is owed Don McKeon, my longtime editor at Brassey's, who has been a continuing source of help and encouragement.

INTRODUCTION

⊷⟹⟸⊶

During his remarkable life, Abraham Lincoln was a man of honesty, wisdom, wit, and compassion. He was also ambitious, working hard at whatever task presented itself. Among other things, he'd been a stockdriver, flatboatman, ferryhand, surveyor, storekeeper, and attorney. In addition, for most of his adult life he was a consummate politician, one who recognized the power of the media.

Today we have radio, television, and the Internet, overloading us with news and information from every direction. In Lincoln's day, however, "media" simply meant the press—newspapers offering a minimum of "news," but a maximum of "politics." It was a time when an editor either sought political office himself or played a major role in deciding who did. The superintendent of the 1860 census, in fact, would classify 80 percent of the country's 2,500 periodicals, including all 373 daily newspapers, as "political in their character." Moreover, newspapers were everywhere. At the start of the Civil War, a town as small as Vicksburg, Mississippi, population 4,500, had six independent journals.[1]

Lincoln, as a rising politician, knew he had to woo editors and use the press—"manipulate" is not too strong a word—to his own advantage. As an orator, he might speak to several hundred people at a time, or (as when he debated Stephen Douglas in 1858) an audience that numbered in the thousands. Yet to reach a *truly* mass audience, he needed the press to report his remarks, and to do so correctly. To make sure, early in his career he might even head for a newspaper composing room to edit personally the manuscript of a speech he'd just delivered.

Later, when he became president, Lincoln had to contend with partisan editors who were openly hostile in their attacks on the administration. As would happen later during the Vietnam War, an adversary culture prevailed in which reporters and editors felt no need to show deference, toward either politicians or the military. The ongoing struggle between the opposition press and the federal government was one of the Civil War's great challenges. Lincoln needed to honor freedom of the press, as guaranteed by the Constitution, yet sustain public support for the war in the face of constant, often vicious, criticism. It made for a difficult balancing act on Lincoln's part. Nevertheless, he carried it off, playing fair with all editors, including the hostile ones, by what he told them directly, by the way he treated their reporters, and by the speeches he made for public consumption. In short, part of his political genius lay in swaying public opinion in a way that would appeal to his friends and not overly antagonize his enemies. Although at times this required deviousness, or what today we call "spin," the basic integrity of "Honest Abe" remained intact.

Especially worth studying are Lincoln's dealings with the New York press, which dominated public opinion in areas loyal to the Union. In Washington, for example, New York City's *Tribune*, *Times*, and *Herald* offered home delivery service, causing *Harper's Weekly* to observe that people in the nation's capital "actually look to the New York papers for news of their own city." The *Philadelphia Inquirer* had a similar reaction, grumbling that those same three papers carried "New York over every railway, sets it down at every station, and extends it everywhere." Throughout the North, editors would grab New York papers off an early-morning train, run to the office, then slice up those papers so printers could run items with headings such as "From the *Tribune*" or "From the *Herald*." That *Tribune* and *Herald* meant New York was taken for granted.[2]

Lincoln was a surprisingly complex individual with a variety of skills. Historians continue to analyze his work in detail, to marvel, and to applaud. Despite that, his ability to use the media has heretofore received insufficient attention. Examining that aspect of Lincoln's career is not only enjoyable, it also provides yet another way to appreciate a great man's talent.

CHAPTER 1

"COOK COUNTY IS FOR ABRAHAM LINCOLN"

On the balmy day of June 15, 1858, enthusiastic Republicans gathered in Springfield, Illinois, for their state convention. After wandering about the square, admiring the handsome little capitol and the new governor's mansion, more than a thousand delegates crowded into the hall of the House of Representatives at the appointed hour. Governor Richard Yates called the meeting to order, and as people settled in their seats, men marched in with a banner proclaiming, "Cook County is for Abraham Lincoln."

That banner created a media event, one of many that would affect Lincoln's career. And, fittingly, it was journalists who had arranged it. Two months earlier, on April 21, four Illinois editors had met and decided that Lincoln was their candidate for the U.S. Senate.[1] Also seeking the nomination, as it turned out, was one of their fellow editors: "Long John" Wentworth, mayor of Chicago and editor of the *Chicago Democrat*. Nevertheless, Wentworth's four rival editors went all out for Lincoln, arranging the demonstration and pushing a resolution that declared Lincoln the meeting's first and only choice for the U.S. Senate. Ordinarily the convention would have nominated men only for state offices. However, Lincoln's supporters were taking no chances; they took the unprecedented step of attaching to the platform a declaration that Abraham Lincoln was the party's nominee.[2] The meeting was then adjourned, but it was announced that delegates would reassemble at eight that evening to hear their candidate's acceptance speech.

Lincoln had designed his remarks more for the nation at large than for those at the convention. He was therefore determined to use the press to maximum advantage. Sitting in his Springfield parlor that afternoon, gathering his thoughts and preparing for the most important speech of his life, he may have recalled what in effect was his original "press release." As a youth running for state office for the first time, he had begun by putting a notice in the local *Sangamo Journal*, closing with a statement:

> Every man is said to have his peculiar ambition. Whether it is true or not, I can say for one that I have no other so great as that of being truly esteemed by my fellow men, by rendering myself worthy of their esteem. How far I shall succeed in gratifying this ambition, is yet to be developed. I am young and unknown to many of you. I was born and have ever remained in the most humble walks of life. I have no wealthy or popular relations to recommend me. My case is thrown exclusively upon the independent voters of this county, and if elected they will have conferred a favor upon me, for which I shall be unremitting in my labors to compensate. But if the good people in their wisdom shall see fit to keep me in the background, I have been too familiar with disappointments to be very much chagrined. Your friend and fellow citizen. A. Lincoln, New Salem, March 9, 1832.[3]

That same self-deprecating tone would become something of a hallmark. Even in the courtroom, attorney Lincoln had a disarming, humble, countrified manner, speaking in simple phrases, never putting on airs, and using homely stories, rather than legal verbiage, to make his points. This often caused people to underrate him. For example, in November 1840, when he gave a speech as a candidate for presidential elector, the *Illinois State Register* said: "Mr. Lincoln's argument was truly ingenious. He has, however, an assumed clownishness in his manner that does not become him, and which does not truly belong to him. . . . We seriously advise Mr. Lincoln to correct this clownish fault before it grows upon him."[4]

That "clownish manner," however, was not only calculated, it would also win over many a jury. Fellow Springfield lawyer Leonard Swett, describing Lincoln's courtroom skill, would say, "Any man who took Lincoln for a simple-minded man would very soon wake up with his back in a ditch."[5]

Lincoln had known for weeks that he would probably receive the nomination. Knowing the importance of this occasion, he had labored long and hard at preparing his remarks, filling scraps of paper and backs of envelopes with stray thoughts, then tossing them into a favorite receptacle, his hat. When the manuscript was in its final stages, he had shown it to people, who said it sounded too radical. Conversely, his law partner, William Herndon, reportedly told him, "Lincoln, deliver that speech as read and it will make you President."[6]

That evening, Lincoln mounted the platform to applause and cheers. He bowed to the chairman, then began, "Mr. President and Gentlemen of the Convention." Before him was a shirt-sleeved audience, hot and perspiring, squirming in their seats. He needed to grab their attention quickly, and he did so with a superb opening paragraph:

> If we could first know where we are, and whither we are tending, we could better judge what to do and how to do it. We are now far into the fifth year, since policy was initiated with the avowed object, and confident promise, of putting an end to slavery agitation. Under the operation of that policy, that agitation has not only not ceased, but has constantly augmented. In my opinion, it will not cease, until a crisis shall have been reached, and passed. "A house divided against itself cannot stand." I believe this government cannot endure, permanently half slave and half free. I do not expect the Union to be dissolved—I do not expect the house to fall—but I do expect it will cease to be divided. It will become all one thing or all the other.

Lincoln went on to assert that slavery must be viewed as a temporary and transitional system, on its way to eventual extinction. The speech ended to thunderous applause. Now Lincoln needed to ensure it was printed correctly. Stepping from the platform, he gave his manuscript to Horace White of the *Chicago Press and Tribune*, asking White not only to bring it to the office of the *Illinois State Journal*, but also to stay there and read proof. That evening in Springfield, delegates continued to mill around, discussing, celebrating, partying. Lincoln stayed with them for a time, then he excused himself and headed for the *Journal* composing room. Joining White, he explained that he wanted to go over the text himself. He had taken great pains with it, he said, and he had to make sure no errors crept in.[7]

Lincoln's efforts paid off. In addition to the *Illinois State Journal*, the *Chicago Press and Tribune* carried the full text of the speech, as did dozens of other western papers. A pamphlet edition was soon issued in Illinois. In the East, where it became known as the "House Divided" speech, Horace Greeley's *New York Tribune* also printed it in full, carrying it to millions of readers. The *Tribune* editorial called it compact, forcible, and admirable, adding, "Mr. Lincoln never fails to make a good speech, when he makes any, and this is one of his best efforts."[8]

⋅→══◉◉══→⋅

Editorial support had not come by chance. For years, Lincoln as a rising politician had worked hard at building press relationships. In Springfield, when he wasn't working at his law practice, he followed national events closely, reading at least a half-dozen newspapers, and making the editorial office of the *Sangamo Journal* his loafing place, telling stories and talking politics. Much of the time, of course, he was away "riding the circuit," serving as an attorney in various courts throughout Illinois. At such times, he made it a point to become friendly with local editors, either through letters or personal contact.[9]

In February 1856, Lincoln was invited to speak at an editors' banquet in Decatur. He began with a tongue-in-cheek apology for his presence among so many distinguished editors, saying it made him feel like an interloper. And as often happened, it reminded him of a story. This time it was about a man "no lady would ever call handsome." The editors, already smiling, assumed Lincoln was referring to himself. Anyway, this man, while riding through the woods, met a lady on horseback. He turned out of the path and waited for the lady to pass. The lady stopped, looked at the man, and said, "Well, for land sakes, you are the homeliest man I ever saw."

"Yes, madam," the man replied, "but I can't help it."

"No, I suppose not," the lady said, "but you might stay at home!"

When the editors stopped laughing, Lincoln said that on this occasion—a banquet for editors—he might with propriety have stayed at home.[10]

In this case, despite his witty comment, the well-known Lincoln was far from an "interloper." After his talk, the smiling editors probably agreed among themselves that this tall young lawyer made an attractive candidate. Voters, they knew, would respond to his humor, common sense, and integrity. They would also find a certain romantic attraction in his poignant life story: a grandfather slain by Indians while clearing the forest; his father building a log cabin in the Kentucky woods; his mother dying when he was nine; his family then moving to another rude cabin in Indiana, living in squalor until a loving stepmother arrived to comb and clean him, feed him, and care for him.

In appearance, of course, he wasn't much to look at. He was uncommonly tall, with a spare, muscular frame that measured some six feet four inches. He had rugged features, deep-set, gray-brown eyes, and a mobile countenance, solemn one moment, all laughter the next. As a circuit lawyer, with little reference to law books or precedents, he had built his reputation on hard work and fair-minded appeals to judges and juries. Moreover—and this was important for a political candidate—he had the knack of presenting issues so clearly that they seemed like common sense to the plainest farmer or the dullest factory worker.

⋯⋙◎⋘⋯

For the coming Senate race, Lincoln's Democratic opponent would be Senator Stephen A. Douglas, the man they called the "Little Giant." Douglas was a savvy political veteran with an established national reputation. It was expected he would use the 1858 senatorial campaign as a stepping stone for a presidential run two years later. Although he was the obvious favorite, Douglas was not underestimating his opponent. In Washington he told a group of Republicans, "You have nominated a very able and a very honest man." On July 24 Lincoln challenged Douglas to a series of statewide debates. It was a shrewd move on Lincoln's part. Joint appearances meant increased publicity, benefiting Lincoln, the lesser-known candidate, far more than Douglas. Somewhat reluctantly, Douglas agreed, but for only seven such meetings.[11]

Thousands of citizens turned out for the debates, larger audiences than any in past American history, both in size and enthusiasm. More important, thanks to the newly invented system of shorthand writing, the candidates' remarks were reported to the nation almost verbatim. Lincoln and his supporters were well aware of this. In Freeport, Illinois, for example, Lincoln was about to begin when a friend stopped him. "You can't speak yet," the friend said. "Hitt ain't here." They waited until Robert R. Hitt, the *Chicago Tribune*'s shorthand reporter, was in his seat and ready.[12]

It was a good precaution. After the first debate, at Ottawa, Illinois, the integrity of the shorthand reports came into question. In the *Chicago Tribune*, Lincoln's remarks were printed as they were written and, presumably, delivered. In the hostile *Chicago Times*, however, they appeared as a horrible, ungrammatical mess, studded with sentences that ran together so as to make no sense. Republicans claimed the *Times*, which had called Lincoln's speech "weak, faltering, childish twaddle," had garbled his words deliberately to embarrass him, perhaps with Douglas's knowledge. On balance, what the public perceived as a "dirty trick" may have actually worked in Lincoln's favor.

One of the debate highlights came at Freeport, when Lincoln asked how Douglas could reconcile popular sovereignty with the Supreme Court's Dred Scott decision, which implied that slavery could not be prohibited in lands belonging to the whole nation. Douglas replied that despite that decision, the people of a territory had the right to admit or exclude slavery, for it "could not exist a day or an hour unless supported by local police regulation." That statement, known as Douglas's "Freeport Doctrine," while applauded in the North, would damage Douglas severely in the South.

As public interest mounted, the remarks became heated, colorful, entertaining, but never personal. The *Missouri Republican,* reporting on the Charleston debate, said, "The joint discussion between the Tall Sucker and the Little Giant came off according to programme." On one occasion,

Lincoln called a Douglas argument as thin as "soup made by boiling the shadow of a pigeon that had starved to death." Douglas, in turn, claimed that the Republicans were inconsistent, sounding more Abolitionist, or "jet black" in the northern part of the state, a "decent mulatto" in the center, and "almost white" in the south. In response, Lincoln said: "I am not, nor ever have been, in favor of bringing about in any way the social and political equality of the white and black races. . . . I am not, nor ever have been, in favor of making voters or jurors of negroes, nor of qualifying them to hold office, nor to intermarry with white people, and I will say in addition to this that there is a physical difference between the white and black races which I believe will forever forbid the two races living together on terms of social and political equality."[13]

Lincoln's expedient statement, repugnant by today's standards, was not inconsistent with his long-held benevolent feeling toward blacks, nor his belief that the institution of slavery should eventually be extinguished. The wisest course, in his opinion, was to let slavery wither away where it already existed, to restrict its expansion, and to convince Americans that it was on its way out. His great difference with Senator Douglas, he said, was that he, unlike Douglas, recognized that slavery was morally wrong. He emphasized this in a speech given at Alton, Illinois:

> The real issue of this controversy, I think, springs from a sentiment in the mind, and that sentiment is this: On the one part it looks upon the institution of slavery as being wrong, and on the part of another class it does not look upon it as wrong. The sentiment that contemplates the institution of slavery as being wrong, is the sentiment of the Republican Party. It is the sentiment around which all their actions and all their arguments circle, from which all their propositions radiate. . . . That is the real cause!—an issue that will continue in this country when these poor tongues of Douglas and mine shall be silent. These are the two principles that make the eternal struggle between right and wrong; they are the two principles that have stood face to face, one of them asserting the divine right of kings; the same principle that says you work, you toil, you earn bread, and I will eat it. It is the same old sentiment, whether it comes from the mouth of a king who seeks to bestride the people

of his nation and to live upon the fat of his neighbor, or whether it comes from one race of men as an apology for the enslaving of another race of men.[14]

An odd feature of the election was the devious position of Horace Greeley, powerful editor of the *New York Tribune*. Earlier, he had even suggested that Republicans let Douglas run unopposed. Greeley, a staunch abolitionist, believed Republicans, and Republican principles, would triumph if the Democrats tore themselves apart over the issue of slavery. To help this along, he decided the *Tribune* would support Stephen Douglas. The "Little Giant" had favored popular sovereignty in Kansas, and proslavery Southerners hated him for it. Cheerfully, Greeley wrote Congressman Schuyler Colfax: "Douglas has broken the back of the Democratic Party. It will hold him responsible for the loss of Kansas, and will never forgive him—never!" Personally, Greeley considered Douglas to be a "low and dangerous demagogue." He reasoned, however, that *Tribune* support for Douglas would be a kiss of death, deepening the impression among Southerners, as he wrote Colfax, that Douglas was "a disguised abolitionist and virtual ally of the Black Republicans. . . . Don't you see they all believe already that he and I are in *cahoots* as they say—secretly leagued to humble and ruin 'the South'?" His supporting Douglas, he believed, would ruin the "Little Giant" in the South, and at the same time keep him a leading figure among Democrats in the North.[15]

That might be well and good for the big picture, but Lincoln for one didn't appreciate it. In late December 1857, he wrote his friend Lyman Trumbull: "What does the *New York Tribune* mean by its constant eulogizing, and admiring, and magnifying Douglas? . . . Have they concluded that the republican cause, generally, can be best promoted by sacrificing us here in Illinois?"

Once Lincoln was nominated, and the *Tribune* continued to praise Douglas while giving Lincoln only lukewarm support, Lincoln told a reporter, "Greeley is not doing me right!" The pro-Lincoln *Chicago Tribune*, for its part, said the Republican convention's endorsing Lincoln was "a remonstrance against outside intermeddling" by Horace Greeley and other easterners favoring Douglas.[16]

On November 2, 1858, Lincoln received a majority of 4,085 votes over Douglas. However, because of a gerrymander situation (Illinois had been divided to give Democrats an electoral majority in a large number of districts while Republican votes were concentrated in as few districts as possible), Douglas controlled a majority of the Illinois legislature. In January the legislature elected Douglas. Lincoln joked that he was like the little boy who stubbed his toe: "It hurts too bad to laugh, and he was too big to cry." That winter Horace Greeley was in Bloomington, Illinois, on a lecture tour. Lincoln also happened to be in town. Supposedly, when their paths crossed, Greeley invited Lincoln to call on him at his hotel. Lincoln did not accept the invitation, which, considering Greeley's political clout, may have been a mistake. If so, it was a media-relations error he wasn't likely to repeat.[17]

Although he'd lost an election, Lincoln remained active politically. In 1859 he made speaking trips to Illinois, Indiana, Ohio, Wisconsin, Iowa, and Kansas. Never once did he hint that he might want to run for president. If the subject came up, he'd usually shrug it off, saying he wasn't fit, or insist that the party had other men who were better qualified. Nevertheless, he continued to seek out and use the power of the printed word. In 1859 a book entitled *Political Debates between Hon. Abraham Lincoln and Hon. Stephen A. Douglas, in the celebrated Campaign of 1858, in Illinois* was published by Follett, Foster & Company of Columbus, Ohio. Several pages of the manuscript (now in the Library of Congress) came from Lincoln's own scrapbook, annotated and corrected in Lincoln's own hand. Although on several occasions a careful Lincoln reviewed newspaper copy, this is the only manuscript he is known to have prepared for book publication.

On March 1, 1859, speaking in Chicago, and perhaps still fuming over Greeley's support for Douglas, Lincoln showed the fallacy of Greeley's position. Lincoln declared he had not said "an unkind word of any one" who thought Illinois Republicans should have supported Douglas. He maintained, however, that such support would have resulted in the destruction of the Republican Party. If Republicans supported Douglas, they would have been perceived as adopting all of Douglas's beliefs, whereas: "The Republican principle, the profound central truth that slavery is wrong and ought to be dealt with as a wrong . . . cannot advance at all upon Judge Douglas's ground; that there is a part of the country in which slavery must always exist; that he does not care whether it is voted up or down." If people thought Republicans accepted that, the party would have lost "the great living principle" upon which they were organized.[18]

During the same period, Lincoln quietly got into the newspaper business himself. In May 1859, with banker Jacob Bunn making the arrangements, Lincoln bought for $400 the weekly German-language newspaper of Springfield, the *Illinois Staats-Anzeiger*. The deal was handled secretly. Under terms of the contract, Lincoln owned the type, press, and other equipment. Theodore Canisius, the editor, would continue to publish a Republican paper in German with occasional articles in English. As pointed out by Lincoln's biographer, Carl Sandburg, the 1860 census would show 700,000 German immigrants in the country, chiefly in the Northern states. In many states they held a political balance of power. Obviously, a candidate with direct access to the German reader had a great advantage, especially if that access was used to convey his views, as was done in this case for Lincoln. On one occasion, for example, Canisius wrote Lincoln, asking where he stood on a Massachusetts law that said no foreign-born naturalized citizen could hold office or vote until two years after his naturalization. Lincoln wrote Canisius he was against it. Canisius promptly published Lincoln's letter, which was widely copied by other papers.[19]

⊷⇒◐⇐⊷

One morning in October 1859, Lincoln came rushing into his law office clutching a letter. He told his partner, William Herndon, that it was an invitation to come east for a speech. It was to be in Brooklyn, at Henry Ward Beecher's Plymouth Church. The subject could be of his choosing, and he would be paid $200 plus expenses. Since people generally knew him only in the western states, he obviously considered this a major opportunity. In his letter accepting the invitation, Lincoln wrote the committee chairman, "I believe, after all, I shall make a political speech of it.[20]

From October to February, Lincoln labored over his speech. Much of his time he spent in the library, studying the words of the Founding

Fathers. On February 23, 1860, he took the train from Springfield. Arriving in New York two days later, he checked into the Astor House. The tall, awkward, generally unkempt westerner seemed out of place at such an elegant establishment. At the moment, however, whether he "belonged" as an Astor guest was the least of his concerns. What *did* concern Abraham Lincoln was the speech he was to give. He had worked hard on it, revising, polishing, revising again. As with his earlier speeches, an appeal to principle would dominate mere debating points. Finally he was satisfied. The planned speech *seemed* correct, but would it be enough to sway sophisticated New Yorkers?

Responsibility for the speech had now been transferred to the Young Men's Central Republican Union of New York and the event's location was changed to the handsome new Cooper Union building. Metropolitan papers, at least those favorable to the Republicans, had given the speech quite a buildup. Greeley's *Tribune*, for example, announced: "ABRAHAM LINCOLN of Illinois will, for the first time, speak in this Emporium, at Cooper Institute, on Monday evening. He will speak in exposition and defense of the Republican faith; and we urge earnest Republicans to induce their friends and neighbors of adverse views to accompany them to this lecture."[21]

Republicans in general tended to like Lincoln, amiably referring to him as "Honest Abe." To most easterners, however, he remained a minor figure, patronizingly described by the *New York Times* as "a lawyer of some local Illinois reputation." In other words, not one to be taken seriously as a presidential contender. To prove the point, just recently the *Philadelphia Press* had listed forty-five men whose names had been mentioned for the presidency; Lincoln's name was not among them. In order to gain credibility, then, Lincoln needed help from the media. And in the nineteenth century, "media" inevitably meant newspapers, particularly those originating in New York.

On Tuesday, February 27, the night of the speech, a snowstorm hit New York City, cutting down on attendance. Nevertheless, some 1,500 people, most of them paying a twenty-five-cent admission fee, managed to make their way through the icy streets and into the spacious hall. They represented the movers and shakers of New York politics, and as the

Tribune commented, "not since the days of Clay and Webster" had there been such an assemblage of New York "intellect and moral culture."

Lincoln was escorted to the platform by his friend and supporter, the eminent attorney, David Dudley Field. The meeting chairman, the distinguished William Cullen Bryant, poet-editor of the *New York Evening Post,* then introduced him to the crowd. Sitting on the platform, listening attentively, was still another editor, that major shaper of Republican opinion, Horace Greeley of the *Tribune.*

The speech contained two main themes. Initially, Lincoln argued persuasively that the Founding Fathers, who had abolished the African slave trade, and had often denounced slavery as an institution, believed that slavery would ultimately perish. Neither the word "slave" nor "slavery" is to be found in the Constitution, Lincoln said, nor even the word "property." The Founders called the slave a "person," one whose master's legal right was phrased as "service or labor which may be due." In other words, they intended "to exclude from the Constitution the idea that there could be property in man."

Lincoln next addressed himself to the Southern people. "We must not only let them alone," he said, "but we must somehow convince them that we *do* let them alone."

Republicans were not radical, he maintained, and "sectional" only because the South did not give them a fair hearing. Although Republicans believed slavery to be morally wrong, they would allow it to stand where it presently existed; they insisted only that it not be spread into the National Territories. Southerners, thinking slavery to be right, were not to blame for desiring its full recognition. But Republicans, thinking it wrong, could not, "while our votes will prevent it, allow it to spread into the National Territories, and to overrun us here in these Free States." He concluded with: "Let us have faith, that right makes might, and in that faith, let us, to the end, dare to do our duty as we understand it."

People rose to their feet, applauding and cheering. Hats went in the air and handkerchiefs waved. Men pushed toward the platform to shake the speaker's hand. The Cooper Union speech had been a triumph. Noah Brooks, a *Tribune* reporter, wrote that "no man ever before made such an impression on his first appeal to a New York audience." Once again, however, Lincoln was taking no chances. As soon as he could free himself, he headed to the offices of the *New York Tribune* to read proofs and ensure his words were reported correctly.[22]

Next morning Lincoln saw that four papers had printed his speech in full. He also learned there would be a pamphlet reprint of it. Papers would also report in full a major speech given a few days later by the leading Republican presidential candidate, William Seward. Both men had been conciliatory toward the South, but few of their words were getting through. By that time, Republican newspapers—the *New York* and *Chicago Tribunes*, the *Springfield Republican*, the *Cleveland Leader*—were being stopped in Southern post offices. Out West, meanwhile, Joseph Medill wrote an editorial for the *Chicago Press and Tribune*, claiming that Lincoln could be elected president that year and Seward could not.[23]

CHAPTER 2

"HONEST OLD ABE"

In Chicago, carpenters were busy erecting a building called "The Wigwam," proudly claimed to be the largest auditorium in the country. The Republican national convention was set to open there on May 16, 1860, and as the delegates gathered, their spirits were high, thanks in large part to their rival party having torn itself apart a month earlier. After a bitter, stormy session, Democrats meeting in Charleston had ended up by nominating Stephen Douglas. This had caused the Southern delegates, who hated Douglas, to bolt the party and leave it in shambles.

Republicans, by contrast, felt united and confident, thanks in large part to a Republican press that was reaching the height of its influence. Editors such as Horace Greeley of the *New York Tribune*, William Cullen Bryant of the *New York Evening Post*, Henry Raymond of the *New York Times*, Samuel Bowles of the *Springfield Republican*, and Joseph Medill of the *Chicago Tribune*, were journalistic heavyweights that Democrats simply could not match. Most powerful of these men was Horace Greeley; his *Tribune* boasted on April 18 that more than twenty-five new Democratic campaign sheets had been started expressly to counteract its influence.[1]

Adding to the Republicans' confidence was the fact that they had a number of credible presidential candidates, men such as Ohio Governor Salmon P. Chase, old-line Whig Edward Bates of Missouri, and Illinois's favorite son, Abraham Lincoln. Despite this array of talent, the odds-on favorite for the nomination was still Senator William H. Seward of New York, a man of experience, proven ability, and with long service to the Free Soil cause. He had what many considered an insurmountable lead, and his campaign manager, Thurlow Weed, publisher of the *Albany* (New York) *Evening Journal*, was telling delegates, "We think we have in Mr. Seward just the qualities the country will need. He is known by us all as a statesman. . . . We expect to nominate him on the first ballot." Weed was already canvassing people about possible vice presidential running mates for Seward, but when delegates picked up copies of the local *Chicago Tribune*, they saw a column headed "Abraham Lincoln, the Winning Man," giving eight reasons why Lincoln should be named.[2]

Right from the start, the contest was as much between journalists as between candidates. Seward's camp included not only publisher Thurlow Weed but also editors such as Henry Raymond of the *New York Times* and James Watson Webb of the *New York Courier and Enquirer*. The crafty Weed and his friends had been lining up Seward support for months, promising political favors right and left.

Seward, however, also had his editorial foes, most notably Horace Greeley, a man who loved politics as much as journalism. Indeed, Greeley's onetime managing editor, John Russell Young, later said that Greeley "would be the greatest journalist in America if he did not aim to be the greatest politician in America."[3] For years, ironically, Greeley had been Seward and Weed's closest political ally. Predictably, though, as one who conferred favors, he had expected something in return, most notably a political office for himself. When it hadn't worked out that way, and adequate favors were not forthcoming, Greeley had written an angry, bitter letter in November 1854 announcing "the dissolution of the political firm of Seward, Weed, and Greeley, by the withdrawal of the junior partner."[4]

Greeley came to the convention determined to stop Seward. Although he still had begrudging respect for his onetime friend, he considered him tainted by Weed. Earlier, for example, Weed had engineered the passage of a corrupt street railway bill, the sole purpose of which, according to Bryant's *Evening Post,* was "to furnish a fund of from four to six hundred thousand dollars, to be expended for the Republican cause in the next presidential election." People sensed they couldn't elect Seward without having Weed come along as part of the bargain.[5]

On the third day of the convention, after a platform was drawn amidst much give and take, it was time to vote for the party's nominee. Although Seward supporters were still confident, Horace Greeley was telling everyone who'd listen that the party could not win with Seward. They must find another candidate, perhaps his own choice, Edward Bates of Missouri. On the floor, Greeley spoke not as a delegate for New York—Weed, who controlled the New York delegation, had refused to include him—but for distant Oregon.

Lincoln's convention managers were *Chicago Tribune* editor Joseph Medill and Judge David Davis, a longtime friend. They too had been busy, going from one delegation to another, making friends and saying nothing to offend. With the West generally for Bates and the East for Seward, they hoped to make Lincoln everyone's alternative choice.

A majority, 234 votes, would be needed to nominate Seward. On the first ballot he had 173½, well ahead of Lincoln, who received 102. Further back, in third, was Pennsylvania's "favorite son," Simon Cameron. Salmon P. Chase of Ohio came next. Greeley's man, Bates, was a distant fifth. With that, the managers and delegates again went to work. A still-confident Weed was twisting arms, seeking votes to put Seward over the top on the next ballot. At the same time, Greeley and others were circulating, still insisting that Seward couldn't win. Neither, it appeared, could Greeley's first choice, Bates. A Kansas delegate asked Greeley what he thought of Lincoln as a candidate. "Lincoln is a very adroit politician," he replied, but Lincoln had no experience in national affairs, and his nomination would be "too risky an undertaking." Still, as Greeley moved around the floor, he found more and more people favoring Lincoln.[6]

Giving up on Bates and switching to Lincoln, Greeley moved from one delegation to another, arguing, cajoling, pleading. Greeley, with his innocent pink cheeks and fringe of white whiskers, was perhaps the most famous man in the country. He was easy to recognize, and wherever he went, he gathered a crowd, people wanting to tell the folks back home that they'd been close to "Uncle Horace."[7] A western delegate later said, "He looked like a well-to-do farmer fresh from the clover fields. He won a place in our hearts at once."[8]

The second ballot showed Seward at 184½, still shy of the needed majority. Many state delegations, having fulfilled their "favorite son" obligation on the first ballot, were switching to Lincoln, who now had 181. He and Seward were nearly even and the momentum had shifted. Earlier, Lincoln had wired Judge Davis, "make no contracts that will bind me." But Lincoln was back in Springfield, and the practical Davis was saying, "Lincoln ain't here, and don't know what we have to meet." Davis probably believed, in fact, that Lincoln knew very well what needed to be done. By getting that "make no contracts" statement on the record, Lincoln was buying insurance in case he later had to renege on some particularly obnoxious agreement. A case in point was a promise, later honored, that Pennsylvania's Simon Cameron, despite an unsavory reputation, could be secretary of war in a Lincoln cabinet.[9]

The jockeying continued. As the third round of balloting got under way, Medill whispered to Cartter of Ohio, "If you can throw the Ohio delegation to Lincoln, Chase can have anything he wants." How did he know that? Medill said he was positive, saying, "I know, and you know I wouldn't promise if I didn't know."[10]

Before the third ballot was counted, Ohio announced it was switching four votes to Lincoln, putting him ahead of Seward. That burst the dam, and the floodgates opened. Other delegations promptly followed suit, bringing Lincoln's total to 354. After a motion by William M. Evarts of New York, the nomination was made unanimous. Abraham Lincoln was now officially the Republican candidate for president of the United States, and much of the credit belonged to the aggressive editor of the *New York Tribune*.

"Greeley has slaughtered Seward, but has saved the Republican Party," shouted the chairman of the Indiana delegation. The correspondent of *Harper's Weekly* wired home that Greeley's triumph had made the *New York Tribune* "the great organ and censor" of the Republican Party. The following day, Greeley's paper had a long editorial headed, "Honest Old

Abe." He was made of "sterling stuff," said the *Tribune*, and could be relied upon "for perfect integrity and constant fidelity to duty." Back in Springfield, Lincoln was typically modest, saying he "almost wished" that the great responsibility "had fallen upon some one of the far more eminent and experienced statesmen whose distinguished names were before the convention."[11]

Henry Raymond, a disgruntled Seward supporter, blasted Greeley in the *New York Times*, giving him "full credit" for Seward's defeat. Citing the 1854 letter "dissolving the political firm of Seward, Weed, and Greeley," Raymond said Greeley's actions had been based on personal enmity. Once Greeley broke with Seward, Raymond said, he "menaced him with his hostility wherever it could be made most effective, for the avowed reason that Gov. S. had never aided or advised his elevation to office." With his motives being questioned, "Uncle Horace" was quick to respond. His reputation needed defending, and moreover, a lively editorial fight was good for circulation! "And if ever in my life I discharged a public duty in utter disregard of personal considerations," wrote Greeley, "I did so at Chicago last month. . . . Need I add that each subsequent day's developments have tended to strengthen my confidence that what I did was not only well meant but well done."[12]

James Gordon Bennett's *New York Herald*, a Douglas supporter, also chimed in. With obvious reference to the fee Lincoln received for his Cooper Union speech, the *Herald* said the Republicans had passed over Seward, Chase, and other statesmen "to take up a fourth-rate lecturer who delivered his hackneyed compositions at $200 a copy." The mud was flying and the campaign was under way.[13]

Eventually Lincoln would honor the promises made to favorite sons Cameron of Pennsylvania and Chase of Ohio, both of whom would receive cabinet positions. However, not knowing, or not wanting to know, what other promises had been made, he needed to get something on the record along the lines of that "make no contracts" wire. Judge Davis had been receiving many letters asking how Lincoln, if elected, would handle office seekers and patronage. Perhaps he was even reminded of promises he'd made during the heat of the convention. In any case, he wrote Lincoln, asking what he should do. Lincoln told Davis how to respond, and even wrote his script for him. Here, he told Davis is "the body of such a letter as I think you should write . . . in your own handwriting." The letter, dutifully copied by Davis, referred to "full and frequent conversations" he'd had with Lincoln, who "says he neither is nor will be, in advance of the election, committed to any man, clique, or faction."[14]

With the campaign under way, Lincoln's supporters in the press went to work, trying to create for him a national image of heroic stature. Lincoln did his part. He gave a long interview to John Locke Scripps, after which, at Scripps's request, Lincoln wrote a 2,500-word autobiography. From this, Scripps prepared a closely printed thirty-two-page "Life of Abraham Lincoln," filled with charming (ever-complimentary) stories. The "Life" received wide distribution, being printed simultaneously, and in full, by both the New York Tribune and the Chicago Tribune. Scripps wrote of a youthful lad who knew about hard work from "splitting rails, pulling the cross-cut and the whip-saw . . . plowing, planting, hoeing, harvesting." He knew about sports. "In wrestling, jumping, running, throwing the maul and pitching the crow-bar, he always stood first among those of his own age."[15]

Lincoln made no personal appearances during the campaign, telling his friends that his positions were already well known. While such a move would seem inconceivable today, it wasn't that unusual in the mid-nineteenth century. Today's personal appearances are significant mainly because statements and images are extended through the magic of radio and television. In Lincoln's day, a mass audience could be reached only through the press. Although he remained close to home, candidate Lincoln was far from inactive. Once again, he courted prominent editors, especially those who had been less than friendly. He started by writing personal letters to Seward supporters Thurlow Weed and Henry Raymond. Then Lincoln's friend Medill made a trip to New York just to urge James Gordon Bennett, a Douglas man, to keep the Herald at least partially neutral.[16]

By remaining silent, Lincoln was following the advice of William Cullen Bryant, respected editor of the New York Evening Post. Referring to himself as "an old campaigner," Bryant wrote Lincoln that "the vast majority of your friends want you to make no speeches, write no letters as a candidate, enter into no pledges, make no promises, nor even give any of those kind words which men are apt to interpret into promises." Lincoln agreed, and if promises happened to be made on his behalf, by remaining silent, he could always disavow them later.[17]

⋆⇒◉⇐⋆

Thanks to the schism of the Democratic Party, there were now three separate candidates opposing Lincoln. In addition to Douglas, there was John C. Breckinridge of Kentucky, a former U.S. vice president, now the candidate of a pro-slavery party formed by southern Democrats. Also, the distinguished John Bell of Tennessee was nominated by the Constitutional Unionists, a party of former Whigs, mainly from the border states, who were trying to appease both the North and South and thereby hold the country together.

By the fall of 1860, Lincoln's election seemed increasingly certain. Throughout the South, men were muttering that this would surely cause a breakup of the Union, almost inevitably followed by war. Southern newspapers foresaw the end of everything held dear. The *Charleston Mercury*, for example, said, "It is the loss of liberty, home, country—everything that makes life worth having." A New York printer, coming to Charleston to work on the *Mercury*, saw firsthand the fanatical sentiment gripping the city. Upon arrival, he was jailed as an "Abolitionist emissary," then freed on his promise to leave the state within twenty-four hours. The alternative was a public flogging and thirty days in jail on bread and water.[18]

Meanwhile, Horace Greeley was trying to assure the South that a Lincoln victory would not mean the end of the world. True, the Republicans would keep slavery out of the Territories, but they had no plans to interfere with the "peculiar institution" where it already existed. If slavery were ever to be overthrown in the South, Greeley maintained, it would have to be by the Southerners themselves—the other states would have no share in the work. Unfortunately, Greeley's soothing words seldom got through. Many Southern postmasters, for example, were refusing even to distribute the *Tribune*.[19]

For his part, Lincoln was following Bryant's advice and keeping quiet, at least publicly. When he wrote his friend Leonard Swett concerning

Weed and others, he ended by saying, "Burn this, not that there is any thing wrong in it; but because it is best not to be known that I write at all." He had stated his positions many times; people didn't need to hear them again. And as he told one correspondent, "Those who will not read, or heed, what I have already publicly said, would not read, or heed, a repetition of it."[20]

By this time, frankly, he expected to be elected, and he didn't want to do anything that might rock the boat. On election night, November 6, Lincoln sat in the Springfield telegraph office as the returns came in. Some time after midnight, it became obvious that things were turning out much as expected. The president-elect told everyone goodnight, then said he better get home to tell his wife, Mary, that "we're elected."

When results were totaled, Lincoln had carried all the Free States except New Jersey, where a fusion ticket gave four electors to Lincoln and three to Douglas. There was no Lincoln ticket in Alabama, Arkansas, Florida, Georgia, Louisiana, Mississippi, North Carolina, Tennessee, and Texas. In South Carolina, electors (chosen by the legislature) were for Breckinridge. There were a relatively small number of votes for Lincoln in Delaware, Kentucky, Maryland, Missouri, and Virginia. Eventually, Lincoln ended up with 180 electoral votes to 123 for the other three candidates, even though his popular vote was nearly a million less than the combined vote of the other three.[21]

Horace Greeley, even as he rejoiced over the election's outcome, was still trying to calm Southern fears. "It is not to be supposed," wrote Greeley, "that the election of Abraham Lincoln as President of these United States—conspicuous and glorious triumph as it is—will at once restore the country to political harmony and quiet, though we are convinced that the agitation raised in the South will gradually and surely subside into peace."[22]

In the Southern states, however, the tone was far different. "The election of Abraham Lincoln has indeed put the country in peril," said the *Richmond Dispatch*. Simultaneously, the *Augusta* (Georgia) *Constitutionalist* screamed, "The South should arm at once." And as expected, the firebrand *Charleston Mercury* was for immediate secession: "In the spirit and temper of the times, a convention of the people of South Carolina, to be held within four weeks, to pronounce upon her remedies in the crisis which is at hand, means disunion—means the separation of South Carolina, whether alone or with others, from the Union which can only be a badge of infamy to her."[23]

Realistically, President-elect Lincoln couldn't do much about the Southern press. As for the rest of the country, he needed to maintain the support of friendly Republicans and do what he could to bring Northern Democrats into line. It wouldn't be easy, especially in the case of James Gordon Bennett and the critical *New York Herald*. In the case of the *Herald*, however, Lincoln had an ally in the person of Henry Villard.

The remarkable Villard had immigrated to the United States from Germany seven years earlier, at the age of eighteen. He'd first wanted to study law, but when funds ran out he'd turned to selling books, then to real estate and various other jobs. Eventually, he'd ended up as a reporter, covering the 1858 Lincoln-Douglas debates for the German-language *New York Staats Zeitung*. One evening during the debates, Villard and Lincoln met by chance at a railroad flag station west of Springfield. Waiting for the train to Springfield, the two were caught in a sudden thunderstorm and took refuge in an empty freight car. In his *Memoirs*, Villard said, "We squatted down on the floor of the car and fell to talking on all sorts of subjects." During the conversation, Lincoln said at one time he doubted his qualifications to be a senator, telling himself, "It's too big a thing for you; you will never get it." Then with a self-deprecating laugh, Lincoln continued: "Mary (Mrs. Lincoln) insists, however, that I am going to be senator and President of the United States, too. Just think of such a sucker as me as President!"[24]

That conversation marked the beginning of a productive relationship—for both parties. The gifted Villard, who had made himself fluent in English, had started writing for papers such as the *Cincinnati Commercial* and the *New York Tribune*. Then, seeing a special opportunity after the election, he presented himself to the *New York Herald* as one who had something of an inside track with Abraham Lincoln. He was hired by Bennett's managing editor, Frederick Hudson, and proceeded to Springfield, where he was welcomed by Lincoln as an old friend and introduced to Lincoln's new private secretary, John G. Nicolay, and to twenty-two-year-old John Hay, correspondent for the *Missouri Democrat*, who was to become an assistant secretary. Soon Villard was sending dispatches from Springfield, in effect introducing the country to this relatively unknown future president. Earlier, the Democratic *Herald* had told Lincoln in no uncertain terms that he should step out of the national picture and stay home. "His withdrawal at this time from the scene of conflict, and the surrender of his claims . . . would render him the peer of Washington in patriotism." Having told Lincoln what to do, the *Herald* then issued a warning: "If he persists in his present position, in the teeth of such results as his election must produce, he will totter into a dishonoured grave, driven there perhaps by the hands of an assassin, leaving behind him a memory more execrable than that of Arnold—more despised than that of the traitor Catiline." With the *Herald* expressing sentiments like this, Lincoln made an extra effort to court the paper's reporter, Villard. To its credit, the *Herald* proceeded to run Villard's stories untouched, allowing James Gordon Bennett to say piously, "We are only endeavoring to give accurate news about Lincoln, no matter how far we disagree with him politically, as part of our duty to the public as a journalist."[25]

With Villard and others on the scene, Lincoln knew his personal life would be closely scrutinized. Clearly, if Lincoln continued to own the *Illinois Staats-Anzeiger*, it might prove awkward. In December 1860, he quietly made a deal to transfer ownership of the paper back to its editor, Theodore Canisius. The obliging Canisius was later appointed the American consul in Vienna.[26]

On February 11, 1861, Lincoln, his wife, Mary, and their eldest son, Robert, left Springfield for Washington. Henry Villard, the only New York reporter climbing aboard their special train, had been granted permission to make the trip by W. S. Wood, railroad superintendent in charge of the train, after Lincoln interceded for him. A crowd had gathered to see Lincoln off, and, stepping onto the train's rear platform, Springfield's favorite son said farewell for the last time to the place he'd come to know and love:

> My friends, no one who has never been placed in a like position, can understand my feelings at this hour, nor the oppressive sadness I feel at this parting. For more than a quarter century I have lived among

you, and during all that time I have received nothing but kindness at your hands. Here I have lived from my youth until now I am an old man. Here the most sacred ties of earth were assumed; here all my children were born; and here one of them lies buried. To you, dear friends, I owe all that I have, all that I am. All the strange, chequered past seems to crowd upon my mind. Today I leave you; I go to assume a task more difficult than that which devolved upon General Washington. Unless the great God who assisted him shall be with me and aid me, I must fail. But if the same omniscient mind, and the same Almighty arm that directed and protected him shall guide and support me, I shall not fail, I shall succeed. Let us all pray that the God of our fathers may not forsake us now. To Him I commend you all— permit me to ask with equal security and faith, you all will invoke His wisdom and guidance for me. With these last words I must leave you—for how long I know not. Friends, one and all, I must now bid you an affectionate farewell.[27]

Henry Villard, caught up in the moment, listened attentively as Lincoln spoke. He was not taking notes, and suddenly he realized he was missing a significant story, one he should send to the *Herald*, and which, under an Associated Press agreement, would later be copied by papers throughout the country. Villard went to Lincoln and explained his problem. Lincoln, as always, wanted to be in a reporter's good graces, particularly a reporter representing the hostile James Gordon Bennett. He borrowed Villard's pen and pencil and wrote down what he had said. Villard began his story with the words written by Lincoln, then added a moving final passage: "Toward the conclusion of his remarks, he himself and audience were moved to tears. His exhortation to pray elicited choked exclamations of 'We will do it. We will do it.' As he turned to enter the car, three cheers were given and a few seconds afterward the train moved slowly out of sight of the silent gathering."[28]

The train slowly proceeded eastward, making frequent stops. At each stop, Lincoln spoke extemporaneously to the local crowd. Making speeches when he had nothing to say, Lincoln told his friend, Ward Lamon, was the hardest work he had ever done. Each talk was duly recorded by Villard for the *Herald*. And as the days went by, Villard's opinion of Lincoln continued to grow. At first he'd seen the man as rather crude, even coarse. He'd been shocked when rough-looking farmers addressed the future president as "Abe," and he'd written that he "felt disgust and humiliation that such a person should have been called upon to direct the destinies of a great nation." By this time, however, having seen more of Lincoln close-up, he was singing a different tune, writing that, "No one can see Mr. Lincoln without recognizing in him a man of immense power and force of character and natural talent. He seems so sincere, so conscientious, so earnest, so simple-hearted, that one cannot help liking him. . . . He seems tremendously rough, and tremendously honest." That was all well and good, but Villard's paper, the *Herald,* was still insisting that Lincoln was showing "no capacity to grapple manfully with the dangers of this crisis."[29]

The special train made numerous stops over the next eleven days, and at each stop, Lincoln continued to meet with local officials and speak at some length to curious citizens who turned out to see him in person. His political instincts were hard at work, and he used every opportunity to endear himself to the average man and woman. At Freedom, Pennsylvania, a coal-heaver in the crowd yelled, "Abe, they say you're the tallest man in the country, but I don't believe you're any taller than I am." Lincoln invited the man to come up on the platform. They stood back to back, and a member of Lincoln's party climbed up on a guard rail, ran his hand over the top of their heads, and announced that they were exactly the same. The crowd cheered. Later, at Westfield, New York, Lincoln asked for Grace Bedell, a little girl who had written a letter advising him to grow whiskers. When she was brought forward, Lincoln said, "You see, I let these whiskers grow just for you, Grace." Then, to the delight of the crowd, he kissed her. The story was repeated far and wide and a headline in the *New York Tribune* read, "Old Abe kissed by Pretty Girl."[30]

When the train reached New York, Villard went to the *Herald* office, said he had grown weary of the "traveling show," and asked to be released from the assignment. As a result, he would miss out on what was really the trip's only major story. There had been many rumors of an assassination attempt, with various hotheads asserting that Lincoln would never reach Washington alive. So far Lincoln had discredited them. When he was in Philadelphia, however, he received a note from Senator Seward telling of a plot to kill Lincoln when he reached Baltimore. Railroad

Detective Allan Pinkerton had received the same information, and, going to Baltimore disguised as a secessionist, he had met a man named Fernandina, who had vowed to plunge a knife into Lincoln's heart, even if it meant losing his own life in the process. Pinkerton suggested that Lincoln either bypass Baltimore altogether or slip through the city incognito under cover of night. Somewhat reluctantly, Lincoln accepted Pinkerton's advice, which was seconded by Ward Lamon and others. From Philadelphia, Lincoln went to Harrisburg, where he spoke to the Pennsylvania legislature. That evening in Harrisburg, he boarded a special train that had been arranged, and after arriving back in Philadelphia, he changed to the regular New York–Washington sleeper. With the cooperation of wire and railroad officials, telegraph wires had been cut to maintain secrecy. Lincoln, accompanied by Lamon and Pinkerton, arrived in Washington without incident around six the next morning.

Joseph Howard, a well-known reporter, had been covering Lincoln for the *New York Times*. Upon awakening in Harrisburg and finding Lincoln gone, he wrote a fantastic story that appeared in the *Times* and was later reprinted by other papers, including the *New York Tribune*. The story said that Lincoln did not want to go, but that Mrs. Lincoln and others had insisted on it. Describing Lincoln's arrival in Washington, he then made up a detail that was seized upon by Lincoln's enemies: "He wore a Scotch plaid cap and a very long military cloak, so that he was entirely unrecognizable." [31]

The *Baltimore Sun*, which one report called "the vilest secession sheet in the U.S.," took that detail, enlarged upon it, and made Lincoln appear ridiculous. "Had we any respect for Mr. Lincoln, official or personal, as a man, or as President elect of the United States," wrote the *Sun*, "the final escapade by which he reached the capital would have utterly demolished it. . . . We do not believe the Presidency can ever be more degraded by any of his successors than it has by him, even before his inauguration." [32]

All over the country, people were laughing and saying, "He wore a Scotch plaid cap and a very long military cloak." Since the story had appeared in the pro-Republican *New York Times*, it was accepted as gospel, even when the *New York Tribune* said, "It should be said that no disguise of any sort was adopted by Mr. Lincoln, all reports to that effect being entirely false." Despite the denials, the story, in modern-day parlance, had "legs." Jokes were made about Lincoln's night ride, silly poems were written, and a cartoonist for *Vanity Fair* drew Lincoln in a kilt. The *Louisville Courier*, not to be outdone, claimed the frightened future president had traded clothing with his wife at Harrisburg and rode through Baltimore in skirts, not a kilt.[33]

For the previous eleven days, Lincoln had made a maximum effort to cooperate with the press, meet the American people, and create a favorable impression on one and all. Despite all his efforts, the trip had ended with a public relations disaster. The threat on his life had been very real, and he had done well to avoid it. Nevertheless, as his friend Ward Lamon lamented: "Mr. Lincoln soon learned to regret the midnight ride to which he had yielded under protest. He was convinced that he had committed a grave mistake in listening to the solicitations of a professional spy and of friends too easily alarmed, and frequently upbraided me for having aided him to degrade himself at the very moment in all his life when he should have exhibited the utmost dignity and composure." Media-wise, it was not a good beginning.[34]

CHAPTER 3

"THE BETTER ANGELS OF OUR NATURE"

On March 4, 1861, standing on the Capitol's east portico, Abraham Lincoln raised his right hand, placed his left on a bible held by Chief Justice Roger Taney, and swore to "preserve, protect, and defend the Constitution of the United States." Following this, the man who was now America's sixteenth president stepped forward to deliver his inaugural address. He had worked on the speech for months, carefully crafting a message that extended an olive branch to the South but emphasized his determination to defend the Constitution.

The proposed speech had been shown to William Seward, the prospective secretary of state, who had made suggestions, a few of which were incorporated into the final version. But only a few. Lincoln didn't much like people tampering with his words. Henry King, a future editor of the *St. Louis Globe Democrat*, could attest to that. As a young reporter, King had been assigned to cover a speech of Lincoln's. Its sentiment and expressions had impressed him, but in reporting it, he used words and phrases he thought Lincoln "should" have used. Proud of his accomplishment, he showed the new version to Lincoln, who said, "Young man, you made a most excellent report of this, but I think you did not quite get my language here and there." Lincoln went over King's copy, changing the reporter's flowery phrases to simple ones. By the time Lincoln finished, King didn't recognize a thing he'd written.[1]

The inaugural speech, in other words, was undeniably Lincoln's own work. As such, it was eloquent, clear, and memorable. Speaking directly to the South, Lincoln concluded his remarks with an impassioned, noble paragraph: "I am loth to close. We are not enemies, but friends. We must not be enemies. Though passion may have strained, it must not break our bonds of affection. The mystic chords of memory, stretching from every battlefield, and patriot grave, to every living heart and hearthstone, all over this great land, will yet swell the chorus of the Union, when again touched, as surely they will be, by the better angels of our nature."[2]

Newspapers North and South raced to get the inaugural address in print, and as Lincoln slept that night, Pony Express riders with copies of the speech were galloping west from St. Joseph, Missouri. In seven days and seventeen hours it would be in Sacramento, California. In all American history, no speech had ever been distributed, analyzed, and scrutinized so intensively. How the message was interpreted, however, depended on the politics of the reader, or perhaps more important, the politics of a particular editor. Horace Greeley, who'd been sitting just behind Lincoln on the inaugural platform, wrote in his *New York Tribune*: "The address cannot fail to exercise a happy influence upon the country. The tone of almost tenderness with which the South is called upon to return to her allegiance, cannot fail to convince even those who differ from Mr. Lincoln that he earnestly and seriously desires to avoid all difficulty and disturbance, while the firmness with which he avows his determination to obey the simple letter of his duty, must command the respect of the whole country, while it carried conviction of his earnestness of purpose, and of his courage to enforce it."[3]

Other papers friendly to Lincoln, including the *Chicago Tribune*, *St. Louis Democrat*, *New York Evening Post*, and *Springfield Republican*, praised the speech, as did the *Boston Transcript*, which liked the fact that not one "fawning expression" could be found in it, and said, "The language is level to the popular mind, the plain, homespun language of a man accustomed to talk with the 'folks' and the 'neighbors,' whose words fit his facts and thoughts."[4]

Lincoln's private secretary, John Nicolay, distributed transcripts of the speech. Meanwhile, his other secretary, young John Hay, was acting as a "secret weapon," writing editorials with what a later day would call "spin." During the 1860 election campaign, soon after he came to work for Lincoln, Hay, using the pen name "Ecarte," had described Lincoln in a series of articles for the *Providence Journal.* Later, still signing himself "Ecarte," he'd submitted items to Springfield's *Illinois State Journal* and the *St. Louis Missouri Republican.* Throughout Lincoln's presidency, Hay would help convey Lincoln's point of view to the American people. And since he did this anonymously, his words had far more credibility than if they were seen as coming directly from the White House. Presumably Lincoln knew what Hay was doing, since the two worked closely on a daily basis throughout the war. In support of this thought, the St. Louis historian and journalist Walter B. Stevens maintained that some of Hay's dispatches were "sent direct from Lincoln's office" and were "inspired by Lincoln." Stevens even said it was a tradition among Missouri journalists that some of Hay's political correspondence was written by Lincoln himself.[5]

On the day of the inaugural address, Hay wrote an item that appeared in the *New York World.* It read in part: "President Lincoln does not regard the Union as dissolved, and he looks not to coerce, but 'to calm thought and reflection,' to bring the disaffected states to again recognize their constitutional obligations. Instead of acts of hostility against those states, calculated to arouse their passions, it will be the aim of his administration to give them a 'sense of perfect security.'"[6]

⬦⟺⬦

Despite Lincoln's placating words, hostile editors such as James Gordon Bennett refused to unbend. His *New York Herald* commented, "It would have been almost as instructive if President Lincoln had contented himself with telling his audience yesterday a funny story and letting them go." However, said the *Herald,* the speech was not a "crude performance," for "it abounds with traits of craft and cunning."[7]

In the South, somewhat predictably, the firmness was noted while the friendliness was ignored. The *Richmond Enquirer* said Lincoln's speech made it clear that peace was now out of the question—"Virginia must fight." Farther south, the *Charleston Mercury* denounced what it called Lincoln's "insolence" and "brutality," declaring, "It is our wisest policy to accept it as a declaration of war."[8]

At the moment, however, Lincoln's greatest concern was not the words of some editorial. South Carolina had seceded from the Union the preceding December 20, soon followed by Mississippi on January 9, Florida on January 10, Alabama on the 11th, Georgia on the 19th, and Texas on February 1. On February 4, 1861, delegates from those states had met in Montgomery, Alabama, and after drafting a provisional constitution for the Confederate States of America, had elected Jefferson Davis as their provisional president.

Even so, there was still a hope that the Southern states would return to the fold of their own accord. Horace Greeley was convinced that secession fever would eventually burn itself out. He wrote in the *Tribune* his belief that time "will be given to the unhappy people, betrayed by an imbecile Government into excesses which four months ago they never contemplated, to return to their allegiance."[9] Despite Greeley's optimism, however, peace was now impossible. Each side had staked out a position, and neither could yield.

The immediate crisis concerned Fort Sumter, in Charleston harbor. South Carolina authorities had demanded the Fort be evacuated, saying that they would resist by force any attempt to bring in arms, provisions, or military reinforcements. Now, on the very day of the inauguration, a message was received in Washington from Major Robert Anderson, the Federal commander at Sumter. According to Anderson, supplies were running low and he could not hold out much longer without help. Providing that help, Lincoln knew, might well precipitate war.[10]

The next morning, March 5, Lincoln sent the Senate his nominations for cabinet positions. For secretary of state, William H. Seward of New York; secretary of the treasury, Salmon P. Chase of Ohio; secretary of war, Simon Cameron of Pennsylvania (Cameron's was a name Lincoln wished he could erase, but promises had been made); secretary of the Navy, Gideon Welles of Connecticut; secretary of the interior, Caleb B. Smith of

Indiana; attorney general, Edward Bates of Missouri; postmaster general, Montgomery Blair of Maryland.

Four of the men—Seward, Welles, Cameron, and Bates—had vied with Lincoln for the presidential nomination. At least two—Seward and Chase—considered themselves far better qualified than Lincoln for the presidency. When someone warned Lincoln, "They will eat you up," he had replied, "They will be just as likely to eat each other up." Whether or not the cabinet selections would prove to be wise, they at least had diversity, which was surely one of Lincoln's aims. As his secretaries Nicolay and Hay put it, "He wished to combine the experience of Seward, the integrity of Chase, the popularity of Cameron; to hold the West with Bates, attract New England with Welles, please the Whigs with Smith, and convince the Democrats through Blair." And proving that the press and politics were interwoven, Lincoln's vice president, Hannibal Hamlin, plus four members of the new cabinet, had been editors at one time or another.[11]

With the cabinet appointments in place, other jobs needed to be filled. At the head of the applicant line, waiting for their reward, stood numerous journalists who had supported Lincoln. They would not be disappointed. Lincoln arranged these appointments:

Charles Wilson, *Chicago Journal*, secretary of legation to London; J. S. Pike, *New York Tribune*, minister to the Hague; W. S. Thayer, *New York Evening Post*, consul to Alexandria; George G. Fogg, *New Hampshire Democrat*, minister to Switzerland; W. H. Fry, *New York Tribune*, secretary of legation to Sardinia; Rufus King, *Milwaukee Sentinel*, minister to Rome; J. E. Harvey, *North American* and *New York Tribune*, minister to Portugal; Rufus Hosmer, *Michigan Republican*, minister to Frankfurt; James Watson Webb, *New York Courier and Enquirer*, minister to Turkey; Richard Hildreth, *New York Tribune*, consul to Tripoli.

Other editors and publishers would get lucrative postmaster jobs. These included: George Dawson, *Albany Evening Journal*; A. M. Clapp, *Buffalo Express*; E. Cowles, *Cleveland Leader*; W. F. Comly, *Dayton Daily Journal*; A. P. Miller, *Chillicothe Scioto Gazette*; A. W. Campbell, *Wheeling Intelligencer*; John L. Scripps, *Chicago Tribune*; Peter L. Foy, *St. Louis Missouri Democrat*.

Other rewards went to Thomas McElrath, *New York Tribune*, appraiser for the New York customhouse; D. P. Holloway, *Richmond* (Indiana) *Palladium*, commissioner of patents; and John D. Defrees, *Indianapolis Atlas*, superintendent of public printing. When Murat Halstead listed all these appointments in the *Cincinnati Commercial*, he called them a "disgrace to journalism." With a sense of outrage, Halstead declared, "The public has a right to suspect the qualifications of men who are continually eager to forsake their legitimate and chosen profession for an office."[12]

During the month of March, three quarters of the correspondence of the typical senator, representative, or cabinet member was about someone who wanted an appointment. The country, and the press, believed the administration had gotten bogged down with office seekers to the point that it was ignoring the crisis at Fort Sumter. On April 3 long editorials in both the *New York Tribune* and the *New York Times* criticized Lincoln for indecision and inactivity. Under the headline "Wanted—A Policy," the *Times* said the president had "spent time and strength in feeding rapacious and selfish politicians, which should have been bestowed upon saving the Union."[13]

They had a point, and when *Times* editor Henry Raymond came to the White House, Lincoln more or less agreed with the *Times* editorial, telling Raymond, "I am like a man so busy in letting rooms in one end of his house, that he can't stop to put out the fire that is burning in the other." Truly the house *was* on fire, but Lincoln still had to contend with administrative matters, all the while hoping war could be avoided. However, not until all the appointments were confirmed, and the special session of Congress ended on March 28, could he give his full attention to the national crisis.[14]

While thinking about everything else, Lincoln could not forget the press. Although formal press conferences were as yet unknown, newsgathering was still centered on the White House. Reporters tried to catch Lincoln on the fly, and he was always willing to talk to reporters who had gained his confidence. A reporter's main difficulty, of course, was to find Lincoln when he had time to talk. Sometimes, if they found him engaged, they would send in their cards, stating in writing what they wanted to know. It gave Lincoln at least some opportunity to manage the news. He might fail to respond if the question was out of bounds. But if a subject were of great interest to Lincoln, he would call the reporter into his office or go to the anteroom and answer the question in detail.[15]

There was also the foreign press to consider. Arriving on the scene about this time was William Howard Russell, a representative of the *London Times*, arguably the world's greatest newspaper. Russell, who'd landed in New York earlier that month, had already met numbers of prominent Americans. He viewed them through the eyes of a supercilious snob. On March 26 Russell wrote his editor, "The men I have met do not much impress me." He went on to dismiss America's two leading journalists by saying, "Gordon Bennett is so palpably a rogue—it comes out so strongly in the air around him, in his eyes & words & smell & voice that one pities the cause which finds in him a protagonist." As for the other, "Horace Greeley is the nastiest form of narrow minded sectarian philanthropy, who would gladly roast all the whites of South Carolina in order that he might satisfy what he supposes is a conscience but which is only an auto-cratic ambition."[16]

Russell traveled to Washington, and at the White House he was intro-duced to Lincoln by Secretary Seward. Lincoln put out his hand and, in his best political style, poured on the syrup: "Mr. Russell, I am very glad to make your acquaintance, and to see you in this country. The *London Times* is one of the greatest powers in the world—in fact, I don't know any-thing which has much more power—except perhaps the Mississippi. I am glad to know you as its minister."[17]

Evidently Lincoln's fulsome praise had some effect. Russell wrote that his meeting with Lincoln went well, and that "Conversation ensued for some minutes, which the President enlivened by two or three peculiar little sallies, and I left agreeably impressed with his shrewdness, humour, and natural sagacity."[18]

Nevertheless, the *London Times* continued to favor the Confederacy. Eventually, George Schneider, editor of the *Illinois Staats Zeitung,* called Lincoln's attention to anti-Union feeling created by the *Times* in northern Europe. The President chose Schneider as consul to Denmark. Arriving in Copenhagen, Schneider called on the editor of the most widely read paper in Denmark, the pro-Confederate *Dag Bladet,* and convinced the paper to change its policy. Schneider later traveled extensively through northern Europe, calling on various editors on behalf of the Union. Shrewdly, Lincoln was waging a media war overseas as well as at home.[19]

All this time, Lincoln had been pondering the probable consequence of any attempt to resupply Fort Sumter. First, however, he needed to know if it was even feasible. He consulted General Winfield Scott, the country's senior military figure, who said supplies at Sumter were running low, and it would be impossible to relieve the fort with existing resources. For that he would need a strong fleet, 5,000 additional regulars, and 20,000 volunteers. Gathering such a force would surely be seen as an act of war. And if war were to come, Lincoln was determined that the other side should fire the first shot. Well then, should he try to send just food to Anderson? Lincoln consulted his cabinet members, and of the seven, five stood against sending food, one was for it, and one was neither for nor against it. Eventually, of course, the decision would have to be solely Lincoln's. As would so often be the case, the buck stopped in the oval office.[20]

The country was on edge, wondering what would happen. The papers, with no solid facts to go on, were relying on conflicting rumors. On April 8, the *New York Tribune* reported that an attempt would be made to provision Fort Sumter; that very day, the *New York Herald* said it had learned that the fort would be evacuated. A *Harper's Weekly* cartoon showed a haggard man, slumped in his chair and surrounded by newspapers. The caption read:

> Our Friend, Mr. Jones, who is deeply interested in the condition of the country, takes all the Papers, and reads them thoroughly. The following Dispatches puzzle him somewhat:
> The Cabinet has issued the orders for the Evacuation of Fort Sumter.—*Herald*.
> It is at last decided that Fort Sumter shall be reinforced.—*Times*.
> Orders were sent off last evening to reinforce Major ANDERSON at all costs.—*Tribune*.
> It is believed that Major ANDERSON Evacuated Fort Sumter by order of the Government last evening.—*World*.[21]

Bennett's *New York Herald* maliciously blamed everything on Lincoln and his administration. "Our only hope now," said the *Herald*, "against civil war of an indefinite duration seems to lie in the overthrow of the demoralizing, disorganizing, and destructive [Republican] sectional party, of which 'Honest Abe Lincoln' is the pliant instrument."[22]

Lincoln considered his duty under the Constitution. He could not voluntarily give up Fort Sumter. However, he had no duty to launch an armed attack against the South. He wisely decided to equivocate by sending a ship loaded only with provisions. A messenger was sent to inform South Carolina Governor Francis Pickens of this, but Pickens found it unsatisfactory. With the blessings of the Confederate government, from Jefferson Davis on down, a surrender ultimatum was sent to Major Anderson. Well-meaning emissaries tried to convince Anderson to leave voluntarily. This he could not do. On the morning of April 12, Confederate Gen. P. G. T. Beauregard, commanding the Charleston batteries, gave the order to open fire. Throughout the 12th and 13th, the Charleston batteries pounded Sumter with all they had. After thirty-three hours of bombardment, with its walls reduced to rubble and provisions exhausted, the fort was forced to send up a white flag of surrender. On Sunday, April 14, in accordance with the terms of capitulation, Anderson fired a fifty-gun salute to his flag. During the ceremony, an ember fell into some powder. The resulting explosion killed one Union soldier, who thus became the affair's lone fatality. Finally, with Southerners extending every courtesy to the gallant Anderson, the garrison marched out with drums beating and colors flying.[23]

Monday morning's *New York Tribune*, while announcing Anderson's surrender, proudly proclaimed, "Fort Sumter is lost, but Freedom is saved. . . . Live the Republic!"[24] That same day, Lincoln called upon the states for 75,000 militiamen to put down the rebellion. Each state was furnished a quota of regiments it was expected to provide. The call was vehemently rejected by the governors of Virginia, North Carolina, Kentucky, Tennessee, and Missouri. There was but a lukewarm response from Maryland and Delaware. Although the other states accepted the call enthusiastically, the reaction of the border states was disappointing. The disappointment grew worse on the 17th, when the Virginia legislature, meeting in Richmond, voted to secede from the Union and join the Confederacy.[25]

In states that remained loyal to the Union, the firing on Sumter had a galvanizing effect. The humiliating loss of the fort, and the firing on Old Glory, was met with outraged shock and indignation. A wave of enthusiastic patriotism swept across the North, not unlike the feeling that would come to America eighty years later, on December 7, 1941, following the attack on Pearl Harbor. By April 18 Major Anderson was back in New York and being toasted as a national hero. On that same day, the *Chicago Tribune* was proclaiming, "Upon the heads of traitors be the dread penalty . . . treason must be put down. . . . There is now every indication that the whole force of ninety-four regiments called for by the President could be readily furnished by Illinois alone, and that the quota of six regiments assigned to Illinois could be obtained in Chicago almost at the tap of the drum."[26]

Thoughtful men, both at home and overseas, suspected that the South had been outsmarted by Lincoln. In his inaugural address, he had said, "You can have no conflict without being yourselves the aggressors." Now, as predicted, they'd been the ones to start the shooting. In England, the pro-South *Manchester Guardian* said cynically, "The only plausible explanation of President Lincoln's account is that he has thought that a political object was to be obtained by putting the Southerners in the wrong, if they could be manoeuvred into firing the first shot." Whether the *Guardian* liked it or not, that was precisely what had happened.[27]

The "generals" of the press were quick to offer advice. Not long before, Horace Greeley, an inherent pacifist, had been arguing that the "erring sisters" should be allowed to depart in peace. On February 23 he wrote, "if the Slave States, the Cotton States, or the Gulf States only choose to form an independent nation, they have a clear moral right to do so. Whenever it shall be clear that the great body of Southern people have become conclusively alienated from the Union and anxious to escape from it, we shall do our best to forward their views."[28] Now that war was a reality, however, Greeley became the shrillest of hawks. Sensing the country's war fever, he told his readers that the chief business of the American people for the year must be to prove "that they have a Government and that Freedom is not another name for Anarchy."[29] With mock humility he declared, "We will not undertake to say what the Government should do at this juncture," and then, almost without pausing, he outlined a six-point policy:

First, Military occupancy of Maryland
Second, Advance upon Richmond and the armed holding of that city
Third, Military Occupancy of Norfolk, Charleston, Savannah, Mobile and New Orleans
Fourth, the proclamation of martial law in all the rebellion States
Fifth, the offering of large rewards for the arrest of Jefferson Davis and his conspirators
Sixth, their trial and execution under martial law.[30]

As the country girded for war, the border states were boiling with violent clashes, neighbor against neighbor, brother against brother. When it was learned that militia regiments would soon be heading for Washington, Baltimore streets were filled with secessionist mobs vowing that no Federal troops would be allowed to pass. Swallowing their pride, Lincoln and the country's senior military man, Winfield Scott, negotiated with the mayor of Baltimore, who promised to restrain the mobs as long as incoming troops bypassed the city, either circling around it or going by water. It was a remarkable spectacle, the president of the United States and his general in chief negotiating with a mayor for the right of Federal troops to march through a neighboring city to save the nation's capital. When Greeley learned of this, he was quick to criticize the administration for appearing weak. At this point, of course, they *were* weak; Lincoln, with virtually no military force at his disposal, was probably being realistic.

It is little wonder that Lincoln, when talking of newspapers, liked telling the story of the man lost in the forest at night during a thunderstorm. Lincoln said editors should pray as did the man in the woods when he went down on his knees and called out, "O Lord, if it is all the same to you, give us a little more light and a little less noise."[31]

Although the press continued to carp and to demand the administration take action, most understood that Lincoln and Scott should determine the timing. As late as June 23, even the aggressive Greeley was counseling that while the coming campaign should be prosecuted with energy, no forward step should be taken that would have to be retracted. Then came a sudden shift. On June 26, a bold proclamation appeared at the top of the *Tribune's* editorial page:

THE NATION'S WAR CRY

Forward to Richmond.   Forward to Richmond!

The Rebel Congress must not be allowed to meet there on the 20th of July. BY THAT DATE THE PLACE MUST BE HELD BY THE NATIONAL ARMY.

Day after day, the headline was repeated. As the "Forward to Richmond" drumbeat continued to pound, popular sentiment was pressuring Lincoln to act. Among other things, many regiments had enlisted for ninety days, and their time was about to expire.

The "Forward to Richmond" slogan had been written by Fitz-Henry Warren, the *Tribune's* Washington correspondent, and heartily approved by the paper's managing editor, Charles Dana. Most people, however, attributed it to Greeley. Lincoln, though, evidently knew it was Warren's. On June 28, he called Warren to the White House and told him his wish was about to be granted.[32]

On June 29, having decided it was time to make a decision, Lincoln called a meeting of his cabinet and principal military officers. General Irvin McDowell, commander of Federal troops in the Washington area, suggested an attack directed against Beauregard's army at Manassas. Winfield Scott, the aged general in chief, said he was opposed. Earlier, Scott had urged a carefully planned campaign down the Mississippi River in the autumn and winter, coupled with a blockade of the eastern seaports, in an over-all enveloping of the South. The impatient press had widely condemned the plan, likening it to slow strangulation and calling it "Scott's Anaconda." Scott still believed that was the best idea, maintaining that for now the greenhorn army was ill-prepared to take the field. However, when he was overruled by Lincoln and the cabinet, the loyal Scott said he would support an offensive effort. With that, McDowell was told to proceed. The war was about to begin in earnest.[33]

⊷⇒◉⇐⊶

CHAPTER 4

"IN THE DEPTHS OF BITTERNESS"

Northern people were screaming for action. Day after day, they were being goaded by the press, seeing Fitz-Henry Warren's "On to Richmond" headlines in the *New York Tribune* or reading inflammatory editorials, such as the one of Warren's that appeared on June 21: "Shall I tell you, frankly and honestly, what I hear all around me and abroad? It is, that there is no intention to press this suppression of the rebellion—that the patience of the people is to be worn out by delay—that the soldier is to have his spirit wasted in the torpor and inaction of the camp, and when, at length, the nation are disgusted and outraged to a proper point, then we are to run after the old harlot of a compromise."[1]

The administration, feeling the pressure, had by early July given Irvin McDowell the go-ahead. Surely, but somewhat ponderously, he prepared to launch his offensive. It seemed, however, that Beauregard, the Southern commander at Manassas, knew each McDowell action almost as soon as it took place. Ironically, Beauregard's best source of intelligence may well have been the Northern press. Inexperienced officers talked freely to reporters, and stories containing military information were printed with little thought of the consequences. A typical item in the *New York Tribune* read: "A regiment left New York for Fortress Monroe; 350 men left New York to join the 69th Regiment at Washington; two regiments of Ohio volunteers, numbering altogether eighteen hundred men, reach Washington."[2]

Security was indeed a major problem, and finally the administration began clamping down. Some who criticized the president for not doing enough were now saying that he did too much. Lincoln authorized simultaneous raids on every telegraph office in the Northern states, seizing copies of all telegrams sent or received during the previous year. With the information obtained, men suspected of being informers were taken from their homes, thrown into jail, and held incommunicado.[3]

John Hay, still writing anonymously, did what he could to explain things to the American public. An item by him in the *New York World*, headed "From Our Special Correspondent," said in part: "The telegraphic correspondents were not a little surprised this morning at the . . . official order of Gen. Scott, prohibiting them from transmitting army movements over the wires. . . . For the past two weeks there has been no government inspector in the office here, and no restrictions on dispatches; consequently, the *Tribune* has run the gauntlet of its *canards*, deceiving the public, and annoying the government. . . . The telegraph company is making efforts to have the embargo raised, but I doubt if it succeeds."[4]

Evidently the new censorship brought a howl from the New York reporters, who insisted on meeting with administration officials. Reporting on this, Hay added some self-serving phrases showing how "zealous" the administration was about respecting the rights of the press:

> Today an interesting meeting of the correspondents of the New-York dailies was held at the capitol for a conference with the government on the publication of important movements of the army. It seems that General Scott and Secretary Cameron have arrived at the conclusion that the details of military movements transmitted to the New-York papers have been of infinite service to the rebel cause, giving them early and reliable information via Louisville of the intentions of the government. In view, therefore, of the impending importance of the movements of troops, it has been necessary to

prevent the transmission of telegraphic dispatches detailing army affairs. But the government, ever zealous of the rights of the press and the rights of individuals, has appealed to the patriotism of the correspondents to co-operate with it in affording themselves as ample liberty as is consistent with the protection desired by the government.[5]

McDowell planned to move against Manassas with the main army. At the same time, another force, under Gen. Robert Patterson, would hold Confederate Joe Johnston in place near Harper's Ferry and keep him from reinforcing Beauregard. It was a good plan, but carrying it out was another story. When McDowell finally got under way, his columns moved almost casually, with soldiers dropping out of ranks to pick berries, others discarding their packs and "spare" equipment. Sightseers from Washington, including congressmen and their ladies, came out to watch the "show," and the whole thing took on a holiday atmosphere. Then everything seemed to go wrong. The men did not have sufficient rations; a day was wasted in correcting the situation. Another day was wasted in reconnaissance, as officers studied maps and considered how best to proceed. Patterson, going in exactly the wrong direction, failed to keep Johnston occupied. By July 20 Johnston had slipped away from Harper's Ferry and linked up with Beauregard.

The attack, when it finally took place on July 21, went well enough at first. Then it shuddered to a halt, partly through the stubborn efforts of a former Virginia Military Institute instructor, Thomas J. Jackson, who would henceforth be known as "Stonewall." With the Union offensive stalled, the Confederates launched a counterattack. Green Federal troops began falling back. Soon it turned into a stampede, and the Bull Run battle became a full-fledged disaster. The English correspondent, William Russell, riding forward on horseback, found himself surrounded by fleeing men. Coming upon a Union officer, he asked, "What does this mean?" The exhausted officer replied, "Why, it means that we are pretty badly whipped." Officers and men, now overcome by panic, continued to flee, discarding equipment and weapons so as to move faster. Those who couldn't run fast enough were throwing up their hands in surrender.[6]

The newspapers printed the grim story, and there was no chance to "spin" this into anything other than an utter, humiliating defeat. A typical account, this one from the *New York World*, said, "The retreat, the panic, the hideous headlong confusion, were now beyond a hope. . . . I saw officers with leaves and eagles on their shoulder-straps, majors and colonels, who had deserted their commands, pass me galloping as if for dear life."[7] While about five hundred Northerners had been killed, and another thousand wounded, exaggerated reports made it sound even worse, with wild tales that literally thousands of dead were left in heaps on the field. As the *New York Tribune* put it: "All was lost to the American army, even its honor. . . . The agony of this overwhelming disgrace can never be expressed in words."[8]

At the War Department, the weary, seventy-five-year-old Winfield Scott spoke in anguish: "I deserve removal because I did not stand up, when my army was not in condition for fighting, and resist it to the last."

Lincoln, hearing the remark, interrupted to say, "Your conversation seems to imply that I forced you to fight this battle."

That undoubtedly was what Scott believed. Out of consideration for Lincoln, however, he replied evasively: "I have never served a President who has been kinder to me than you have been."[9]

In the dark hours following Bull Run, papers such as *Harper's Weekly* urged the public to stand behind Lincoln. "We cannot too often repeat," said *Harper's,* "that the first duty of the citizen at this juncture is to give the President a generous, confiding, and cordial support."[10]

At the *Tribune,* however, managing editor Charles Dana looked for someone to blame. He charged the "shipwreck of our grand and heroic army" squarely to the administration, confessed his inability to conjecture what apology the government could offer "to the humiliated and astounded country," and declared that whatever apology would be offered would "be found altogether insufficient and unsatisfactory. . . . We have fought and been beaten. God forgive our rulers that this is so. . . . The 'sacred soil' of Virginia is crimson and wet with the blood of thousands of Northern men, needlessly shed. . . . A decimated and indignant people will demand the immediate retirement of the present Cabinet."[11]

Rival papers were claiming that the *Tribune* had forced the battle by its demand for precipitous action. The *Philadelphia Press*, for example, after saying "our army has been routed and many of its regiments demoralized," went on to describe "a premature advance on the enemy without sufficient force, which may be attributed to the clamors of politicians and newspapers like the *New York Tribune*."[12]

The *Tribune* editorial made the situation even worse. And though Dana was the author, most readers believed it came directly from the pen of Horace Greeley. At least Greeley got the blame, and Bennett's *Herald* had a field day at his expense. Protesting his innocence, Greeley wrote: "I wish to evade no responsibility [which is *exactly* what he was trying to do] but to repel a personal aspersion. . . . I wish to be distinctly understood as not seeking to be relieved of any responsibility for urging the advance of the Union grand army into Virginia, though the precise phrase, 'Forward to Richmond!' is not mine and I would have preferred not to iterate it. . . . If I am needed as a scapegoat for all the military blunders of the month, so be it. Individuals must die that the nation may live. If I can serve her best in that capacity, I do not shrink from the ordeal."[13]

With irrational egotism, Greeley believed the *Tribune* had brought on the battle almost by itself, and he was stunned by the thought that he might be responsible for needless deaths. Completely shaken, he went to bed with what the doctors called "brain fever." Then he took pen in hand and wrote directly to the president. By any standard it was a weird letter, and in later years he would say he was "almost insane" when he wrote it: "Dear Sir: This is my seventh sleepless night—yours, too, doubtless—yet I think I shall not die, because I have no right to die. I must struggle to live, however bitterly. You are now considered a great man, and I am a hopelessly broken one. . . . If our recent disaster is fatal—do not fear to sacrifice yourself to your country. . . . If the Union is irrevocably gone, an armistice for thirty, sixty, ninety, one hundred and twenty days—better still for a year—ought to be proposed with a view to a peaceful adjustment. . . . Yours in the depths of bitterness, HORACE GREELEY."[14]

It was advice Lincoln could not accept. A lengthy armistice would provide the South the stature it needed for international recognition. That must not happen. The war had to be pursued without letup, and Lincoln knew it. No doubt shaking his head, he pigeonholed Greeley's letter.

One of the most devastating accounts of the battle did not appear immediately. It was written by the Englishman, William Russell, for the *London Times,* so his article had to cross the Atlantic, be printed, then return. When it finally appeared in the States, it became a bombshell. Russell described Washington as a city in panic, "crowded with soldiers without officers, who have fled from Centreville, and with 'three months' men,' who are going home. . . . The streets, in spite of the rain, are crowded with people with anxious faces, and groups of wavering politicians are assembled at the corners, in the hotel passages, and the bars." With pompous assurance, he declared that unless the North put "its best men into the battle . . . she will inevitably fall before the energy, the personal hatred, and the superior fighting prowess of her antagonists. . . . In my letters, as in my conversation, I have endeavored to show that the task which the Unionists have set themselves is one of no ordinary difficulty, but in the state of arrogance and supercilious confidence, either real or affected to conceal a weakness, one might as well have preached to the Pyramid of Cheops."[15]

It was all right for Americans to criticize themselves, even understandable. But it was *outrageous* for a foreigner to do so! Moreover, Russell had made an even greater blunder—he had ridiculed the American press, referring to "journals conducted avowedly by men of disgraceful personal character—the bewhipped and be-kicked and unrecognized pariahs of society in New York."[16] Attacking the press, in any century, is not something one does with impunity. Lincoln knew this, and acted accordingly. Russell undoubtedly knew it too, but Russell, from his high English perch, simply didn't care.

Soon the press was responding to the man now derided as "Bull Run" Russell. A reporter for the *Chicago Tribune* claimed that Russell never saw the battle itself and only witnessed the ensuing retreat. "The imaginative correspondent left the battle-ground before any confusion occurred," said the *Tribune* man. "Hearing the exaggerated stories of what came to be a flight, after he got to Washington on Monday, while the excitement was at its height, he wove them into his letter as facts of his own observation. The rout was disgraceful enough . . . but it was not what Mr. Russell describes. As we asserted, he did not see it."[17]

Letters to the editor came pouring in, all denouncing the Englishman who dared to criticize our gallant boys in blue. A writer signing himself "Union" told the *Washington Star*, "he saw nothing of the battle . . . saw not a shot fired; saw not one soldier of the rebel army, horse or foot, but was a spectator merely of the panic and the rout." How dare he, then, "heap derogatory comments upon the character of the conflict he did not witness at all, and upon the behavior of the troops, successfully engaged for hours before and up to the time of his arrival."[18]

Similar letters appeared in papers throughout the North. Russell had definitely worn out his welcome. The chill evidently extended to the White House, for a chagrined Russell later made the following entry in his diary: "September 8: Going home, I met Mr. and Mrs. Lincoln in their new open carriage. The President was not so good-humored, nor Mrs. Lincoln so affable, in their return to my salutation as usual."[19]

Throughout the North, people shocked by the Bull Run casualty figures were finally acknowledging that a bloody and very "real" war was under way. The press became filled with pessimistic, defeatist articles, one that made the Union cause seem hopeless. Many of the stories, in Lincoln's mind, bordered on outright treason. While he had always respected the freedom of the press, he decided he couldn't sit still while hostile journalists tore the country apart. The Congress agreed, and passed legislation authorizing the president to stop transportation of aid and comfort to those in rebellion.

One of the worst offenders was the *Philadelphia Christian Observer*. The Reverend Amasa Converse, editor of the *Observer*, published among other things some probably bogus letters, supposedly written by a Virginian. This one is typical: "Reunion is an utter impossibility. The gross, brutal, fiendish, demoniac outrages perpetrated by the chicken stealers sent here to ravage the country, pillage the houses and burn them, outrage the women, and shoot down for amusement peaceable citizens, and even children, on the streets, have greatly exasperated the people."[20]

Desperate times called for desperate measures. A month after Bull Run, using the authority Congress had given him, Lincoln sent federal marshals to storm the office of the *Observer* and seize the type. Editor Converse had flown, having previously written in the *Observer* that "the next issue will be the last." That same day, the local district attorney ordered that copies be seized of several disloyal New York newspapers, including the latest issue of the *Observer*. Elsewhere, a military officer arrived at the *Chicago Times* to shut down the paper and seal its presses. In New York, the antiwar *Journal of Commerce*, the *Morning News*, and the *Freeman's Journal* were shut down. The latter, a Roman Catholic weekly, saw its editor jailed without a trial and held in the government's prison in New York harbor.[21]

A new crisis arose in September. This time the culprit was Gen. John C. Fremont, commander of the Department of the West, with headquarters in St. Louis. The high-handed Fremont rashly issued a proclamation saying that any person taken with arms in their hands within his lines would be tried by court-martial and if found guilty would be shot. The proclamation also declared that the property of all persons taking up arms against the United States would be confiscated and any slaves they held would be set free. Many papers, including the *New York Times*, the *New York Tribune*, and the *Chicago Tribune*, printed the proclamation in full and applauded Fremont's action. Even Bennett's *New York Herald* was in favor of it. Lincoln, however, quickly realized the pitfalls. He wrote Fremont a tactful note, urging him to withdraw the proclamation, and saying by way of explanation, "I think there is great danger that the closing paragraph, in relation to the confiscation of property and the liberating of slaves of traitorous owners will alarm our Southern Union friends and turn them against us; perhaps ruin our rather fair prospect for Kentucky."[22]

Fremont refused to take the way out that Lincoln had offered. Instead, he sent his wife, the politically savvy Jessie Benton Fremont, to plead his case. The meeting did not go well, and Lincoln stood firm, ordering Fremont to withdraw the order. Eventually, after further missteps by the man who'd won fame as the "Pathfinder," Lincoln relieved him and sent Gen. Henry Wager Halleck to take his place.

Longtime Abolitionists such as Greeley were disappointed by Lincoln's action, and papers such as the *Chicago Tribune* were quick to denounce it. Conversely, Bennett's *Herald,* normally no friend of the administration, said, "The President, who has always been known as an upright man, of late months has justly earned the reputation of a wise and energetic states-man. . . . The moderate and effective rebuke contained in his letter to Major General Fremont is eminently worthy of admiration . . . for the death blow it strikes at all attempts of badly advised commanders to over-step the legitimate sphere of their military duties."[23]

It was a tricky situation for Lincoln, particularly with respect to Gree-ley, who in 1856 had helped make Fremont the Republican candidate for president. By relieving a man Greeley had supported for years, Lincoln was crossing swords with "Uncle Horace." Greeley didn't like it, but he nevertheless conceded editorially that "the President has doubtless done what appeared to him not only expedient but urgently necessary."[24]

Hoping to improve things in the Army of the Potomac, Lincoln re-placed McDowell with the youthful Gen. George Brinton McClellan, a man who had waged a successful campaign in western Virginia and given the Union one of its few bright moments. McClellan, an able adminis-trator who was highly popular with the troops, set about aggressively to restore the eastern Army's discipline and morale. Meanwhile recruits were pouring in. The Union volunteer forces as a whole, East and West, were nearing half a million. McClellan's Army of the Potomac had numbered 50,000 in July; by late October it was three times that. As weeks went by, however, and no offensive action was initiated, the country grew restless.

McClellan was personally courageous, but he proved overly cautious, even fearful, where the Army was concerned. He was determined to do battle only on his own terms. "A long time must elapse before I can do this," he wrote his wife, "and I expect all the newspapers to abuse me for delay, but I will not mind that." Unlike Lincoln, the haughty McClellan failed to understand that this was a people's war, and as such, the people's will had constantly to be consulted to ensure popular support.[25]

On November 1, the aging Gen. Scott was allowed to retire and Lin-coln named McClellan general in chief of the entire Union Army. He hoped the cocky general realized what was being asked of him. "Draw on me," Lincoln said, "for all the sense I have, and all the information. In addition to your present command, the supreme command of the Army will entail a vast labor upon you."

"I can do it all," McClellan assured him.[26]

━━◉◖━━

Relations with the unpredictable Horace Greeley continued to blow hot and cold. Bryant, the distinguished editor of the *New York Evening Post*, who was not above criticizing Lincoln himself, had once sent the president a friendly note, saying not to let Greeley worry him, that the *Tribune* editor was moved by "vagaries."[27] Nevertheless, Lincoln decided it was time to mend fences with the powerful *Tribune* editor. Consequently, he entered into a rather weird arrangement through his friend Robert J. Walker, a former territorial governor of Kansas. For the undertaking, which shows Lincoln at his slyest, the intermediary would be James R. Gilmore, Walker's partner in a new magazine enterprise. In a letter to Walker (but intended for Greeley's eyes), Lincoln wrote:

> Dear Governor: I have thought over the interview which Mr. Gilmore has had with Mr. Greeley, and the proposal that Greeley has made to Gilmore, namely that he (Gilmore) shall communicate to him (Greeley) all that he learns from you of the inner workings of the administration, in return for his (Greeley's) giving such aid as he can to the new magazine and allowing you (Walker) from time to time the use of his (Greeley's) columns when it is desirable to feel of, or forestall, public opinion on important subjects. The arrangement meets my unqualified approval, and I shall further it to the extent of my ability, by opening to you—as I do now—fully the policy of the Government—its present views and future intentions when formed—giving you permission to communicate them to Gilmore for Greeley; and in case you go to Europe I will give these things directly to Gilmore. But all this must be on the express and explicit understanding that the fact of the communications coming from me shall be absolutely confidential—not to be disclosed by Greeley to his nearest friend, or any of his subordinates. He will be, in effect, my mouth-piece, but I shall not be known to be the speaker.

I need not tell you that I have the highest confidence in Mr. Greeley. He is a great power. Having him firmly behind me will be as helpful to me as an army of one hundred thousand men. That he has ever kicked the traces has been owing to his not being fully informed. Tell Gilmore to say to him that, if he ever objects to my policy, I shall be glad to have him state to me his views frankly and fully. I shall adopt his if I can. If I cannot, I will at least tell him why. He and I should stand together, and let no minor differences come between us; for we both seek one end, which is the saving of our country. Now, Governor, this is a longer letter than I have written for a month— longer than I would have written for any other man than Horace Greeley.
Yours very truly, Abraham Lincoln

When someone brought the letter to Greeley, his eyes lit up and he exclaimed of Lincoln, "He is a wonderful man—wonderful. . . . You must let me keep this letter . . . I want to look at it when I am downhearted."[28]

The honeymoon was short-lived. When it appeared that exclusive information was not forthcoming, Greeley resumed his criticism. As a good journalist, he had always been suspicious of those in authority, whether they were politicians or generals. Months earlier he had said as much in a letter addressed to young men seeking to enter politics: "The moral I would inculcate is a trite one, but none the less important. It is summed up in the Scriptural injunction, 'Put not your trust in princes.' Men, even the best, are frail and mutable, while principle is sure and eternal." That was Greeley's creed. If he did not always live by it himself, at least he always preached it to others.[29]

For the moment, the *Tribune*'s particular target was McClellan. His continued inaction, Greeley said, had allowed the rebels to close the Potomac east of Washington and disrupt the Baltimore and Ohio railroad west of the city. What was he waiting for? Didn't he realize that winter was the best fighting season in the South? "Let us end the war!" Greeley thundered.[30]

The next crisis involved England. With all the problems at home, Lincoln surely didn't need to provoke the British, who were already leaning toward the Confederacy. He was well aware of this, and at one point he sent an emissary, Thurlow Weed, to ask the *New York Herald* to tone down its anti-British rhetoric. The plea fell on deaf ears, and James Gordon Bennett continued to have fun, twisting the tail of the British lion by writing scathingly of all things English. Then, in November, a situation arose that involved far more than newspaper insults. Navy Captain Charles Wilkes of the cruiser *San Jacinto* stopped a British mail ship, the *Trent*, on the high seas, boarded her, and seized two Confederate commissioners traveling as passengers. The men, James Mason of Virginia and John Slidell of Louisiana, were imprisoned at Boston's Fort Warren, and Wilkes was hailed as a national hero. The English were outraged by what was deemed an affront to British honor and a clear violation of international law. Lord Palmerston's government promptly dispatched a note to Secretary of State Seward demanding the commissioners' release.

Lincoln's first thought was to approve Wilkes's action. Upon reflection, however, and after conferring with Seward, he began having second thoughts. "I fear the traitors will prove to be white elephants," he said, and he impressed on Seward that one war at a time was enough. He knew, however, that an immediate release of the prisoners would not sit well with the public. After a series of cabinet meetings, and after public opinion had cooled, Seward carefully crafted a note with Lincoln's blessing, a note accepting no blame for America, but nevertheless releasing Mason and Slidell on a technicality. The honor of both countries was upheld, the public was mollified, and the crisis had passed.[31]

As Greeley continued to carp at the administration, Lincoln reminded James R. Gilmore of the scheme whereby he would provide inside information to Walker and Gilmore, and they would relay that information to Greeley. That was supposed to elicit Greeley's cooperation, but it wasn't working out that way. "I infer from the recent tone of the *Tribune*," Lincoln said, "that you are not always able to keep Brother Greeley in the traces." Gilmore said he had handed Greeley the memoranda sent on by Walker, but it had not done much good. When he showed the memo to the *Tribune*'s Sydney Gay, however, it had softened Greeley's wrath on several occasions. "What is he wrathy about?" asked the president. Gilmore said the war was going too slow to suit Greeley, and worse yet, the administration was not attacking slavery as it should.

"Why does he not come down here and have a talk with me?" Lincoln asked. Gilmore said such an interview had been proposed, but Greeley said he wouldn't let the president act as an advisory editor of the *Tribune*. "I have no such desire," said Lincoln. "I certainly have enough now on my hands to satisfy any man's ambition. Does not that remark show an unfriendly spirit in Mr. Greeley?" Gilmore said he thought not, insisting that Greeley still had a strong personal regard for Lincoln.[32]

Despite Greeley's disappointment in the Gilmore pipeline, the *Tribune* was securing plenty of inside information through the inept secretary of war, Simon Cameron. The responsible party was the *Tribune's* crafty Washington correspondent, Sam Wilkeson. When he arrived in Washington, Wilkeson had written Sydney Gay in the home office, "[I] soon shall fasten my grapples on the necessary influences here. I *shall have* them, Sydney."[33]

Wilkeson then proceeded to butter up Cameron in the most outrageous fashion. It was common knowledge in Washington that Cameron was a wretched administrator; the War Department under his haphazard direction would buy almost anything at any price. Nevertheless, Wilkeson wrote a story saying, "Secretary Cameron gives day and night to the service of his country. The contracts made by him will defy the most unfriendly scrutiny." Wilkeson clipped the piece, then sent it to Cameron with an accompanying note, "The satisfaction of doing justice to a wronged statesman, is not equalled by the pleasure with which I sincerely pay a tribute of respect to a maligned good man."[34]

While other correspondents were being frustrated by the censors, a note soon went from Cameron to H. E. Thayer, chief censor at the War Department:

> My Dear Sir:
>   It is my wish that you neither suppress nor alter the telegrams of Mr. Samuel Wilkeson. Please send them as they are written and signed by him.
> Respectfully, Simon Cameron[35]

Unfortunately for Wilkeson, Cameron's Washington days were numbered. For some time, the secretary had advocated the arming of slaves. It was something Lincoln was not yet ready to say, since it was a political question as much as a military one, and the uncertain status of the border states made such a statement highly indiscreet. Nevertheless, part of

Cameron's annual report read: "Those who make war against the Government justly forfeit all rights of property. . . . If it shall be found that the men who have been held by the rebels as slaves are capable of bearing arms and performing efficient military service, it is the right, and may become the duty, of the Government to arm and equip them, and employ their service against the rebels."[36]

To make matters worse, Cameron had mailed copies of the report to postmasters for distribution to leading newspapers. Lincoln, upon reading the report, ordered Cameron to suppress the offending paragraph. Cameron argued, but Lincoln's word was final, and a corrected version was dispatched. It was too late, however. While both the *New York Times* and *Herald* carried the amended version, the *New York Tribune* published it in the secretary's original form.[37]

Regardless of which version was printed, it was obvious to editors everywhere that there was dissension within the administration. "What a fiasco!" said C. H. Ray of the *Chicago Tribune*.[38] By this time, the War Department under Cameron was a chaotic shambles. Charges were made, not only of gross inefficiency, but also of internal corruption. Cameron had to go, but Lincoln knew an abrupt dismissal would cause a political uproar. With an eye to public relations, Cameron was named ambassador to Russia, permitting him to exit with dignity. His surprising replacement was Edwin M. Stanton, a hardnosed attorney and a lifelong Democrat. Stanton's appointment was well received, especially after a *Tribune* editorial credited him with "the highest qualities of talent, courage, and uncompromising patriotism."[39]

Making Stanton responsible for the War Department was a step in the right direction. However, as Lincoln surveyed the overall situation, he saw nothing to encourage him. Talking to Quartermaster General Montgomery Meigs, he moaned, "What shall I do? . . . The bottom is out of the tub."[40]

CHAPTER 5

"AS DEEP AS A WELL"

As 1862 began, the administration's media problems continued to grow and fester. Underlying everything was the slavery question, and the president was walking a tightrope. While he needed the support of the Abolitionists, he couldn't afford to antagonize border states like Kentucky, Maryland, and Missouri.

To mollify these wavering slave-holding states, Lincoln had suppressed Secretary of War Cameron's idea about arming African-Americans. Similarly, he had stepped in when John Fremont made a move to free the slaves of disloyal Missourians. By now, both men were gone. Fremont had been relieved and Cameron had left the country as minister to Russia. Getting rid of Cameron had been a delicate maneuver. Not wanting to offend the man's political supporters, Lincoln exchanged courteous notes with the former Pennsylvania governor, then released those notes to the press.

Nevertheless, the problem was not going away. *Harper's Weekly* put it bluntly: "If anybody supposes that Slavery is going to survive this war he seems to us not rightly to understand human nature. The military hand, which knows no rule but necessity, will loosen its roots; and the hand of law will afterwards tear it up and cast it into the fire. Probably there is no man in the country who sees this more clearly than the President."[1]

The eminent historian, George Bancroft, also got in the act, writing Lincoln to remind him that the slavery question could not be ignored. "Civil war is the instrument of Divine Providence to root out social slavery," Bancroft wrote. In his reply, Lincoln made it clear that he needed no reminding: "The main thought . . . in your letter is one which does not escape my attention, and with which I must deal in all due caution, and with the best judgment I can bring to it."[2]

Yet abolitionists such as Greeley saw no need for "due caution." "We do not see how the Union and Slavery can both be upheld," Greeley wrote.[3] Freeing the slaves, in his opinion, was not only morally right, it was also a practical step toward victory. "Do you ask how to put down the rebellion?" he wrote. "Destroy Slavery. Do you ask how to prevent European intervention? Destroy Slavery."[4]

When it was announced that Greeley would lecture at the Smithsonian to a crowd packed with abolitionists, the *New York Tribune*'s William Croffut asked Lincoln if he planned to attend. "Yes, I will," Lincoln said. "I never heard Greeley, and I want to hear him. In print every one of his words seems to weigh about a ton; I want to hear what he has to say about us."

At the lecture, Lincoln was on the platform as Greeley proclaimed that "the destruction of slavery" was the one sole purpose of the war. As he said this, he looked directly at Lincoln. The audience cheered at what appeared to be a direct challenge to the president. Lincoln sat impassively.[5]

Greeley was indeed an impatient man. "He thought the world might be reformed in a day—in his day," wrote Beman Brockway in 1891 of his old friend Greeley. "When a thing is to be done, his idea was that it should be done now—this very day and hour."[6] Greeley's impatience must have been frustrating for Lincoln, who detested slavery as much as any man, but who knew if he acted prematurely, emancipation could be seen as the desperate act of a weakened government. "What's the matter with Uncle Horace?" Lincoln asked *Tribune* correspondent Homer Byington. "Can't he restrain himself a little?" Then he added, "Well, I do not suppose I have any right to complain; Uncle Horace goes with me pretty often after all; I reckon he is with us at least four days out of seven."[7]

Greeley, who continued to underestimate Lincoln, told the *Tribune's* James Gilmore, "It is said that but for my action in the convention, Lincoln would not have been nominated. It was a mistake—the biggest mistake in my life." He then asked Gilmore what *he* thought of Lincoln. Gilmore replied, "Now, Mr. Greeley, you have asked my impression of Lincoln, and I have told you only the half. He has the reputation of being the frankest of men, but there never was a bigger mistake. With all his apparent transparency, he is as deep as a well."[8]

Lincoln had gone to war to save the Union. Greeley recognized this, but like many present-day Americans, he still considered slavery the war's main issue. In Europe, most people saw it differently. One London editor said he wasn't surprised "that the South is tempted to regard the clamour of the North against slavery as something very like hypocrisy, and to resent with bitterness a cry which it knows to be injurious and believes to be insincere." The writer went on to say that "we have seen that he [Lincoln] was prepared to give slavery more protection than it had ever before enjoyed. Another editor echoed that sentiment, saying, "If slavery were alone, or principally, in issue, the conduct of the South would not only be unreasonable, but unintelligible."[9]

The British, generally pro-Confederacy, were also disdainful as they read about America's heavy-handed suppression of the press. Writing in the *London Times*, the man Americans now derided as "Bull Run" Russell said: "There is no one in Congress, there is not in Senate, in House of Representatives, in pulpit, or stump, or in the forum, man who has a word to say in this year of grace 1862 against a war against the press compared with which there has been nothing known. . . . And the American people are very glad of it; leastways, they don't appear at all dissatisfied."[10]

With no apparent progress in the war effort, the public was becoming disenchanted with those who were running things. The press called Lincoln appointees either inefficient or corrupt—sometimes both. And most were considered "old fogeys." A *New York Tribune* cartoon showed Rip Van Winkle sleeping in the Washington Ordnance Bureau, guarded by two giants, Red Tape and Routine. When disturbed, he mutters, "Keep him out!—inventor!—new idea!—can't come in here!—Routine! Red Tape!"[11] In a like vein, Edward Everett, in the *Atlantic Monthly*, referred to "miscreants" who had "robbed the people directly or disguised their thefts under the euphonism of 'commissions.'"[12]

Lincoln did what he could to shore up public support, and he now had help from his new secretary of war, Edwin Stanton. On January 24, 1862, soon after he took office, Stanton wrote Greeley's managing editor, Charles Dana: "I know the task that is before us—I say *us*, because the *Tribune* has its mission as plainly as I have mine, and they tend to the same end. . . . This army has got to fight or run away; and while men are striving nobly in the West, the champagne and oysters on the Potomac must be stopped. But patience for a short while only is all I ask, if you and others like you will rally around me."[13]

Thanks in large part to the hawkish Dana, the *New York Tribune* usually supported the war effort. That wasn't true of Bennett's *New York Herald*, whose support of the war was lukewarm at best. That was all the more reason for Lincoln to be concerned when the secretary of the navy let several reporters accompany a ship down the Potomac, but refused a pass to a *Herald* reporter seeking to do the same. When this was brought to Lincoln's attention, he wrote Bennett an apologetic note in his own hand: "It was too late at night for me to see the Secretary, and I had to decline giving the permission, because he, the Secretary, might have a sufficient reason unknown to me." He then added, "I write this to assure you that the Administration will not discriminate against the *Herald*, especially while it sustains us so generously, and the cause of the country as ably as it has been doing." Writing that last smooth sentence, which ignored the *Herald's* frequent hostility, must have been hard—even for a canny politician.[14]

In seeking public support, Lincoln didn't ignore the influence of books. He once called Harriet Beecher Stowe, author of *Uncle Tom's Cabin*, "the little woman who wrote the book that made this great war."[15] He also wrote a letter thanking Mary Louise Booth for translating, from the French, *The Uprising of a Great People*, which in early 1862 was being distributed to hundreds of thousands of Americans. The author, Count Agenor de Gasparin, stressed slavery as the cause of the war and urged all civilized nations to support the North. In a closing page he wrote: "Ah! courage, Lincoln! the friends of freedom and America are with you. Courage! You have to resist your friends and to face your foes; it is the fate of all who seek to do good on earth. Courage! You will have need of it tomorrow, in a year, to the end; you will have need of it in peace and in war." Those were words Lincoln could appreciate.[16]

The public continued to grow restless, both with the war and with the *New York Herald*'s favorite general, George McClellan. There was a growing suspicion that too many Democrats, including McClellan, conservative on the slavery question, were directing the war. McClellan had three times as many men as his Confederate opponent, Joe Johnston, yet he still didn't act. In Lincoln's opinion, the general had "the slows."[17] Nevertheless, while urging action, he told the arrogant McClellan, "you must not fight until you are ready."[18]

In February some encouraging news came from the West, where a heretofore obscure general named Ulysses Grant captured Forts Henry and Donelson, Confederate strongpoints on the Tennessee and Cumberland Rivers. An elated press was finally able to report a Union victory. A *Chicago Tribune* reporter said the town "was on the rampage . . . was crazy with delight and insane with jubilation upon receipt of the glorious news from Ft. Donelson."[19] The *New York Herald* shouted: "Fort Donelson has surrendered! . . . Our army has captured fifteen thousand prisoners." In its editorial, the *Herald* called it "the most important victory yet achieved by the armies of the government," and predicted it would "probably prove to be the most disastrous defeat which the rebel cause has suffered."[20] The *New York Times*, not to be outdone, sang the praises of Grant, this new Union hero: "Certainly a more gallant and determined officer never led an invincible soldiery to victory and his prestige is second now to that of no General in our army."[21]

The press particularly liked Grant's note to Simon Bolivar Buckner, the Donelson commander, demanding "unconditional and immediate surrender." Moreover, the words "unconditional surrender," according perfectly with his initials, and composed, although unconsciously, with the skill of a public relations artist, caught the imagination of the entire country. One paper, for example, referred to "the signature, which he gives to all his official papers—thus, U. S. GRANT. The puzzle is with a great many, what is shadowed forth by U. S. One suggests that it means United States GRANT; another, that it represents Union Savior GRANT; while a third, deriving some countenance from his answer to Gen. Buckner, insists that the letters stand for Unconditional Surrender GRANT. This ought to be satisfactory, inasmuch as it has passed into history."[22]

The unassuming Grant took the newfound notoriety in stride. To him, far more pleasing was the news that Abraham Lincoln had promoted him to major general.

Perhaps emboldened by the Donelson victory, Lincoln resurrected a long-held favorite idea, that of freeing slaves by compensating their owners. On March 6, 1862, he sent Congress a proposal recommending "that the United States ought to cooperate with any state which may adopt gradual abolishment of slavery, giving to such state pecuniary aid, to be used by such state in its discretion to compensate for the inconveniences public and private produced by such change of system." The press discussed the proposal at length, and generally in favorable terms. One dissenter, however, was the New York Times, which thought the plan too expensive.[23]

On March 9 Lincoln wrote a rebuttal to the Times's editor, Henry Raymond, pointing out that the cost of eighty-seven days of the war would pay for all the slaves in Delaware, the District of Columbia, Kentucky, Maryland, and Missouri at $400 "per head."[24]

After the New York Tribune printed Lincoln's proposal in its entirety, Greeley said he had never printed a state paper with "more satisfaction." With a burst of enthusiasm, the volatile Greeley said, "we thank God that Abraham Lincoln is President of the United States, and the whole country, we cannot doubt, will be thankful that we have at such a time so wise a ruler."[25]

In a separate message, written to Speaker of the House Schuyler Colfax and relayed to Lincoln, Greeley assured the president that the Tribune would support him in his emancipation effort if he would advise its editor what to do. Lincoln replied directly to Greeley, expressing gratitude for the "generous sentiments" and saying, "Of course I am anxious to see the policy proposed in the late special message go forward, but you have advocated it from the first, so that I need to say little to you on the subject. If I were to suggest anything it would be that as the North is already for the measure, we should urge it persuasively, and not menacingly, upon the South."[26]

⋆⟶●⟵⋆

Although war in the East was at a standstill, major things kept happening out West. On April 5 Island Number 10, a Confederate strongpoint on the Mississippi, surrendered to Gen. John Pope. Then at Shiloh, in southwestern Tennessee, Ulysses Grant fought a fierce and bloody battle on April 6 and 7. After a setback on the first day, Grant, reinforced by the forces of Gen. Don Carlos Buell, counterattacked and drove the Confederates from the field. The *New York Herald*, after saying, "We have fought and won the hardest battle ever fought on this continent," added editorially, "The appetite for news has been satisfied today with the intelligence of the surrender of Island No. 10 and the splendid victory of General Buell and General Grant near Pittsburg Landing."[27]

Lincoln seized the moment by issuing a proclamation and sending copies to the press. "It has pleased Almighty God," Lincoln wrote, "to vouchsafe signal victories to the land and naval forces engaged in suppressing an internal rebellion, and at the same time to avert from our country the dangers of foreign intervention and invasion." He went on to ask the people, in their accustomed places of public worship, to "render thanks to our Heavenly Father for these inestimable blessings."[28]

Editors had first painted Shiloh as a glorious victory. Then, as their papers began printing the staggering casualty lists, they decided there must have been serious blunders. The *Chicago Times*, among others, said the Army had been completely surprised. So did the *Chicago Tribune*, which described an attack while men were at breakfast and told of refugees at Pittsburg Landing who "utterly refused to fight."[29]

The press was soon ganging up on Grant. Even Greeley, who shortly before had been praising him effusively, now wrote, "There was no more preparation by General Grant for an attack than if he had been on a Fourth of July frolic."[30] Finally, the *New York Herald* was moved to say, "There is no mistaking the universality of the sentiment that General

Grant was accountable for the reverse of Sunday . . . a word in his defense is scarcely to be heard in any quarter. . . . If he be not amenable to the charges . . . he is the best abused man in the country."[31]

With Grant under fire, a group of prominent Republicans met and decided, both for Lincoln's sake and the good of the party, that Grant had to go. Not surprisingly, they chose an editor, A. K. McClure of the *Philadelphia Times*, to act as their spokesman. Late one night, McClure came to the White House, where he told Lincoln that the "tide of popular sentiment" was against Grant. It was the "almost universal conviction of the President's friends," McClure said, that Grant must be relieved. After a long silence, Lincoln gave his measured reply: "I can't spare this man—he fights!"[32]

To maintain popular support, Lincoln had more than the press to contend with; there were also many nervous politicians and financiers. If the war were to be won, it was becoming clear that more men and more money would be needed. That April they approached Secretary Seward, demanding to know the president's plans for pursuing the war. Lincoln wrote a letter that Seward could use to respond to such queries, generally outlining his military plans, then offering what sounded like a solemn vow: "I expect to maintain this contest until successful, or till I die, or am conquered, or my term expires, or Congress or the country forsake me." Then, showing his awareness of the public mood, he said he would appeal to the country at once for new forces "were it not that I fear a general panic and stampede would follow, so hard it is to have a thing understood as it really is."[33]

Another emancipation crisis arose in May, when Union Gen. David Hunter, responsible for coastal parts of South Carolina, Georgia, and Florida, issued an order freeing slaves who had come under his control. William Cullen Bryant's *Evening Post* praised Hunter's action, but it was condemned by moderate journals such as the *Philadelphia North American*, the *New York Times*, and the *Boston Morning Journal*. Lincoln, although he was not angry with Hunter, promptly annulled the order. However, he used the situation to urge border states to accept his idea of compensated emancipation: "This proposal," he wrote, "makes common cause for a common object, casting no reproaches upon any. . . . Will you not embrace it? So much good has not been done, by one effort, in all past time, as in the providence of God, it is now your high privilege to do. May the vast future not have to lament that you have neglected it." Nevertheless, although both houses of Congress had passed the proposal, no state acted upon it.[34]

In March McClellan had begun his long-awaited offensive. His plan was to secure a base of operations on the Virginia Peninsula at Fort Monroe, then to advance along the Yorktown-Williamsburg Road to Richmond. Lincoln, relieved that McClellan was finally moving, supported him fully, only stipulating that a sufficient force be left behind to protect Washington. Stonewall Jackson had been waging a vigorous campaign in the Shenandoah Valley, with the potential of threatening the Northern capital. It was Lincoln's belief, shared by many, that were Washington to be captured, England would move to recognize the Confederacy, and the war would be lost.

Moving the Army of the Potomac to the Peninsula required a massive logistical effort, and McClellan handled it well. By early April he was on the Peninsula with an army many times greater than that of the Confederates opposing him. Once the advance started, however, the ever-cautious McClellan moved too slowly. Rather than attacking vigorously, he became bogged down at Yorktown for a full month, giving Confederates a free gift of the time they needed to bring up more troops. In a series of messages, McClellan pleaded for more men, including those troops guarding Washington. Lincoln's crisp reply showed he was losing patience: "You now have over one hundred thousand troops with you independent of General Wool's command. I think you better break the enemies' line from Yorktown to Warwick River at once. They will probably use time, as advantageously as you can. A. Lincoln."[35]

McClellan plodded ahead, and the Confederates withdrew slowly and stubbornly until they were close to the gates of Richmond. The campaign came to a climax the last week in June, with a series of bitter, inconclusive battles known to history as the "Seven Days." At one point, a jubilant McClellan had wired Washington: "Victory of to-day complete and against great odds. I almost begin to think we are invincible."[36] Hours later, however, he ordered a withdrawal and sent a paranoid message that, in the words of one author, gave "compelling and damning evidence of how unfit for *any* command the Young Napoleon was."[37]

McClellan's message concluded, "I have lost this battle because my owns force was too small. I again repeat that I am not responsible for this. . . . In addition to what I have already said, I only wish to say to the President that I think he is wrong in regarding me as ungenerous when I said that my force was too weak. I merely intimated a truth which to-day has been too plainly proved. . . . As it is, the Government must not and cannot hold me responsible for the result. . . . I have seen too many dead and wounded comrades to feel otherwise than that the Government has not sustained this army. If you do not do so now the game is lost. If I save this army now, I tell you plainly that I owe no thanks to you or to any other persons in Washington. You have done your best to sacrifice this army." Fortunately for McClellan, who might otherwise have been charged with treason, a quick-witted censor in Washington deleted those last two sentences.[38]

Lincoln, acting as his own general in chief, wired McClellan: "Save your army at all costs. Will send re-inforcements as fast as we can. . . . If you have had a drawn battle or a repulse it is the price we pay for the enemy not being in Washington."[39] The Army of the Potomac withdrew to Harrison's Landing, admitting in effect that the campaign had been a failure. One soldier, probably speaking for many, said he didn't know whether "we have made an inglorious skedaddle or a brilliant retreat."[40] Meanwhile, Richmond was saved, and the South's Army of Northern Virginia, now led by Robert E. Lee, breathed a sigh of relief. The Confederacy's secretary of the navy, Stephen Mallory, wrote his wife that the Seven Days made up "a series of the grandest Battles that was ever fought on the American continent," and exulted that "the great McClellan the young Napoleon now like a whipped cur lies on the banks of the James River crouched under his Gun Boats."[41]

Toward the end of June, Lincoln visited the aged Winfield Scott at West Point. Rumors started circulating—was he asking Scott to recommend a replacement for McClellan? On his way back to Washington, Lincoln told a crowd in Jersey City: "I can only say that my visit to West

Point did not have the importance which has been attached to it, but it concerned matters that you understand quite as well as if I were to tell you all about them. Now, I can only remark that it had nothing whatsoever to do with making or unmaking any general in the country." Then he added, with mock seriousness: "The Secretary of War, you know, holds a pretty tight rein on the press, so that they shall not tell more than they ought to; and I'm afraid that if I blab too much, he might draw a tight rein on me."[42]

Lincoln had been gaining in military know-how, but he'd had enough of being his own general in chief. On July 11, at Lincoln's request, Stanton summoned to Washington Henry Wager Halleck, a man known throughout the army as "Old Brains": "The President has this day made the following order, which I hasten to communicate to you: Ordered: That Major General Henry W. Halleck be assigned to command the whole land forces of the United States, as general-in-chief, and that he repair to this capital as soon as he can with safety to the positions and operations within the department under his charge."[43]

McClellan was irritated that he'd not been told of the move in advance. Moreover, he said it grated on him to serve under the authority of a man "whom I know to be my inferior."[44] Although in many ways Halleck would prove a disappointment, his coming east had a happy by-product, for it left Ulysses S. Grant as the senior man in the Western Department. While Lincoln didn't realize it at the time, Grant's elevation would have fortunate and far-reaching effects.

A few months earlier, fearing an adverse reaction from the press and public, Lincoln had been reluctant to call on the states for masses of troops. Now, with the Peninsular Campaign seemingly lost, it was time to jar the country into action. Lincoln had a knack for sensing the public mood, and unlike later-day politicians, he needed no opinion polls to reach a decision. When a call went out for 300,000 volunteers, the reaction was positive—at least from those who believed in the war effort. The War Department fixed state quotas according to population, and the public responded; its sentiment was reflected in John S. Gibbons's stirring verse, published in Bryant's *Evening Post:* "We are coming, Father Abraham, three hundred thousand more!"[45]

It was decided to unite McClellan's Army of the Potomac with the army of John Pope, now holding a line in northern Virginia along the Rappahannock. However, McClellan protested vigorously when he received the order recalling him from the Peninsula. He wired Halleck: "Our true policy is to reinforce [this] army by every available means and throw it again upon Richmond. Should it be determined to withdraw it, I shall look upon our cause as lost." All along, McClellan had been claiming he was opposed by 200,000 Confederates, whereas the true number was closer to 85,000. Lincoln may have suspected something of the kind, for when he heard McClellan's reaction to the withdrawal order, he told Halleck that if by some magic he could reinforce McClellan with 100,000 troops, he'd be delighted and would promise to capture Richmond tomorrow. But the next day he'd say the enemy had 400,000, and he couldn't advance until he got *another* 100,000 men![46] The withdrawal order stood, and all available vessels were dispatched to bring the Army of the Potomac back from the Peninsula.

And so it went, that fateful summer of 1862. As young men in blue and gray fought and bled on the fields of battle, there was another struggle going on. This one was in the soul of Abraham Lincoln as he wondered how best to cope with the crucial issue of slavery. Only a few recognized Lincoln's dilemma and appreciated the way he was handling it. One of these, a *Harper's Weekly* editor, said, "In the President of the United States Providence has vouchsafed a leader whose moral perceptions are blinded neither by sophistry nor enthusiasm—who knows that permanent results must grow, and can not be prematurely seized—a man who, whatever he has not, has that inestimable common sense which is the last best gift of Heaven to all who are clothed with great authority."[47]

Not many were so understanding. Two antislavery Unitarian ministers came to the White House one morning to tell Lincoln that merely saving the Union wasn't good enough. They asked if Lincoln thought the American people would be satisfied, if at the end of the war, the Union survived with slavery still in it. "Yes," Lincoln said, "if they were to see that slavery was on the downhill." But, they said, that's what the Founding Fathers had thought when *they* compromised on slavery. And that had brought on the war. That might be so, Lincoln said. He pointed out, however, that the good ministers, feeling so strongly about slavery, naturally met a good many people who agreed with them. He, however, met an equal number who cared little for the negro and wanted only to win the war. Nevertheless, he thanked them for their views and promised that "When the hour comes for dealing with slavery, I trust I will be willing to do my duty though it cost my life. And gentlemen, lives will be lost."[48]

Lincoln told a caller about three powerful congressmen, Charles Sumner, Henry Wilson, and Thaddeus Stevens, who relentlessly put pressure on him to issue an emancipation proclamation, "They are coming and urging me, sometimes alone, sometimes in couples, sometimes all three together, but *constantly* pressing me." Sumner, this time acting alone, had come to the White House on July 4, urging Lincoln to "reconsecrate" the day by a decree of emancipation. Lincoln replied that that would be "too big a lick." It might also send three more states—Kentucky, Maryland, and Missouri—into the Confederacy.[49]

On another occasion, a Quaker woman came to the White House requesting an audience. After Lincoln told his secretary, "I will hear the Friend," she told him she'd been sent by the Lord to inform him that he was the minister appointed to do the work of abolishing slavery. Then she fell silent. "Has the Friend finished?" Lincoln asked. She said she had, and Lincoln replied: "I have neither the time nor disposition to enter into discussion with the Friend, and end this occasion by suggesting for her consideration the question whether, if it be true that the Lord has appointed me to do the work she has indicated, it is not probable he would have communicated knowledge of the fact to me as well as to her?"[50]

If he issued an emancipation proclamation, there was also a question of practicality. Why publish an order one can't enforce? Lincoln told a group of Chicago ministers that he didn't want to issue a directive that the whole world would consider pointless. "Would just my word free the slaves, when I cannot even enforce the Constitution in the rebel states?"[51]

Regardless of what Lincoln said or thought, the pressure wasn't going away. Day by day, it was wearing him down, and often it showed. The poet Walt Whitman, seeing the president as he traveled to a favorite spot of tranquillity, the Soldiers' Home, noted the sad, weary expression on a face that grew increasingly lined. Once, when the pressure got too much,

Lincoln spoke harshly to a wounded officer who'd come to the White House. The officer's wife, it seemed, had come south by boat to care for her husband, but tragically there had been an accident and the woman had drowned. The officer sought permission to take her home for burial, and Lincoln abruptly refused, saying the man should have petitioned the War Department, rather than bothering an overworked president. Chastened, the man returned to his hotel room. Late that evening, there was a knock on the hotel room door. It was Lincoln, coming in person to apologize for his rudeness and to grant the officer's request.

Joseph Medill, who'd acted as the president's campaign manager, and whose political instincts were as good as any man's, told Lincoln that in effect he'd painted himself into a corner with that early "House Divided" speech. He'd told not only his Republican supporters, but actually the whole country, that slavery eventually had to go. Why did he ever put that on the record? "Well," Lincoln said, "after you fellows had got me into that mess and began tempting me with offers of the presidency, I began to think, and I made up my mind that the next president of the United States would need to have a stronger antislavery platform than mine. So I concluded to say something." In other words, he had come up with something dramatic to separate himself from the other candidates. Then realizing what he'd just said in an unguarded moment, Lincoln asked Medill not to quote that directly, since it could be interpreted as his having taken that position solely on a basis of practical politics.[52]

To escape the constant stream of White House callers, Lincoln often went to the War Department telegraph office to read the latest bulletins from the front. Like the Soldiers' Home, it had become a favorite place of refuge. The telegraph operators also saw him, from time to time, scribbling away at something, writing and rewriting. They didn't realize that history was being made. Abraham Lincoln was putting together the country's most important document since the Declaration of Independence.

On July 22 Lincoln called a cabinet meeting. Once the group had assembled, he showed them a draft he'd prepared of an emancipation proclamation. He had resolved to take such a step, he said, and this meeting wasn't for the purpose of asking the group whether or not to do so. Instead, he merely wanted to lay the subject matter of a proclamation before them. After they had heard it read, of course, suggestions would be in order. Their reactions were varied. Treasury Secretary Salmon P. Chase, a strong Abolitionist, said he thought the proclamation should be made stronger. Postmaster General Montgomery Blair, always the politician, said he hoped Lincoln realized that a document like this could cost the Republicans the fall elections. These were points of view that Lincoln had already considered. Only Secretary of State William Seward, after referring to McClellan's setbacks in Virginia, brought up a new point. It was a good one. "While I approve the measure," Seward said, "I suggest, sir, that you postpone its issue until you can give it to the country supported by military success, instead of issuing it, as would be the case now, upon the greatest disasters of the war."[53]

Eight days later, the *Press* of Philadelphia, in an editorial by John Forney, came out with a declaration for a policy of national emancipation. Insiders recognized it as a Lincoln trial balloon. Forney was known to be not only a Lincoln confidant, but also a White House voice. People suspected that Forney would not have published such a declaration without Lincoln's blessing.[54]

CHAPTER 6

⊸⟫◉⟪⊶

"I WOULD SAVE THE UNION"

For many weeks, letters complaining about Lincoln's inactivity had been pouring into the offices of the *New York Tribune*. Sidney Gay, who had replaced Charles Dana as the *Tribune's* managing editor, became convinced that the president had lost touch with the public. On July 30, the day of Lincoln's "trial balloon," Gay addressed a letter to the White House:

> Sir—
>
> I take the liberty of sending you herewith a communication intended by the writer for publication in the *Tribune*. . . .
>
> I am receiving daily many similar letters from all parts of the country for the paper, evincing a deep-seated anxiety on the part of the people. I do not publish them because I know they would exercise a most serious influence on the public mind.
>
> I cannot, however, justify it to myself that the public of the *Tribune* should at this moment be denied the privilege of being heard through its columns and the Government at the same time left in ignorance of that which so many thousands of people desire it should

hear. Taking a middle course, therefore, I send you one letter as a specimen of all the rest. . . .

The letter Gay enclosed said, "the President . . . hangs back, hesitates, and leaves the country to drift." Lincoln was impressed by Gay's frankness. He responded immediately, wiring Gay: "Please come and see me at once." He also suggested that Gay bring with him the man from Auburn, New York, who wrote the letter. Gay replied that a death in the family kept him from coming at once, but Lincoln didn't let it drop. Nine days later he wired: "When will you come?" On August 10 Gay arrived at the White House. The angry letter writer was not with him; having told Gay it would be "a waste of time and money."[1]

One suspects Lincoln would have been a master had there been press conferences such as we know today. In their absence, the meeting with Gay was the kind of face-to-face media contact that he enjoyed. To begin with, Lincoln was friendly by nature and liked exchanging views and stories. As a good politician, he also believed he could win people over by personal contact. That was often true when he met with reporters, although probably not as much as he believed. Many reporters, of course, basically agreed with his positions, so it was no problem to have them write what he wanted. Others, especially those working for cynical, frequently hostile editors like James Gordon Bennett and Henry Raymond, were seldom influenced by personal contact or cajolery, even when they appeared receptive on the surface.

Evidently the meeting with Gay went well, for not long afterward Lincoln told a White House caller, "I believe Mr. Gay is a truly good man, and a wise one." There had been a friendly give and take, with Gay pressing the argument for emancipation. Although Lincoln wasn't yet ready to show all his cards, a few days later he let a *Tribune* man send a message to Gay that "the President had an emancipation proclamation prepared three weeks ago and would have issued it, but for the opposition of Seward and Blair."[2]

Undoubtedly Gay shared all this with Greeley, but the impatient "Uncle Horace" still wasn't satisfied. He had been pleading with Lincoln for months to issue an emancipation order. Now, but a few days after

Lincoln's message to Gay, Greeley's plea turned into a demand. He wrote a shrill, lengthy editorial in the form of an open letter to Lincoln, calling it "The Prayer of Twenty Millions." It was composed, Greeley said, "only to set succinctly and unmistakably before you what we require, what we think we have a right to expect, and of what we complain." In column after column, he cited the nation's reasons for the *immediate* abolition of slavery.[3]

This was a direct, open challenge, and Lincoln decided to answer it publicly. A less astute man might have blurted out an angry response. Instead his reply, one of deliberate moderation, showed Lincoln's media skill at its best:

Executive Mansion
Washington, August 22, 1862

Hon. Horace Greeley

Dear Sir:

I have just read yours of the 19th, addressed to myself through the *New York Tribune*. If there be in it any statements or assumptions of fact which I may know to be erroneous, I do not, now and here, controvert them. If there be in it any inferences which I may believe to be falsely drawn, I do not, now and here, argue against them. If there be in it an impatient and dictatorial tone, I waive it in deference to an old friend whose heart I have always supposed to be right.

As to the policy I "seem to be pursuing" as you say, I have not meant to leave any one in doubt.

I would save the Union. I would save it in the shortest way under the Constitution. The sooner the national authority can be restored, the nearer the Union will be "the Union as it was." If there would be those who would not save the Union unless they could at the same time save slavery, I do not agree with them. If there would be those who would not save the Union unless at the same time destroy slavery, I do not agree with them. *My paramount object in this struggle is to save the Union, and is not either to save or to destroy slavery*. If I could save the Union without freeing any slave, I would do it; if I could save it by freeing all the slaves, I would do it; and if I could save it by freeing some and leaving others alone, I would also do that. What I do about slavery and the colored race, I do because I believe it helps to save the Union; and what I forbear, I forbear because I do not believe it would help to save the Union. I shall do less whenever I shall believe whatever I am doing hurt the cause and I shall do more when-ever I believe doing more will help the cause. I shall try to correct errors when shown to be errors, and I shall adopt new views as fast as they shall appear to be true views.

I have here stated my purpose according to my view of official duty, and I intend no modification of my oft-expressed personal wish that all men everywhere could be free.

Yours, A. Lincoln[4]

The *New York Times*, among others, approved of the way Lincoln had handled the situation. It also used the opportunity to take a slap at Gree-ley, calling his claim to represent twenty million readers a "bold assump-tion." Of Lincoln's reply, the *Times* said: "It is in infinitely better taste, too, than the rude epistle to which it is an answer. . . . The President not yet seeing the propriety of abdicating in behalf of our neighbor, consoles him with a letter that assures the country of abundant sanity in the White House." The *Times* continued with some interesting background data: "Several days ago the President read to a friend a rough draft of what appears this morning as a letter to Horace Greeley. He said that he had thought of getting before the public some such statement of his position on the slavery question in some manner and asked the opinion of his friend as to the propriety of such a course and the best way to do it. The appear-ance of Greeley's 'Prayer' gave him the opportunity."[5]

Horace Greeley probably thought his "Prayer of Twenty Millions" was putting the president on the spot. In truth, however, it gave him a welcome chance to use the media to his advantage. Greeley soon recognized that he'd been outmaneuvered. He told an associate, "Lincoln added insult to injury by answering my 'Prayer of Twenty Millions,' which asked only for the honest enforcement of an existing law, as if it had been a demand for the abolition of slavery; thus utterly using me to feel the public pulse, and making me appear as an officious meddler in affairs that properly belong to the government. No, I can't trust your 'Honest Old Abe.' He is much too smart for me." Three years later, in fact, Greeley expressed the belief that Lincoln had his statement ready written, and seized the opportunity to promulgate it.[6] Whether or not that was true, Lincoln, with carefully crafted phrases, had taken both the North and the South into his confidence. His thoughtful reply said he personally wished all men could be free, but in the interim he'd be willing to liberate some, all, or none of the people now held in slavery. His goal, in other words, was simply to save the Union, whatever it took.

Lincoln had made sure his response was well received, and given a proper forum. Rather than first sending it to Greeley's abolitionist *New York Tribune*, he contacted James C. Welling, political editor of the *Washington National Intelligencer*, a paper that made no secret of its sympathy for the slavery system. Welling came to the White House and went over the letter with Lincoln, word for word. In a flattering gesture, Lincoln even eliminated one particular sentence when Welling suggested it. Lincoln as always was a master communicator, and when he released the letter for publication he insisted it be printed accurately, even stipulating which words he wanted italicized. It appeared on Saturday, August 23, 1862, at the top of the *Intelligencer's* editorial column, under the heading, "A Letter from the President." The editor added: "We suppose he [Greeley] had little idea that his communication, if ever reaching the eye of his distinguished correspondent, would receive from that correspondent the honor of a response. . . . We hope, however, that when Mr. Greeley has duly pondered the pithy sentences of the President's letter, he will be able to rejoin, if he proposes to continue the 'correspondence' in a spirit which shall be slightly less arrogant, dictatorial, and acrimonious."[7]

Lincoln's letter, which was soon printed in all major papers, was telling the world that the war was *not* about slavery. Abolitionists on all sides, however, convinced it *should* be, weren't at all satisfied with that kind of neutral position. They weren't bashful about saying so.

Maj. Gen. John Pope, the conqueror of Island Number 10, had been brought east to command the Army of Virginia. He was already known as one who tried to manipulate the press, and a *Tribune* reporter who'd known him in the West urged his colleagues to be wary of "Pope's lying."

Despite that, or perhaps because of it, *Tribune* reporter George Smalley recognized that here was a man who could be flattered into granting special favors. In August, Smalley wrote his managing editor: "Pope personally corrects! the dispatches—is very good natured, etc. but will have facts his own way." And again, "I have written this letter at Pope's request. . . . Pope was rather worried by the Times and World's attacks & asked me if I would send you for editorial use such points as he desired made."[8]

At the War Department, people were saying that Smalley's dispatches "betrayed an unusual intimacy with the General." That was too much for "Old Brains," the new general in chief. He fired off a wire to Pope saying: "You will immediately remove from your army all newspaper reporters and you will permit no telegrams to be sent over the telegraph lines out of your command except those sent by yourself. You will also suspend the transmission of any mail matter other than that of official communications. Halleck."[9]

Smalley sent a special messenger to Washington with the news. When he learned of this, an irate Halleck telegraphed Pope: "I think your staff is decidedly leaky. The substance of my telegrams to you is immediately telegraphed back here to the press. . . . Clean out such characters from your headquarters."[10]

It appears that Halleck had become an enthusiastic ally in Lincoln's "good cop/bad cop" strategy. While permitting Halleck and Stanton to be seen as the press's mortal enemies, Lincoln liked to portray himself as the press's friend. He once told a correspondent for the *Herald:* "You gentlemen of the press seem to be pretty much like soldiers, who have to go wherever sent, whatever may be the dangers or difficulties in the way. God forbid I should by any rudeness of speech or manner, make your duties any harder than they are. . . . If I am not afraid of you, it is because I feel you are trustworthy. . . . The press has no better friend than I am—no one who is more ready to acknowledge . . . its tremendous power for both good and evil."[11]

Lincoln's friendly attitude toward the press didn't sit well with some cabinet officers. Gideon Welles, for example, not realizing that Lincoln acted that way for a purpose, thought it a sign of weakness that "he permits the little newsmongers to come around him and be intimate."[12]

⤙═◉═⤚

In late August, John Pope's Army of Virginia fought what became the Second Battle of Bull Run. It turned into a severe Union defeat, and many blamed McClellan for not coming more rapidly to Pope's aid. To some, it appeared that McClellan, still sulking, actually *wanted* to see Pope beaten. Evidently Lincoln said as much to McClellan, who wrote in his report: "The President informed me that he had reason to believe that the Army of the Potomac was not cheerfully co-operating with and supporting General Pope. . . . I replied, substantially, that I was confident that he was misinformed; that I was sure, whatever estimate the Army of the Potomac might entertain of General Pope, that they would obey his orders, support him to the fullest extent, and do their whole duty."[13] Despite the "Young Napoleon's" protestations, senior cabinet members, notably Chase and Stanton, again urged Lincoln to sack the temperamental general. For the moment, Lincoln's hands were tied, for he saw no suitable candidate to take McClellan's place. Speaking to John Hay, Lincoln summed up the situation in a single sentence: "McClellan has acted badly in this matter, but we must use what tools we have."[14]

On September 17 McClellan met Lee's invading army at Antietam Creek in Maryland, near Sharpsburg. It became the bloodiest day yet, with more than 12,000 casualties on each side. In many ways it was a draw. Lee's army was so weakened by the battle, however, that he realized his invasion gamble had been a failure. Marylanders, rather than flocking to him, had basically remained on the sidelines. The handful of recruits gathered in Maryland did not even equal his desertions. Reluctantly, Lee gave the order to retreat; for the next few days, unmolested, his weary Army of Northern Virginia wound its way back across the Potomac.

Shortly after the battle, Lincoln wired McClellan: "God bless you, and all with you. Destroy the rebel army, if possible."[15] Much to Lincoln's disappointment, that was not to be. Although many Union officers believed a vigorous pursuit would have dealt a death blow to Lee's army,

McClellan seemed content with driving Lee out of Maryland and back to Virginia. One disgusted reporter wrote: "We were the conquerors, and yet our property—small arms and accoutrements by the hundred—was the only property thrown away to waste upon the field. . . . The enemy outwit us under our very noses." The cautious McClellan was still convinced the enemy outnumbered him. He continued to call for more troops, more supplies, more horses. Late the following month a frustrated Lincoln wired him: "I have just read your despatch about sore-tongued and fatigued horses. Will you pardon me for asking what the horses of your army have done since the battle of Antietam that fatigues anything?"[16]

Meanwhile, the Army was being plagued by problems with absenteeism and desertion. When a group of women came to the White House they commented on this, and one of them asked Lincoln: "Is not death the penalty for desertion?" Lincoln said that was so.

"And does it not lie with the President to enforce this penalty?" Again Lincoln said that was true.

"Why not enforce it then?" the lady asked.

The president's reply showed not only his compassionate nature, but also how attuned he was to the public's reaction: "Oh no, no! This cannot be done. It would be unmerciful, barbarous."

"But is it not more merciful to stop desertions, so that when a battle comes off it may be decisive, instead of being a drawn game, as you say Antietam was?"

"It might seem so. But if I should go to shooting men by scores for desertion, I should have such a hullabaloo about my ears as I have not heard yet, and I should deserve it. . . . People won't stand it and they ought not to stand it. No, we must change the condition of things some other way."[17]

⋆⟫◍⟪⋆

Although the Antietam battle had been inconclusive, Lincoln decided it gave him an opening. On September 22 he assembled his cabinet members, showed them the emancipation proclamation, and said: "I have thought all along that the time for acting on it might probably come. I think the time has come now. I wish it were a better time. I wish that we were in a better condition. The action of the army against the rebels has not been quite what I should have best liked. But they have been driven out of Maryland, and Pennsylvania is no longer in danger of invasion. When the rebel army was at Frederick, I determined as soon as it should be driven out of Maryland, to issue a proclamation of emancipation, such as I thought most likely to be useful. I said nothing to anyone; but I made the promise to myself and to my Maker. The rebel army is now driven out, and I am going to fulfill that promise."[18] Two days later, on September 24, the proclamation was published:

> I, Abraham Lincoln, President of the United States of America, and Commander-in-Chief of the Army and Navy thereof, do hereby proclaim and declare that hereafter, as heretofore, the war will be prosecuted for the object of practically restoring the constitutional relation between the United States and the people thereof, in which States that relation is, or may be, suspended or disturbed; and that, with this object, on the 1st day of January, 1863, all persons held as slaves within any State, or any designated part of a State, the people whereof shall then be in rebellion against the United States, shall be then, thenceforward, and for ever, free.[19]

The proclamation was limited in scope, saying that not until January 1 would it take effect, and only then would it be decided who it affected. This pleased some, displeased others, and the press reacted more or less along party lines. The conservative *New York Times* defended the policy on the grounds of political necessity; the *New York Herald* said Lincoln had given "a sop to the Abolitionists"; the *New York World* said Lincoln was "adrift on a current of radical fanaticism" and that the South, rather than being terrorized by the proclamation, "would now fight harder than ever." Horace Greeley's *New York Tribune*, quite understandably, greeted it with abolitionist applause: "God Bless Abraham Lincoln!"[20]

The *Chicago Tribune* perhaps came closest to viewing the proclamation as it is seen today. Joseph Medill's editorial said: "The President has set his hand and affixed the great seal to the grandest proclamation ever issued by man. He has declared after the first day of January next all the slaves in the then rebellious states shall be free. . . . From the date of this proclamation begins the history of the Republic, as our Fathers designed to have it—the home of freedom, the asylum of the oppressed, the seat of justice, the land of equal rights under the law, where each man, however humble, shall be entitled to life, liberty, and the pursuit of happiness."[21]

Abolitionists were quick to point out that the proclamation omitted the loyal or semiloyal slave states—Delaware, Maryland, Kentucky, and Missouri—plus the whole rebel state of Tennessee, as well as the Federally occupied portions of Virginia and Louisiana. However, Lincoln had made it clear that the proclamation was a military edict, prompted by expediency. Secretary of State Seward emphasized that fact, calling the proclamation "a just and proper military act," one which he believed would be approved by "all the good and wise men of all countries."[22]

In Lincoln's mind, it was an act of necessity, almost of desperation. Some months later he explained his reasoning: "Things had gone from bad to worse, until I felt we had reached the end of our rope on the plan we were pursuing; that we had about played our last card, and must change our tactics or lose the game. I now determined upon the adoption of the emancipation policy."[23]

Some said the proclamation could set off a slave revolt, an event that for generations had been the South's worst nightmare. On the eve of his election as governor of New York, the Democrat Horatio Seymour said he feared as much and called the proclamation an act of unparalleled atrocity. In contrast, the *North American Review* said if a revolt were to happen, then so be it: "It may be that the slaves thus armed will commit some atrocities. We shall regret it. But we repeat, this war has been forced upon us. We have sent to the field our bravest and our best. . . . We hesitate not to say, that it will be better, immeasurably better, that the rebellion should be crushed, even with the incidental consequences attendant on a servile insurrection, than that the hopes of the world in the capacity of mankind to maintain free institutions should expire with American liberty."[24]

Abroad, the *London Spectator* said the proclamation did Lincoln no credit: "The principle is not that a human being cannot justly own another, but that he cannot own him unless he is loyal to the United States." The *Manchester Guardian*, equally critical, said: "To the few surviving chiefs of that great anti-slavery struggle in England [1834], and the representatives of those who are gone, will have nothing to do with the hypocritical adoption of their cherished principles as a pretext in the last resort for further shedding of human blood." The *London Times*, for its part, called it "a very sad document," which the South would "answer with a hiss of scorn."[25]

When he wrote his response to Greeley, Lincoln had sought the support of the *National Intelligencer*. The paper's pro-slavery editors had praised that response, thinking it showed an unwillingness to tamper with slavery. The preliminary proclamation showed they were mistaken, and it was seen almost as a betrayal. They said they expected no good to come of it, and would be "happy to find that no harm has been done." From that time on, the *Intelligencer* was an avowed enemy of Lincoln.[26]

Nevertheless, Lincoln had set the ground rules—the proclamation was issued to save the Union. If people wanted to attack him about it, they would have to do it on that basis, not about its Constitutionality or morality, but on the question of winning the war. The Emancipation Proclamation, by freeing slaves only where the Federal power could not reach, had little *actual* effect at the time, and many Lincoln scholars have pointed out the irony—that coming generations would remember Lincoln not so much for being the Preserver of the Union, which he was, but as the Great Emancipator, which he was not. At least not yet. Nevertheless, by signing that immortal proclamation, Lincoln had issued slavery's death warrant.

⋯⟫═◉═⟪⋯

McClellan was still not moving. Messages from Halleck, urging him to go on the offensive, were having little effect. It was small wonder, for McClellan treated his superiors' ideas almost with contempt. He had called Lincoln's Emancipation Proclamation an "outrage," and he was already talking to the Democratic mayor of New York, Fernando Wood, about possibly running for president. Moreover, he considered Stanton and Halleck to be only stumbling blocks, and he tried his best to get rid of them. "An opportunity has presented itself," he wrote his wife Mary Ellen, "through the Governors of some of the states to enable me to take my stand—I have insisted that Stanton be removed & that Halleck shall give way to me as

Comdr in Chief. I will not serve under him—for he is an incompetent fool—in no way fit for the important place he holds."[27]

Wanting to judge the situation for himself, Lincoln decided to visit the Army of the Potomac. As he said later, "I went up to the field to try to get [McClellan] to move." The meeting was cordial enough, but inconclusive as far as results. McClellan, who always spoke of the Army of the Potomac as "my" army, once spoke of it to a member of his staff, saying, "We have grown together and fought together. We are wedded and should not be separated."[28] The army felt that way too, and Lincoln knew it. He suspected that removing Little Mac would cause an uproar in the Army of the Potomac, perhaps in the country as a whole. Who knew how it might affect the coming midterm elections? He'd already been advised that McClellan's inactivity would cost the Republicans votes in those elections. However, relieving him might be even worse. No, if he were to relieve McClellan, which was becoming increasingly likely, it would have to be *after* the elections.

One evening during his visit to the army, Lincoln called to an Illinois friend, O. B. Hatch, and asked him to walk with him. From a hilltop, they could see the neatly aligned tents of the mighty army, stretching almost to the horizon. Gesturing in their direction, Lincoln asked, "What is all this?"

Hatch, somewhat confused, said, "Why, Mr. Lincoln, this is the Army of the Potomac." Lincoln shook his head. "No, Hatch, no. This is General McClellan's bodyguard."[29]

Before returning to Washington, Lincoln reviewed the troops and later visited the hospital wards. Passing a house in which there were Confederate wounded, Lincoln asked to go in. He stood gazing for a few minutes, then said he would be pleased to take them by the hand if they had no objections. A correspondent quoted him as saying they were "enemies through uncontrollable circumstances." He bore them no malice, he said, and could take them by the hand with sympathy and good feeling. After a silence, the Confederates came forward and without words, took the hand of the president. Some were unable to walk or sit up. The president went among these, took some by the hand, and said they should have the best of care. In the words of a Baltimore correspondent who was present, Lincoln's

attention was drawn to a young Georgian—a fine, noble-looking youth—
stretched out on a humble cot. He was pale, emaciated, and anxious, far
from kindred and home, vibrating, as it were, between life and death.
Every stranger that entered was caught in his restless eyes, in hope of their
being some relative or friend. President Lincoln observed this youthful
soldier, approached and spoke, asking him if he suffered much pain. "I do,"
was the reply. "I have lost a leg, and feel I am sinking from exhaustion."

"Would you," asked Lincoln, "shake hands with me if I were to tell
you who I am?" The response was affirmative: "There should be no enemies in this place," remarked the young Georgian. Then said the distinguished visitor, "I am Abraham Lincoln, President of the United States."
The young sufferer raised his head, looking amazed, and freely extended
his hand, which Mr. Lincoln took and pressed tenderly for some time.
The correspondent wrote, "Beholders wept at the interview, most of the
Confederates, even, were moved to tears." The resulting newspaper story
was probably good for Lincoln's "image," but this was no public relations
ploy. It was, rather, the unrehearsed, instinctive act of a decent man, one
whose heart was torn every day by the nation's suffering, both North and
South.[30]

As the election approached, political oratory became heated. Many
complaints were lodged about McClellan's inactivity. For the Democrats,
civil liberties also became a main issue. Horatio Seymour wrote Manton
Marble of the *New York World* that they "must be made *the* issue." There
were widespread protests against the suspension of the writ of habeas corpus, arbitrary arrests, and interferences with the press. The Democrats had
a point, and the Republicans were vulnerable with respect to principles
that every true American revered. Lincoln understood this, of course, but
his main concern was for the nation's survival. As he later wrote, a limb
must often be amputated to save a life, but a life must never be given to
save a limb. "I felt that measures, however unconstitutional, might become
lawful by becoming indispensable to the preservation of the constitution
through the preservation of the nation."[31]

The 1862 elections, held in October and November, were by and
large a setback for the Republicans. The number of Democratic congressmen nearly doubled, going from forty-four to seventy-five. In five states

where two years earlier Lincoln had won the electoral vote, his party now lost. The *New York Times* said it showed a "want of confidence" in the president. The *New York Herald* put it differently, saying the Republican Party was "rebuked and repudiated," while the "original wise and patriotic policy of Lincoln is approved." The voters were serving notice, in other words, that they approved a war for the restoration of the Union, but not for "the bloody extermination of slavery."[32]

Two Republican congressmen came to the White House shortly after the election. William D. Kelley of Philadelphia had been reelected, which wasn't expected. He told Lincoln it was because he had clamored so loudly for McClellan to be replaced. Edward McPherson, of the Gettysburg district, supposedly a safe Republican seat, had been defeated. Lincoln asked what happened, and McPherson responded politely, saying the responsibility was his. At that Kelley interrupted: "Mr. President, my colleague is not treating you frankly; his friends hold you responsible for his defeat." Lincoln thanked Kelley for his forthrightness, then said, "Tell me frankly what cost us your district. If ever there was an occasion when a man should speak with perfect candor to another it is now, when I apply to you for information that may guide my course in grave national matters."

"Well, Mr. President," McPherson answered, "I will tell you frankly what our friends say. They charge the defeat to the general tardiness in military movements, which result, as they believe, from McClellan's unfitness for command. The enforcement of the draft occurred during the campaign, and of course our political enemies made a great deal of capital out of it; but in my judgment, not enough to change the complexion of the district."[33]

Lincoln nodded and thanked the men for their frank advice. However, it was advice he didn't need, for he'd already made up his mind. On November 5 an order went forth to McClellan's headquarters: "By direction of the President, it is ordered that Major-General McClellan be relieved from the command of the Army of the Potomac; and that Major-General Burnside take command of that army."[34]

CHAPTER 7

·◦▰◦═◦▰◦·

"A WORSE PLACE
THAN HELL"

After George McClellan was relieved, he wrote his wife, "They have made a great mistake—alas for my poor country—I know in my innermost heart she never had a truer servant."[1] He was being sincere, for despite his failings, and despite being a Democrat, he had prosecuted the war as best he saw fit. Many Republicans, however, suspected that Democrats did *not* give their support to the war, or if they did, that the support was only lukewarm. They also harbored a suspicion that Lincoln, for political expediency, had given too much authority to Democrats. The German immigrant, Carl Schurz, said as much in a letter to the president. The fall elections were "a most serious reproof to the Administration," Schurz wrote, "for placing the nation's armies in "the hands of its enemies," meaning Democrats. Ignoring the fact that he himself was a Republican "political" general, he wrote: "What Republican has ever had a fair chance in this war? . . . Let us be commanded by generals whose heart is in the war."

That was too much for Lincoln, who came right back at Schurz: "I have just received and read your letter of [November] 20th. The purport of it is that we lost the late elections and the Administration is failing because the war is unsuccessful, and that I must not flatter myself that I am not justly to blame for it. I certainly know that if the war fails, the Administration fails, and that I will be blamed for it, whether I deserve it or not. And I ought to be blamed if I could do better. You think I could do better; therefore you blame me already. I think I could not do better; therefore I blame you for blaming me."[2]

Republicans and Democrats were *both* needed to support the war, and Lincoln knew it. That applied whether they were in the military, the press, or the Congress. In the latter, a Democrat like Colonel William Ralls Morrison was particularly helpful. Morrison, a regimental commander, had been wounded at Fort Donelson. He had first intended to run for Congress after his wounds healed. When he changed his mind and returned to duty, the people had elected him nonetheless. He then submitted his resignation from the Army so that he could serve in Congress, but Ulysses Grant wrote on his resignation: "Resignation not accepted. Colonel Morrison is too good a soldier to spare." Lincoln, however, overruled Grant so as to bring to Washington a needed War Democrat with wound stripes. While Grant and others were waging a shooting war, Lincoln had his own battles to fight, one where adversaries might lurk in newspaper offices, the halls of Congress, or even the Army.[3]

Lincoln knew that McClellan's departure had rankled the Army of the Potomac, perhaps turning many of the soldiers in that force against the administration. To ease the situation, he called on John Forney, a frequent White House visitor who was as near to Lincoln as any man in journalism or politics. Forney, publisher of the *Philadelphia Press*, had for the last year also published the Washington *Sunday Morning Chronicle*. When McClellan was relieved, Lincoln urged Forney to convert his Washington paper into a daily. Soon 10,000 copies of the new *Daily Morning Chronicle* were going to the Army of the Potomac every day, filled with items favorable to the administration. The *Chronicle's* pages were also filled with Federal notices and advertising, giving evidence of ample government patronage.[4]

McClellan's replacement, Ambrose Burnside, was a good and honorable man but a mediocre general. However, Abraham Lincoln, not knowing this, had given him command of the Army of the Potomac. Before accepting that command, Burnside had three times refused it, arguing that he wasn't qualified to lead such a large force. McClellan agreed. Earlier he'd said: "I *ought* to rap Burnside, and probably will—yet I hate to do it. He is very slow and not fit to command a regiment." Later, when Burnside assumed command of the army, McClellan wrote his wife: "Poor Burn feels dreadfully—almost crazy. I am sorry for him."[5]

Unfortunately, Burnside was right when he said he wasn't qualified. At Fredericksburg, on December 13, 1862, he proved it. He knew McClellan had been removed for failing to take action, and come what may, he was determined to go on the offensive. One reporter, Richardson of the *New York Tribune*, sized up Burnside correctly. He wrote his editor: "I am very sure of one thing: Whenever he gets a positive order to Go; he will Go if it breaks his neck." It became an eerie prophecy.[6]

Burnside sent his army across the Rappahannock to seize Fredericksburg and assault Confederates on the overlooking Marye's Heights. Lee's men were well prepared, and even after it became obvious that their position along a sunken road was too strong, Burnside kept pouring men in. Gen. Joseph Hooker—the papers called him "Fighting Joe"—argued against continuing the attack, as did other senior commanders. The orders stood; Hooker's men went forward and were cut down unmercifully. Finally, "finding that I had lost as many men as my orders required me to lose," he suspended the attack. Hooker later said his soldiers "were put to do a work that no men could do." At day's end, the icy ground of Marye's Heights was littered with Union dead and wounded. That night many of the latter froze to death where they lay. Burnside would have renewed the attack the next day, but his senior commanders dissuaded him. The casualties were staggering, especially by contrast. The Federals had lost 12,653 men; Lee's casualties were only a third of that, about 4,200. One Ohio correspondent wrote: "It can hardly be in human nature for men to show more valor, or generals to manifest less judgment, than were perceptible on our side that day."[7]

After the battle, Henry Villard (now working for Greeley's *Tribune*) made his way to Washington, where he filed a story so gloomy and disheartening that his editors held it up until it was confirmed. Lincoln invited Villard to the White House, where he repeated his story about

Union blunders. Lincoln questioned him at length, and though he was careful not to appear to be criticizing anyone, it was clear he felt Villard was telling the truth.[8]

The following day, Burnside wrote a letter to Halleck assuming full responsibility for the outcome of the battle. The *New York Times* printed the letter and claimed it was written at the dictation of, or in connivance with, the government. The *Times* went on to blame Lincoln, Stanton, and Halleck for forcing Burnside to fight against his better judgment.[9] When the honorable Burnside read this, he told his staff he'd put a stop to that sort of thing at once. By God he'd send a statement to the Associated Press, making it clear that he alone was responsible for what had occurred. Officers friendly to Burnside cautioned him against acting too hastily. After all, they argued, it was not his place to undertake a defense of the government. Why not consult with Lincoln before issuing any such statement? They may have believed the president, while appreciating the gesture, would say it wasn't necessary. Lincoln told Burnside, however, that he was the first man he'd found who was willing to relieve the president of a particle of responsibility. He appreciated this, and he gave full approval to having the general issue such a statement.[10]

Burnside's honorable words contrasted sharply with those written earlier by McClellan. John Hay doubtless reflected Lincoln when he wrote: "There seems to be one General, at least, . . . who holds himself bound by the same principles of integrity in his intercourse with the government as in that with his friends and equals. I mean General Burnside. If the unfortunate occurrences at Fredericksburg have no other ray of light to relieve them, we may still congratulate ourselves that they have shown us a General who prefers justice to unfounded praise, and refuses to allow blame to rest upon the undeserving through his reticence."[11]

Nevertheless, Burnside's days were numbered. Even as he prepared to launch another operation, his subordinates were telling people in Washington, including the press, that the Army lacked confidence in Burnside and that any operation led by him was bound to fail. Burnside knew what was happening. He came to the White House, met with Lincoln, and hours later wrote a long, poignant letter to the president. "I am convinced," he wrote, "after mature deliberation, that the army ought to make another movement . . . but I am not sustained in this by a single grand division commander in my command. . . . Doubtless this difference of opinion between my general officers and myself results from a lack of confidence in me. In this case it is highly necessary that this army should be commanded by some other officer, to whom I will most cheerfully give way."[12]

Lincoln asked Gen. Halleck to visit the Army of the Potomac, evaluate Burnside's situation, and make a recommendation. "General Burnside wishes to cross the Rappahannock with his army, but his grand division commanders all opposed the movement. If in such a difficulty as this you do not help, you fail me precisely in the point for which I sought your assistance. . . . In a word, gather all the elements for forming a judgment of your own, and then tell General Burnside that you do approve or that you do not approve his plan. Your military skill is useless to me if you will not do this."[13]

The letter clearly shows Lincoln's frustration. He was a military amateur, asking an experienced professional to make a decision, to in effect tell him what he should do. Halleck, however, did not see decision making as part of his job description. On New Year's Day 1863, offended by Lincoln's letter, Halleck wrote Secretary Stanton that he was "led to believe that there is a very important difference of opinion in regard to my relations toward generals commanding armies in the field, and that I cannot perform the duties of my present office satisfactorily at the same time to the President and to myself. I therefore respectfully request that I may be relieved from further duties as General-in-Chief."[14]

In Halleck's mind, Lincoln was simply passing the buck, wanting political cover in case something went wrong. There may have been some truth to this; after all, the president had let Burnside accept full blame for the Fredericksburg debacle. Did he want Halleck to be the scapegoat if the *next* operation ended in failure? Whatever the case, Lincoln was within his rights in asking his senior military man to make a military decision.

Somewhat surprisingly, Lincoln refused to accept Halleck's resignation, even though he must have been tempted. Part of Burnside's letter, for example, had said Lincoln was not well served by Halleck and Stanton, and their loyalty to him was questionable. Earlier, McClellan had said much the same thing, and Lincoln was beginning to agree, at least where Halleck was concerned. Subsequently he described his general in chief as "little more . . . than a first-rate clerk."[15]

Despite his personal feelings, Lincoln was well aware that Henry Halleck's departure would be seen as yet another administration failure. The hostile press would have a field day, and in the last week of 1862, that was something Lincoln could ill afford. In the West, Grant's Vicksburg campaign seemed to be going nowhere. According to the New York Times, he remained "stuck in the mud of northern Mississippi, his army of no use to him or anybody else."[16] Meanwhile in Tennessee, one of the war's bloodiest battles was opening at Murfreesboro, along Stone's River, between the Union Army of Gen. William Rosecrans and Confederates under Braxton Bragg. On the first day, Rosecrans's men were driven back two miles, and Bragg wired Richmond, "God has given us a happy New Year." He was premature. There would follow two more days of fierce, inconclusive fighting, after which Bragg would withdraw. Union casualties were 12,906; the Confederates lost 11,739. People on both sides of the Mason-Dixon Line had reason to mourn.[17]

On January 1, 1863, the Emancipation Proclamation took effect, despite conflicting views about its advisability and earlier Washington rumors that it might be withdrawn. Lincoln's friend from Illinois, Senator Orville Browning, was reflecting the view of his constituents when he said it was "fraught with evil, and evil only." He believed the "useless and mischievous" document would serve "to unite and exasperate" the South, and to "divide and distract us in the North." Lincoln, however, was undeterred. After shaking hands for hours in the traditional New Year's reception, he went to his office, signed the edict, and told Secretary of State Seward, "I never in my life felt more certain that I was doing right."[18]

After newspapers published the proclamation, salutes of a hundred guns were fired in Pittsburgh, Buffalo, and Boston. Still, the sorrows of war overshadowed everything else, and the nation's joy was far from universal. And on a day when Lincoln deserved applause, his critics' voices were harsher than ever. The Democratic press, heartened by substantial gains in the fall elections, was quoting men like Ohio Congressman Clement L. Vallandigham, who told Republicans in the House, "Money you have expended without limit, and blood poured out like water. Defeat, debt, taxation, and sepulchers—these are your only trophies." *Harper's Weekly* said the "loyal North was filled with sickness, disgust and despair" over "unequivocal evidences of administration imbecility. . . . Matters are rapidly ripening for a military dictatorship." In many cases, criticism aimed at the president was both personal and abusive. Orestes Brownson, the prominent Boston author, said of Lincoln: "He is thickheaded; he is ignorant; he is tricky, somewhat astute, in a small way, and obstinate as a mule. . . . He is wrong-headed, the attorney not the lawyer, the petty politician not the statesman, and in my belief, ill-deserving of the sobriquet of Honest. I am out of all patience with him."[19]

"If there is a worse place than Hell, then I am in it," Lincoln moaned.[20] Nevertheless, the war had to go on, and his immediate problem was dealing with Ambrose Burnside and the faltering Army of the Potomac. On January 20 the men of that army listened to brave words from Burnside, who proclaimed, "The auspicious moment seems to have arrived to strike a great and mortal blow to the rebellion, and to gain that decisive victory which is due to the country." Then they broke camp and set out, a long, winding column of infantry, accompanied by scores of artillery pieces and a ponderous baggage train. Their plan was to cross the Rappahannock at Banks Ford, get behind Lee's left flank, and then move south to cut the Confederates' lines of supply and communications. The morning march started out well enough, but that afternoon it began to rain, a steady downpour that turned the roads into wallows of oozing mud. That night the rain continued, soaking men and equipment and making the roads even worse. Cannons and wagons became bogged down; ropes were attached and men (as many as 150 at a time) tried pulling them out. It was, in short, an unholy mess. "The roads were oceans of deep mire," one soldier wrote, "and the heavy rain had made the ground a vast mortar bed." Another recalled that "it was no longer a question of how to go forward, but how to get back." Finally accepting the inevitable, Burnside ordered a return to camp.[21]

Criticism from Hooker and others became louder and more public, completely shattering whatever confidence the army might still have in its commander. For Burnside, that was the last straw. He set off for

Washington to provide Lincoln the names of generals who had been undermining him. He put it in the form of an ultimatum; either they had to go, or he did. As much as he admired Burnside's integrity, Lincoln knew what he should do. On January 25 General Orders No. 20, Army of the Potomac, stated, by direction of the president of the United States, that Maj. Gen. A. E. Burnside, at his own request, was relieved from the command of the Army of the Potomac. Gen. Joe Hooker, who had helped bring about Burnside's downfall, was named to replace him.[22]

Plainly speaking, Hooker had a big mouth. He boasted of his own abilities and castigated others behind their backs, especially those in authority. Lincoln already knew of this, and not only from Burnside. A New York Times reporter, who had recently been with Hooker, told Lincoln what the general said about the administration's shortcomings and the country's need for a dictator. Lincoln did not act surprised. "That is all true," he said, "Hooker does talk badly."[23]

As he rewarded Hooker with this new command, Lincoln decided it was important to let Hooker know where he stood. He took pen in hand and composed a lengthy letter. He never wrote a better one:

I have placed you at the head of the Army of the Potomac. Of course I have done this upon what appear to me to be sufficient reasons and yet I think it best for you to know that there are some things in regard to which I am not quite satisfied with you. I believe you to be a brave and skillful soldier, which, of course, I like. I also believe you do not mix politics with your profession, in which you are right. You have confidence in yourself, which is a valuable, if not an indispensable, quality. You are ambitious, which, within reasonable bounds, does good rather than harm; but I think during Burnside's command of the army you took counsel of your ambition, and thwarted him as much as you could, in which you did a great wrong to the country and to a most meritorious and honorable brother officer.

I have heard, in such a way as to believe it, of your recently saying that both the Army and the Government, needed a dictator. Of course, it was not for this, but in spite of it, that I have given you the command. Only those generals who gain successes can set up dictators. What I now ask of you is military success, and I will risk the dictatorship.

The Government will support you to the utmost of its ability, which is neither more nor less than it has done and will do for all commanders. I much fear that the spirit which you have aided to infuse into the army of criticizing their commander and withholding confidence from him, will now turn upon you. I shall assist you as far as I can to put it down. Neither you nor Napoleon, if he were alive again, could get any good out of an army while such a spirit prevails in it.

And now beware of rashness. Beware of rashness, but with energy and sleepless vigilance go forward and give us victories.

Yours, very truly,

A. LINCOLN

Hooker's appointment made for a tricky situation, especially where the press was concerned. Reporters belonged to a gossipy clique, and if one man knew of Hooker's disloyalty to Burnside, then they all did. Would they think Lincoln approved of such actions? Or at least overlooked them? Lincoln wanted the press to understand his reasoning, and he decided to take them into his confidence. He showed the Hooker letter to Noah Brooks, a jovial Maine reporter with whom he was on close personal terms. The two had met in Illinois many years before the war, and recently Brooks had come east from California to represent the *Sacramento Union*. Since then, the trusted Brooks had been a frequent caller at the White House and had often accompanied Lincoln on trips to the front.

During the first week of April, Brooks was along when Lincoln visited Hooker and the Army of the Potomac. One night, when no one else was present, Hooker said to Brooks, "The President tells me that you know all about the letter he wrote to me when he put me in command of this army." Brooks said that was correct. Nevertheless, Hooker thought Brooks might like to hear it again. Pulling the letter from his pocket, Hooker began to read. After replacing the letter in his pocket, Hooker said, "That is just such a letter as a father might write to his son. It is a beautiful letter, and, although I think he was harder on me than I deserved, I will say that I love the man who wrote it."[24]

⊶⊜⊷

Lincoln continued to worry about public sentiment, not just at home, but also abroad. The English government was generally favorable to the Confederacy for a variety of reasons. Perhaps foremost was the economic damage to English textile mills through the cutting off of their basic raw material, Southern cotton. Knowing all this, Lincoln did what he could to win approval from the English public. Going over the heads of government, Lincoln wrote letters addressed directly "To the working-men of Manchester" and "To the working-men of London." Earlier he'd received gratifying messages of support from these people, letters that condemned the institution of Southern slavery. Now Lincoln wrote to thank them: "I know and deeply deplore the sufferings which the working-men at Manchester, and in all Europe, are called to endure in this crisis. . . . Under the circumstances, I cannot but regard your decisive utterances upon the question as an instance of sublime Christian heroism which has not been surpassed in any age or any country."[25] That was laying it on pretty thick; nevertheless, it was a master stroke. After these words appeared in the English press, Lord Palmerston and his ministers knew they'd have a hard time generating public support for the Confederacy.

In the last days of April, Hooker sent the main body of his army northwest to cross the Rappahannock and Rapidan rivers far upstream, while General Sedgwick, with 20,000 men, demonstrated on Lee's front, near Fredericksburg. The complicated maneuver was well executed, and Hooker believed he had Lee in a trap. For a change, the army was feeling good about itself, and an enthusiastic *Tribune* reporter sent a dispatch that described an army "bouyant with hope and overflowing with ecstasy." The over-confident Hooker boasted to his troops that, "the enemy must either ingloriously fly, or come out from behind his defenses and give battle on our own ground, where certain destruction awaits him."[26]

"Fighting Joe" was being premature, to say the least. Lee refused to behave as Hooker expected, and he surely had no intention of "ingloriously flying." Discovering the danger, Lee wheeled about, confronted

Hooker with a portion of his force, and gave the remainder to the trusty Stonewall Jackson. After a dramatic, daring march along back roads, Jackson suddenly appeared on Hooker's right flank. The attack, which cost Jackson his life, was a brilliant success, and so crippled Hooker that he was never able to regain the initiative. Although he still greatly outnumbered Lee, "Fighting Joe" gave the order to fall back across the Rappahannock. It was yet another "skedaddle" for the Army of the Potomac.

In Washington, Lincoln waited anxiously for news of the battle. Secretary Welles came to the White House on May 4, and wrote of Lincoln, "He said he had a feverish anxiety to get facts, was constantly up and down, for nothing reliable came from the front." That evening the prominent George Templeton Strong wrote in his diary that "We have had about two hundred and fifty rumors good and bad, all of them 'authentic.'" Another diarist wrote, "It would seem that Hooker has beaten Lee, and Lee has beaten Hooker; . . . that Hooker has cut off Lee's retreat, and Lee cut off Sedgwick's retreat, and Sedgwick has cut off everybody's retreat generally, but has retreated himself although his retreat was cut off. . . . In short, all is utter confusion."[27]

It *had* been a confusing affair, much of it fought in tangled underbrush in a region known as "The Wilderness." Reporters had been hard-pressed to make much sense of the battle, and for days Lincoln didn't know if it had been a Union victory, a defeat, or another draw, like Antietam. When the true story became known, it appeared that Hooker, at the crucial moment, had simply lost his nerve. For those who knew him best, it was not unexpected. "He could play the best game of poker I ever saw," said a cavalry officer, "until it came to the point when he should go a thousand better, and then he would flunk."[28]

On May 5 reporter Noah Brooks came to the White House, where he found the president "anxious and harassed beyond any power of description" and, despite having no positive information, certain in his own mind that "Hooker had been licked."

An hour later, Brooks said, he was in an adjacent room when "the door opened and Lincoln came into the room. He held a telegram in his hand, and as he closed the door and came toward us I mechanically noticed that his face, usually sallow, was ashen in hue. . . . He gave me the telegram, and

in a voice trembling with emotion, said, 'Read it—news from the army.'"
Then, Brooks recalled, "Clasping his hands behind his back, he walked
up and down the room, saying, 'My God! My God! What will the country
say! What will the country say!'"[29]

A cynic might have wondered about that first reaction of Lincoln's. It
wasn't an expression of shock about the military defeat, nor a lamentation
for the Chancellorsville casualties, but rather a concern for public opinion. Obviously he was worried about the military situation, and he was far
from callous about the expected casualty lists. However, he was a man
with a life-defining purpose—saving the Union. To do that, he needed
the Northern public to sustain him. If the people ever gave up on him, the
war would be lost, and the inseparable Union, the noble dream of the
Founding Fathers, would be but a memory.

The following month, Lincoln, accompanied by Halleck, visited the
Army of the Potomac. While he was there, he talked to one of Hooker's
generals, George Gordon Meade. They spoke of Chancellorsville, Meade
recalled, and Lincoln said that the result was, in his judgment, most unfortunate, that he did not blame anyone—he believed everyone had done all
in his power—and that the disaster was one that could not be helped. Nevertheless he thought its effect, both at home and abroad, would be "more
serious and injurious than any previous act of the war."[30] As in the past,
Lincoln realized that the public's *perception* of the war's progress was nearly
as important as actual events on the battlefield.

CHAPTER 8

"I'LL COPY THE SHORT ONE"

I n the early days of 1863, eastern reporters focused on the struggle between the Army of the Potomac and Robert E. Lee's Army
of Northern Virginia. In the West, however, correspondents with
Grant's army had *two* wars to cover, one against the rebels, the other
against the irascible redhead, William Tecumseh Sherman.

Lincoln's plate was already full; he didn't need a media conflict piled
onto everything else. Nevertheless, he soon had one on his hands, and
Sherman was at the bottom of it. Throughout his career, "Cump" Sherman never accepted the workings of a free press. Newsmen in general he
considered a nuisance, and he reserved a special hatred for those providing information of value to the enemy. "You fellows make the best paid
spies that can be bought," he once told a startled journalist. "Jeff Davis
owes more to you newspaper men than to his army."[1]

Sherman expressed similar thoughts in a letter to his wife: "So long
as our camps are full of newspaper spies revealing each move, exaggerating
our difficulties, success cannot be expected." In his camp, he wrote, were
"some half-dozen little whippersnappers who represent the press, but are

in fact spies, too lazy, idle, and cowardly to be soldiers."[2] Soon after the start of the Vicksburg campaign, Sherman issued an order letting reporters know where they stood: "Any person whatever . . . found making reports for publication which might reach the enemy, giving them information, aid and comfort, will be arrested and treated as spies."[3]

When Tom Knox, a reporter for the *New York Herald,* wrote an especially obnoxious story, Sherman ordered the man's arrest. He wrote a trusted colleague, Admiral David Porter: "I am going to have the correspondent of the N.Y. Herald tried by a court martial as a spy, not that I want the fellow shot, but because I want to establish the principle that such people cannot attend our armies, in violation of orders, and defy us, publishing their garbled statements and defaming officers who are doing their best."[4] The court found Knox guilty of disobeying Sherman's orders and ordered him evicted from army lines. Sherman probably thought the man was getting off too easy. Newsmen, however, believed the sentence was not only too harsh, but that it set a dangerous precedent.

In Washington, John Forney and others signed a petition asking that Knox be reinstated. On the evening of March 10, 1863, two New York reporters, Albert Richardson of the *Tribune* and James Winchell of the *Times,* presented the petition to Lincoln. The president, after listening patiently, said it appeared "our newspaper friend has been a little too severely dealt with." Assuring the reporters of his friendship, he said he was willing to intervene and would write something to that effect. His note reinstating Knox, however, said Knox could remain only "if Gen. Grant shall give his express consent."[5] As Lincoln probably expected, Grant left the matter up to Sherman, who told Knox, "Come with sword or musket in your hand . . . and I will welcome you as an associate; but come . . . as the representative of the press, which you yourself say makes no slight difference between truth and falsehood, and my answer is, Never." Sherman may have won his battle with Knox, but the press had won the war. Lincoln's desire to placate the media was obvious, and after this, Sherman gave up on trying to muzzle the press. Nevertheless, his opinions were unchanged, and he wrote Grant in disgust, "Mr. Lincoln, of course, fears to incur the enmity of the Herald, but he must rule the Herald or the Herald will rule him; he can take his choice."[6]

It wasn't as simple as Sherman thought, and it wasn't a question of "ruling" or "being ruled." As Lincoln well knew, to win the war he needed support from private citizens as well as soldiers. And for that citizen support, he needed the media. It was a constant struggle, and the unrelenting pressure was beginning to show. Reporter Noah Brooks saw Lincoln in church about this time and said he no longer resembled the "happy-faced Springfield lawyer" that Brooks remembered. "His hair is grizzled," Brooks wrote, "his gait more stooping, his countenance sallow, and there is a sunken, deathly look about the large, cavernous eyes, which is saddening to those who see there the marks of care and anxiety, such as no President of the United States has ever before known."[7]

Before long another media crisis arose, and this time it involved Ambrose Burnside. After being relieved as head of the Army of the Potomac, Burnside had been shunted off to Cincinnati to command the Department of the Ohio, basically the Middle West plus Kentucky. His area of responsibility was out of the war's mainstream, and there seemed little chance that Burnside could cause further problems for Lincoln. But he did.

In parts of the Midwest, people were speaking out openly against the war, even expressing support for the embattled Confederates. The loudest protestors, known as Copperheads, were led by Clement L. Vallandigham, a former congressman and one-time editor of the Dayton (Ohio) Western Empire. While still in Congress, the pro-slavery Vallandigham said he had a vision of the "gospel of peace" replacing "the gospel of abolition and hate."[8] And once out of Congress, he continued to rail against the war, leading protests that sympathized with the South and served to encourage army desertions. Several western newspapers joined him in proclaiming these antiwar sentiments, the most notorious being Wilbur Storey's Chicago Times. Storey printed items attributed to an anonymous "Washington correspondent" that claimed Lincoln was an "outrageous criminal" who would soon be impeached.[9]

The patriotic Burnside, just weeks away from the bloody sacrifices of the battlefield, saw such actions as not only disloyal, but treasonous. On April 13, 1863, he issued General Order No. 38, which read in part:

"Hereafter all persons found within our lines who commit acts for the benefit of the enemies of our country will be tried as spies or traitors, and if convicted will suffer death. . . . The habit of declaring sympathies for the enemy will no longer be tolerated in this department. Persons committing such offenses will be at once arrested, with a view to being tried as above stated or sent beyond our lines into the lines of their friends."[10]

Vallandigham said General Order 38 was a base usurpation of arbitrary power. On May 1, at Mount Vernon, Ohio, he challenged it openly. At a well-publicized mass meeting of Peace Democrats, many of whom were wearing Copperhead badges, Vallandigham said, among other things, that the "wicked and cruel war" was an attempt "to erect a Republican despotism on the ruins of slavery." Furthermore, he said, those who meekly submitted to the Conscription Act did not deserve to be called free men. That was enough for Burnside. In a burst of excessive zeal, he sent a company of soldiers to Vallandigham's Dayton home in the middle of the night. After rousting him out of bed, the soldiers placed him under arrest and took him directly to a Cincinnati jail.[11]

Vallandigham was tried promptly by a military commission and sentenced to imprisonment for the duration of the war. This caused an immediate uproar from all quarters. Protest meetings took place throughout the North, with one of the largest held in New York City's Union Square. At the capitol in Albany, New York Democrats passed a resolution that said: "We denounce the recent assumption of a military commander to seize and try a citizen of Ohio . . . for no other reason than words addressed to a public meeting, in criticism of the course of the Administration, and in condemnation of the military orders of that general"[12] Back in Ohio, William T. Logan, editor of the *Dayton Empire*, denounced the action in a scathing editorial. He too was arrested, and soon joined his hero Vallandigham in the Cincinnati prison.

It wasn't just Democratic journals crying out; many Republican papers were also criticizing the sentence. The *Louisville Journal* pointed out that these papers, including the prominent *New York Tribune* and *New York Evening Post*, didn't agree with Vallandigham's "peculiar views." What they resented was the implied threat to the right of free speech and print, plus the fact that a military rather than civilian court had tried Vallan-digham. The sentiment was shared, said the *Journal*, "by at least three-fourths of the Republican Party itself."[13]

The *Cincinnati Gazette*, while acknowledging the uproar, said, "Our eastern contemporaries, who have commented on this arrest as unneces-sary, do not appreciate the entire situation.[14] However, said the *Gazette*, "General anxiety has been expressed here lest the decision of the court-martial in Vallandigham's case should have the effect to make a martyr of him."[15]

Lincoln also knew the danger of turning Vallandigham into a hero, especially after the man cleverly urged the people of Ohio to help him defend the Constitution, the laws, the Union, and liberty. Vallandigham had demanded a civil trial, applying for a writ of habeus corpus. A federal judge, hearing the case, reminded the prisoner that the president, exercis-ing his wartime authority, had suspended that right. That was true; it was also publicity Lincoln didn't need. New York's Democratic governor, Hor-atio Seymour, declared that Vallandigham's arrest had "brought dishonor upon the country" and predicted that Lincoln's handling of the case would determine "whether this war is waged to put down rebellion at the South or destroy free institutions at the North."[16]

Lincoln was faced with a "damned if you do, damned if you don't" dilemma. As president, he was charged with protecting a man's Constitu-tional rights. As commander in chief, however, he was responsible for the actions of Burnside, his military subordinate. Upholding the sentence would please many loyal supporters, including most of the military, but it would turn Vallandigham into a martyr. Conversely, setting Vallandig-ham free would be met with howls of outrage. "All the Cabinet," Lincoln wired Burnside, "regretted the necessity of arresting . . . Vallandigham, some perhaps doubting there was a real necessity for it; but being done, all were for seeing you through with it."[17]

Lincoln's decision was worthy of Solomon. Commuting the sentence, he ordered the Copperhead Democrat sent not to prison, but south to the Confederacy, thus turning the posturing ex-congressman into a figure of mockery. Vallandigham was turned over to a rebel outpost, where he told the amused Confederates that he was "surrendering himself as a prisoner of war."[18]

Some, of course, thought Vallandigham shouldn't have received *any* punishment. Lincoln had a good answer for them, asking, "Must I shoot a simple-minded soldier boy who deserts, while I must not touch a hair of a wily agitator who induces him to desert?"[19]

So far, so good—then Burnside did it again. First he took on the antagonistic *New York World,* banning its circulation in his department. Then he targeted the *Chicago Times* and its vituperative editor, Wilbur Storey, a man who had denounced the Emancipation Proclamation as "the most wicked, atrocious and revolting deed recorded in the annals of civilization." On the night of June 2, Burnside sent a squad of soldiers to enter the *Chicago Times*'s offices and stop the paper's publication. Almost immediately the Illinois legislature called the seizure "so revolutionary and despotic" that it was "equivalent to the overthrow of our government."[20]

Lincoln had tried hard to be a friend to journalists. Now the entire press corps, Republican as well as Democrat, rose up against him. In New York, fifteen newspaper and magazine editors met and selected Horace Greeley as their chairman. Whatever they thought of Storey personally, and most of them could not stand the man, the group unanimously affirmed "the right of the press to criticize firmly and fearlessly the acts of those charged with the administration of the Government, also those of all their civil and military subordinates."[21]

Lincoln acted swiftly. In no uncertain terms, he had Stanton tell Burnside to get those soldiers out of that newspaper office. And get that editor Logan out of jail! Soon the *Chicago Times* was back in business and Wilbur Storey was proclaiming victory, telling his readers that "the right of free speech has not passed away . . . we have, then, still a free press."[22]

Once again, Lincoln had walked a public relations tightrope without losing his balance. A few Peace Democrats, egged on by Vallandigham, had somewhat naively convinced themselves that the Abolitionists were really the problem. If only the administration would cancel the Emancipation Proclamation and forget about freeing the slaves, then Southerners would return to the fold and peace would again reign over the land.

However, it had gone too far for that. Although some might dream that renouncing abolition would bring Southerners back into the Union, it was just that—only a dream. Confederates believed in their cause and by this time their desire for Southern independence was rock solid. Moreover, the Copperhead demonstrators had not established a peace party—it only looked like one. True, they feared the loss of civil liberties and suspected the war was permanently crushing American ideals. Nevertheless, they believed in the Union, and as long as victory seemed possible without losing those ideals, they were willing to keep on with the war until the other side gave in. It was up to Lincoln to convince them that they were on the right course. And for that, he needed the press. He also needed some cheerful news from the battlefronts.

Good news, however, was hard to come by that spring of 1863. More than once, Lincoln was heard to say, "In God's name! If anyone can do better in my place than I have done, or am endeavoring to do, let him try his hand at it, and no one will be better contented than myself." Lincoln was suffering a form of depression, and reporters sometimes reported his disposition as "kind of cheerful melancholy." At other times, he couldn't conceal the sadness, and they used expressions like "gloomy" or "low frame of mind." Late one evening Lincoln told an Associated Press reporter, "I can't sleep tonight without hearing something." The reporter walked with him as he headed for the War Department telegraph office. On the way, a messenger handed him a telegram, and he stopped under a street light to read it. "Bad news, bad news," he said slowly, then added, "Don't say anything about this—don't mention it."[23]

However, when the news was good that spring, Lincoln was eager to share it, particularly with a sympathetic organ like Forney's *Chronicle*. His feelings toward the *Chronicle* were well known, and writing to Stanton, he spoke of it as "my paper, as you jokingly call it." Nevertheless, Forney was disappointed when he looked for special White House favors. When he went to see Lincoln, Forney complained, "he just asks me what is the last good joke I have heard."[24]

All the same, when *Chronicle* reporter Joseph A. Ware called on Lincoln one evening, he was greeted heartily. "Here are two dispatches," Lincoln said, "one from Rawlins and one from Hurlbut. Don't stop to read them, but I'll copy the short one while you copy the long one, as you can write faster than I." The president and the reporter than sat down, working side by side, to transcribe the messages in time for the morning *Chronicle*.[25]

During that period, Lincoln was almost desperate in his thirst for news. There was the situation in Mississippi, for example. Did Grant know what he was doing? And did the general have a drinking problem? Significantly, Lincoln called on a member of the media to help answer those questions. He and Stanton sought the aid of a brilliant journalist, Charles Dana, former managing editor of Greeley's *Tribune*. They asked him to go to Grant's army, make daily reports on the military situation, and, in Stanton's words, "give such information as would enable Mr. Lincoln and himself to settle their minds as to Grant."[26]

"The ostensible function I shall give you," Stanton told Dana, "will be that of special commissioner of the War Department to investigate the pay service of the Western armies, but your real duty will be to report to me every day what you see." Soon Dana was with Grant, sending messages to Stanton that were passed on to the White House. Dana was assured that they were read with "deep interest."[27]

On most nights, Lincoln would walk from the White House to the War Department building at the corner of Pennsylvania Avenue and Seventeenth Street. Upon arriving, he would climb to the telegraph office on the second floor, greet the operators on duty, and take a seat at a large flat-topped desk. He would then go through yellow tissue copies of the latest telegrams received. The chattering telegraph key was his link to the Union armies, and he might linger by its side for hours. Sometimes he would spend the night in the room he called his other "office," especially if a battle was in progress.

The telegraph room was a place of refuge, offering temporary relief from the frantic hubbub of the White House. "I come here to escape my persecutors," he told one operator. The military dispatches, and now the messages from Dana, were obviously essential for Lincoln's keeping abreast of important happenings. The media also had their role to play, of course, but by now it was mostly a one-way street, administration informing the media, rather than the other way around. Lincoln read the New York papers when he could, particularly the *Herald* so as to learn what the opposition was saying. Mostly, however, according to his secretary John Hay, "excepting the Washington City dailies, in which he carefully reads the telegraphic dispatches, the President rarely ever looks at any papers, simply for want of leisure to do so."[28]

⟶⟹⟸⟵

A thorny question was bubbling to the surface about this time—the recruitment of black soldiers for combat regiments. It was not a new idea. Many friends of the administration, particularly Abolitionists, had consistently advocated such a step. Early in the war, however, when Northern blacks in several cities volunteered for the Union army, the War Department rejected them. Then, in December 1861, Lincoln had squelched Secretary of War Cameron's reference to arming slaves in occupied areas. And in the summer of 1862, the administration refused at first to accept the organization of black regiments in Kansas and occupied Louisiana. It was not that Lincoln didn't realize the military benefits to be gained. He was aware, though, that the slaveholding border states would be violently opposed to such a step. Arming blacks, moreover, would intensify the Democratic press's backlash against emancipation, and might well exacerbate racial tensions in the military.

Early in 1863, a bill passed the House, obviously referring to blacks, which authorized the president "to enroll, arm, equip, and receive into the land and naval service of the United States, such numbers of volunteers as he may deem useful to suppress the present rebellion." The Senate returned the House bill as unnecessary, because the president already had such power under previous acts. In effect, the ball was in Lincoln's court; the Senate wasn't going to take the blame if arming blacks proved to be too unpopular.[29]

By this time, however, the question was moot. Black regiments were already in existence and were beginning to make their mark. The colonel of one such regiment, Thomas Higginson, wrote a glowing report of his soldiers' performance during a raid on the South Carolina coast, saying, "Nobody knows anything about these men who has not seen them in battle. No officer in this regiment now doubts that the key to the successful prosecution of the war lies in the unlimited employment of black troops." His report, as intended, made its way into the newspapers. The *New York Tribune* applauded, saying such reports "were sure to shake our inveterate Saxon prejudice against the capacity and courage of negro troops."[30]

With much of the press on board, Lincoln knew the time had come to lend full support to the recruiting of black regiments. In March he wrote Andrew Johnson, military governor of Tennessee: "The bare sight of fifty thousand armed, and drilled black soldiers on the banks of the Mississippi, would end the rebellion at once. And who doubts that we can present that sight, if we but take hold in earnest?"[31]

+→══◯═══←+

Of all Lincoln's media relationships during the war, the most fascinating is the one between him and Horace Greeley. In years when he had the time, Lincoln had been a faithful reader of Greeley's *New York Tribune*. He admired the editor's journalistic talent and recognized him as a sincere crusader. At the same time, he knew him to be a little, well, "peculiar." A rival editor once said Greeley "sought notoriety by the strangeness of his theories and practices. . . . He lays claim to greatness by wandering through the streets with a hat double the size of his head, a coat after the fashion of Jacob's of old, with one leg of his pantaloons inside and the other outside of his boot, and his boots all bespattered with mud."[32] Those things might all be true, but Greeley was still the most prominent figure in American journalism, rivaled only by James Gordon Bennett, editor of the *New York Herald*.

For years the Greeley-Bennett rivalry had titillated the nation's readers. Not by chance, it had also boosted circulation for *both* their papers. Early in the war, when the colorful, aggressive *Herald* gained readers at the expense of the *Tribune*, a gloating Bennett "bemoaned" the *Tribune's* financial problems, and wrote with a mock sigh: "Alas for Greeley." Saying the *Herald* had not had Greeley's "sad trials in pecuniary matters," Bennett facetiously offered to "give him $1,000 to send him south, if he will only go."[33] Greeley's financial problems were short-lived, however. Circulation soared after the *Tribune* acquired a first-rate group of reporters to cover the war.

Maintaining rapport with both the Republican *Tribune* and the Democratic *Herald* was one of Lincoln's greatest challenges. In a way, he was following the advice he once gave General John Schofield in Missouri: "If both factions, or neither, shall abuse you, you will probably be about right. Beware of being assailed by one and praised by the other."[34]

The *Tribune's* coverage of Lincoln was generally favorable, although "Uncle Horace" never ceased his haranguing, cautioning, and "advising" of the president. Although the volatile Greeley blew hot and cold where Lincoln was concerned, he usually tried to be fair. Consequently he resented James Brooks, editor of the *New York Express*, when he accused Lincoln of deliberately prolonging the war. Brooks, a Democrat recently chosen to represent a portion of New York City in Congress, had written that "The Proclamation of January 1 put an end to all hope of peace from this Administration. . . . The War Administration has since been so conducted, as if purposely to strengthen the South and to weaken the North . . . weakening the ardent expectations of both Conservative Republicans as well of Democrats for the early restoration of the Union, upon the principle of compromise and concession."[35]

Greeley rose to Lincoln's defense, referring to Brooks's accusation as an "utter, inexcusable untruth." He said Lincoln's inaugural address, for example, "was one continuous, beseeching appeal for Peace—Peace." Never before, Greeley maintained, had an Executive of any nation so pleaded and entreated that the country be spared the horrors of civil war. "From that hour to the present," Greeley continued, "every Message, every utterance of President Lincoln has attested his anxiety for the earliest possible restoration of Peace."[36]

Nevertheless, whatever people thought of Lincoln personally, many were displeased with his conduct of the war. One evening a delegation of excited clergymen arrived at the White House to voice their concern. In responding to them, Lincoln referred to the famous tightrope walker, Blondin: "Gentlemen, suppose all the property you were worth was in gold, and you had put it in the hands of Blondin to carry across the Niagara River on a rope, would you shake the cable, or keep shouting out to him, 'Blondin, stand up a little straighter!—Blondin, stoop a little more—go a little faster—lean a little more to the north—lean a little more to the south'? No! You would hold your breath as well as your tongue, and keep your hands off until he was safe over. The Government is carrying an immense weight. Untold treasures are in their hands. They are doing the best they can. Don't badger them. Keep silence, and we'll get you safe across." An approving reporter made sure Lincoln's reply appeared in the press.[37]

For the moment, Horace Greeley had no problem with Lincoln. His main concern, rather, was for the long-range political outlook. With the way things were going, Lincoln might choose not to run again in 1864, and even *were* he to run, Greeley didn't think he could be reelected. "Uncle Horace," it must be remembered, was one of the founding fathers of the Republican Party, and like most nineteenth-century editors, his first love was politics. As mentioned earlier, a *Tribune* managing editor, James Russell Young, once said Greeley, not content to be a great journalist, also aimed "to be the leading politician in America."[38] Whether that was true or not, Greeley's political instincts were razor sharp. He knew the midterm elections of 1862 had been a disaster for Lincoln and the Republicans. Five key states, New York, Pennsylvania, Ohio, Indiana, and Illinois—ones Lincoln had carried in 1860—had sent a majority of Democrats to Congress just two years later. Moreover, many influential figures had given up on the president. In March of 1863, the popular writer Richard Henry Dana wrote Charles Francis Adams, Lincoln's ambassador to Great Britain: "As to the politics of Washington, the most striking thing is the absence of personal loyalty to the President. It does not exist. He has no admirers, no enthusiastic supporters, none to bet on his head. If a Republican convention were to be held tomorrow, he would not get the vote of a State."[39]

Meanwhile, the Democrats were waiting in the wings, ready to mount a 1864 presidential campaign with a peace platform. Their presumed candidate was none other than the "Young Napoleon," George McClellan. When he was relieved of command for a second time, McClellan had joined his wife, Ellen, at her home in New Jersey. In Trenton, he was welcomed as a hero home from the wars. According to the *New York Express*, "No such demonstration, political or otherwise, was ever before witnessed in Trenton."[40] The administration clearly had no plans to give him another field command; anything other than the Army of the Potomac would be viewed as a slap in the face. He could have been ordered to Washington, of course, perhaps to replace Halleck as general in chief. However, neither Lincoln nor Stanton wanted the discontented McClellan in Washington. Once in the capital, the egotistical McClellan would probably start criticizing the administration's handling of the war. When he did, eager reporters would be sure to seize on any juicy tidbits.

After a week in New Jersey, McClellan moved to New York City, the largest Democratic stronghold in the North. He took up residence in the Fifth Avenue Hotel, and on the day he arrived, a crowd gathered in front of the hotel, hoping to catch a glimpse of its favorite general. His appearance on the hotel balcony, said the *Herald*, "was the signal for an outburst of enthusiasm simply impossible to describe."[41]

Before long, McClellan was being wooed by New York's leading Democrats, including the governor, Horatio Seymour; August Belmont, the party's national chairman; and big money men like John Jacob Astor. Significantly, he was also becoming close to two leading Democratic editors, Manton Marble of the *New York World* and William C. Prine of the *New York Journal of Commerce*.[42]

Nearby, from his cluttered third-story office in the *Tribune* building, Horace Greeley watched these developments with growing concern. The Peace Democrats evidently were grooming their candidate for a presidential run in 1864. Were he to be elected, he'd undoubtedly work out some compromise with the South. That might bring Southern states back into the Union, but only by accepting their right to hold slaves. Alternatively, it might result in an acceptance of Southern independence. In either case, it would mean the war's sacrifices had been in vain, and Greeley's dream of full emancipation would have been shattered.

Since he'd given up on Lincoln as a viable candidate, Greeley went looking for a better one, preferably a successful Union general whose record would contrast with that of McClellan. He decided that William Rosecrans best fit the bill. The previous fall, after the battle of Corinth, *Tribune* headlines had proclaimed a "GREAT VICTORY BY ROSE-CRANS."[43] The *Tribune* had also reported the fierce battle of Stones River, where Rosecrans faced off against Braxton Bragg, as a Union victory, although it was mainly inconclusive.

With all that in mind, Greeley decided that "Old Rosy" was the Republicans' best bet for 1864. True, the man was a Catholic, which might bother some people, but his candidacy would probably secure the Irish vote for the Republicans. First, though, Greeley needed to find out if Rosecrans was "sound" on the slavery question. He sent his friend, James R. Gilmore, to find out. Gilmore hesitated, saying he didn't want to undermine Lincoln, for whom he had a "strong personal liking." Greeley said that he himself liked Lincoln personally, but he would sacrifice his best friend, cut off his right arm, if it would serve the country in its extremity.

"You are just the man for the job," Greeley told Gilmore, and named many prominent Republicans who would go along with him. "I will give you my word," Greeley said, "that if you find Rosecrans the man that is needed, I will go personally to Lincoln and force him to resign." Vice President Hannibal Hamlin, assuming the presidency, would then give Rosecrans command of all Union armies. Thus the war would be finished promptly and Rosecrans would be the natural Republican candidate for the presidency in November 1864. It was a fantastic scheme, and although "Uncle Horace" had tremendous influence, it's hard to believe that anyone, even Greeley, could have taken such a plot seriously.[44]

Gilmore met with Rosecrans and satisfied himself that Rosecrans was "sound" on slavery. He then mentioned Greeley's desire to support Rosecrans for the presidency. The honorable Rosecrans emphatically declined. Recalling his cadet days at West Point, he said: "My place is here. The country gave me my education, and so has a right to my military services; and it educated me for precisely this emergency. So this, and not the presidency, is my post of duty, and I cannot, without violating my conscience, leave it. But let me tell you, and I wish you would tell your friends, who are moving in this matter, that you are mistaken about Mr. Lincoln. He is in his right place, I am in a position to know, and if you live you will see that I am right about him." A few months later, when Rosecrans performed poorly at Chickamauga, leaving his subordinate George Thomas to save the day, Greeley no doubt was happy that his offer had been rejected.[45]

CHAPTER 9

⊷══◎══⊷

"The Very Best I Can"

After the Chancellorsville disaster, an anguished Lincoln asked, "What will the country say?" At first they couldn't say much; news of the battle had been suppressed. Hooker, the Union commander, had ordered his chief of staff, Major General Dan Butterfield, to refrain from reporting anything. Finally, early on the afternoon of May 3, 1863, Butterfield wired Lincoln: "From all reports yet collected, the battle has been most fierce and terrible. Losses heavy on both sides."[1]

A few hours later came an ominous wire from Hooker: "We have had a desperate fight yesterday and today, which has resulted in no success to us."[2] Lincoln didn't need an interpreter to realize "no success" was a euphemism for "defeat," especially after Hooker's next message, three days later, reported: "Have this moment returned to camp."[3]

The public meanwhile was still up in the air. Stanton, the hard-nosed secretary of war, had had enough of reporters leaking information to the enemy; for the first time in the war, Washington telegraphers could transmit only things approved by military censors. To avoid those censors, several reporters left the army and headed directly to New York. On Monday, May 4, according to the *Tribune*, a reporter arrived with such a dire account of the battle that his paper refused to believe it.[4] By Tuesday afternoon, however, the *Tribune* office knew the truth—Hooker's army had been whipped. "My God! It is horrible—horrible," Greeley said, "and to think of it, 130,000 magnificent soldiers so cut to pieces by less than 60,000 half-starved ragamuffins."[5]

Nevertheless, it was days before the public learned the full extent of the disaster. The *Boston Journal* editor probably spoke for all his peers when he wrote: "There never has been during the war such an important series of events, about which the public were so imperfectly informed."[6]

Once again reporters were unhappy with the administration, and they tended to blame the president personally. Still, Lincoln had to persist, and as he told a friend, "I do the very best I know how—the very best I can; and I mean to keep doing so until the end. If the end brings me out all right, what is said against me won't amount to anything. If the end brings me out wrong, ten angels swearing I was right would make no difference."[7] About this time an old Springfield acquaintance asked Lincoln how it felt to be president. Lincoln used a story to punctuate his reply, telling of a man who was tarred and feathered and ridden out of town on a rail. When asked how he liked it, the man said that if it wasn't for the honor of the thing, he would much rather walk! That said it all.[8]

Reporters might complain about being kept in the dark, but even Lincoln had trouble learning the truth about the Army of the Potomac. He decided to see things for himself, and on May 6, he and General Halleck headed for Hooker's headquarters. Two days later, after face-to-face consultations, they were back in Washington and Lincoln was writing Hooker a carefully crafted message:

> The recent movement of your army is ended without effecting its object, except, perhaps some important breakings of the enemy's communications. What next? If possible, I would be very glad of another movement early enough to give us some benefit from the fact of the enemy's communications being broken. . . . An early movement would also help to supersede the bad moral effect of the recent one, which is said to be considerably injurious. Have you already in your mind a plan wholly or partially formed? If you have, prosecute it without interference from me. If you have not, please inform me, so that I,

incompetent as I may be, can try and assist in the formation of some
plan for the army[9]

Reading between the lines, one suspects Lincoln was building a case
against Hooker should he later decide to fire him. After all, "Fighting Joe"
had powerful friends in Congress and he had worked hard at cultivating
the press corps. For weeks, papers such as the *New York Tribune*, the *New
York Times*, and Forney's *Washington Chronicle* had done their best to
defend him, as when a *New York Times* reporter, William Swinton, wrote a
scathing indictment of Hooker, saying his course of action at Chancellorsville "was ill-advised and unfortunate throughout. It was not only
bad—it was the worst possible, and in all the cardinal operations, where
there were a half-dozen different modes of operation, he not only chose a
bad course—he chose the *only bad course.*" Before printing the story, *Times*
editor Henry Raymond sent a copy to Lincoln to see whether he would
approve. He definitely did *not,* and Raymond was told that were he to publish such a statement, the author might well find himself behind bars the
next morning. Raymond prudently decided to suppress Swinton's article.[10]

In addition to his other problems, Lincoln had to concern himself
with important political events that spring of 1863, including elections in
New Hampshire and Connecticut. Peace Democrats running for governor
in those states, taking a page out of Vallandigham's book, were screaming about Lincoln's suspension of habeus corpus and his attack on civil
liberties.

Lincoln took his case directly to the people, writing two letters on civil
liberties that were published far and wide by the newly established Union
League and Loyal Publication Society. Replying to his Democratic critics,
Lincoln said that the rebels, "under cover of 'liberty of speech,' 'liberty of
the press,' and habeus corpus, hoped to keep amongst us a most efficient
corps of spies, informers, suppliers, and aiders and abbettors of their cause."
Thus the whole country was a war zone, and military arrests far from the
fighting front were justified. He did not believe, Lincoln said, that he was
setting a dangerous precedent by suspending certain civil liberties in
wartime, no more "than I am able to believe that a man could contract so

strong an appetite for emetics during temporary illness, as to persist in feeding upon them through the remainder of his healthful life."[11]

The Peace Democrats lost the gubernatorial elections in New Hampshire and Connecticut, but only by a whisker. Lincoln's letter may have made the difference. Somehow he had the knack of writing words that reached peoples' hearts, and one who appreciated that ability was no less an authority than Henry Raymond, who wrote: "No one can read Mr. Lincoln's state papers without perceiving in them a most remarkable faculty of 'putting things' so as to command the attention and assent of the common people. His style of thought as well as of expression is thoroughly in harmony with their habitual modes of thinking and speaking. . . . He uses language for the sole purpose of stating, in the clearest and simplest possible form, the precise idea he wishes to convey."[12]

⋆⟶⟦⟧⟵⋆

In June of 1863, Robert E. Lee launched an invasion of the North, marching up the Shenandoah and Cumberland Valleys, heading for Maryland and Pennsylvania. The decision to invade seems to have been Lee's alone. He knew further victories in northern Virginia would be of little help in the long run, and he could never hope to win a war of attrition. His best bet was to threaten Northern cities, even capture a major one such as Philadelphia or Baltimore. Such a blow would strengthen Northern antiwar factions, perhaps enough to make them sue for peace. As Lee continued to march, many in the North wondered apprehensively if this was the beginning of the end, an end that would bring Southern independence. *Harper's* early history of the war described the situation as the North perceived it that spring: "During the first six months of the year 1863 it seemed as though the tide of success had fully set in favor of the Confederacy, and it appeared that nothing but a successful invasion of the North was wanting to secure its final triumph, recognized by all the great powers of Europe. The invasion once determined upon, the entire disposable strength of the Confederacy was placed at the disposal of Lee. . . . The advance of this great army was made with a deliberation in strong contrast with the hurried invasion of Maryland the year before."[13]

The Army of the Potomac followed Lee's army, maintaining what Lincoln called the "inside track." Hooker's orders were to keep between Lee and the nation's capital. "If the enemy should be making for Maryland," Hooker wired Lincoln on June 14, "I will make the best dispositions in my power to come up with him."

Lincoln's reply showed a growing confidence in his own military know-how. He let Hooker know that "making dispositions" simply wasn't good enough: "If the head of Lee's army is at Martinsburg, and the tail of it on the Plank road between Fredericksburg and Chancellorsville, the animal must be very slim somewhere. Could you not break him?"[14]

Hooker was an opportunist. He had little respect for Halleck, and since Lincoln was calling the shots, he communicated directly with the president, bypassing both Halleck and Stanton. So far Lincoln had made the mistake of letting him get away with it. His next message set things straight: "To remove all misunderstanding, I now place you in the strict military relation to General Halleck of a commander of one of the armies to the general-in-chief of all the armies. I have not intended differently, but as it seems to be differently understood, I shall direct him to give you orders and you to obey him."[15]

Hooker resented taking orders from Halleck and truly believed he needed more freedom of action. Finally, in exasperation, he asked Halleck to relieve him. In reply, Halleck said: "As you were appointed to this command by the President, I have no power to relieve you. Your dispatch has been duly referred for Executive action."[16]

What Halleck's reply *didn't* say was that orders had already been cut, relieving Hooker and naming Gen. George Gordon Meade as his replacement. Early on the morning of June 28, James A. Hardie, a colonel from the War Department, handed the order to Meade, saying, "General, I'm afraid I've come to make trouble for you." Meade read: "You will receive with this the order of the President placing you in command of the Army of the Potomac. Considering the circumstances, no one ever received a more important command; and I cannot doubt that you will fully justify the confidence which the Government has reposed in you."[17]

The order was signed by Halleck, but clearly Lincoln had made the decision. Changing commanders on the eve of a crucial battle was a calculated risk. Only days before, having heard rumors that Hooker might be fired, Meade had written his wife about "the ridiculous appearance we present of changing our generals after each battle."[18] Lincoln had tried to prepare the press for this eventuality, but he doubtless wondered how they would react. Horace Greeley, for one, was supportive: "We believe that every decided failure by a commander should be promptly followed by his displacement. . . . In judging the President harshly, people forget the truth that the human race has in all history produced but a few really great generals. Mr. Lincoln has been required to make brick, straw or no straw."[19]

A *New York Herald* reporter, T. C. Grey, wrote his editor: "The relieving of Hooker is received with a kind of apathetic indifference by the army, although many are loud in denouncing the act *at this particular moment.*"[20] Such was the tone adopted by the *Herald*, that switching from Hooker to Meade made little difference to the man in the ranks. Meanwhile, the *Herald* couldn't resist putting in a plug for McClellan, the paper's Democratic favorite, both as a general and as a potential candidate for the presidency: "Many liked General Hooker and had faith in him; most believe in the ability of General Meade to fill his place. It may come inopportunely, but I must say that General McClellan is the man the rank and file of the army want at their head. They cannot get over worshiping him and clamoring for him."[21]

As Lee's army advanced into Pennsylvania, shrill Northern headlines sounded almost panicky. The *Philadelphia Inquirer* shouted: "To Arms! Citizens of Pennsylvania! The Rebels Are Upon Us!"[22]

The *New York Tribune* was equally breathless: "Men of the North! Pennsylvania, Jerseymen, New Yorkers, New Englanders! the foe is at your doors! Are you true men or traitors? If you are patriots deserving to be free, prove it by universal rallying, arming, and marching to meet the Rebel foe! Prove it now!"[23]

On July 1 the two mighty armies clashed at Gettysburg, an obscure Pennsylvania town, whose crossroads would give it geographic significance and lasting fame. The public's first news of the battle came from a dispatch written hastily by the chief correspondent of the *New York Times*, L. L. Crounse:

Near Gettysburg, July 1—A heavy engagement has been going on since nine o'clock this A.M. between the rebel forces of Longstreet and Hill and the First and Eleventh Corps under Gens. Reynolds and Meade.

The locality of the fight is beyond Gettysburg, on the Chambersburg Pike. Portions of the fight have been very severe, and with heavy loss. . . .

I regret to say that General Reynolds was mortally wounded, and has since died.[24]

For three days the battle raged, as people North and South worried, waited, and prayed. Lincoln, desperate for news, haunted the War Department telegraph office, pacing the floor and hovering near a silent telegraph key. For hours, nothing came through from the Army of the Potomac—Jeb Stuart's cavalrymen had cut most of the wires. Finally, one enterprising newsman, Aaron Homer Byington of the *New York Tribune*, rounded up a local telegrapher, patched a break in the line, and filed a dispatch covering the first two days of the battle. A mighty struggle was under way; the gallant Gen. John Reynolds had been killed early on the first day; casualties were heavy; and the issue was still in doubt. When the message came through, Lincoln asked, "Who is Byington?" No one knew, and a return message said: "Dispatch about a battle received. Who are you?"

Byington replied and gave Gideon Welles as a personal reference. Welles, whose long white beard gave him the look of an Old Testament patriarch, was the secretary of the Navy Lincoln called "Father Neptune." Fortunately, the secretary, after being roused from his bed at midnight, was able to vouch for the reporter. Before the war, both men had been media figures in Connecticut, when Byington had edited the *Norwalk Gazette* and Welles wrote editorials for the *Hartford Press*. Now that Byington was properly identified, the War Department asked him to turn over his line to military traffic. His own copy, he was told, could be sent during breaks in transmission.[25]

As the battle raged, Greeley's *Tribune* agonized: "These are the times that try men's souls! The peril of our country's overthrow is great and imminent."[26]

Hour after hour, men fought and died on fields that became soaked with blood. Seldom had a battle seen such fierce combat, with fighting often hand-to-hand, and seldom did so many men on both sides endure slaughter so bravely. After two days, names like the Wheat Field, the Peach Orchard, and Little Round Top had been forever engraved in American history. On the morning of the third day, cannons roared in what was to that time the mightiest artillery duel in American history. Around three in the afternoon, the Northern guns fell silent so as to let them cool and conserve ammunition. Confederates considered this a hopeful sign, and some 15,000 proud, gallant men, including the colorful Gen. George Pickett, formed ranks and started forward. Northern artillery, roused from their slumber, opened up in force; Northern infantrymen, line after line, took up position and opened fire as the enemy came within range. Artillery shells and musketry tore into the Southern ranks, riddling them unmercifully. Within minutes, Pickett's charge had become a glorious failure. Of those who started out so bravely, only a pitiful handful reached the Federal line, there to die or surrender. Lee nobly accepted the blame, saying the fault was his alone. Next day, sadly and reluctantly, he had his army start falling back toward Virginia.

On July 4 a Lincoln message told the country that news had arrived covering with honor the Army of the Potomac, promising great success to the cause of the Union, and offering condolence to those who had fallen. The president especially desired, said the message, "that on this day He whose will, not ours, should ever be done be everywhere remembered and reverenced with profoundest gratitude."[27]

Gettysburg, however, was not the triumph that Lincoln might have wished. The cautious Meade failed to pursue Lee's battered army, letting them slip across the Potomac and back to the security of friendly Virginia. Meade's sluggish tactics, Lincoln said, reminded him of an old woman trying to shoo a flock of geese across a creek. At the telegraph office, where the president devoured every scrap of news as it came over the wires, someone saw him reading Meade's congratulatory order to his troops. His face dropped, the observer noted, when he saw the phrase, "drive the *invaders* from our soil."

"My God! Is that all?" Lincoln groaned. Didn't Meade realize what he was saying? If the Union were to survive, everyone, especially every Union general, should be thinking in terms of one *inseparable* country. Next day Lincoln sent a message to Halleck saying he had left the telegraph office "a good deal dissatisfied." A few days later, in a similar vein, Lincoln told John Hay, "This is a dreadful reminiscence of McClellan. The same spirit that moved McClellan to claim a great victory because Pennsylvania and Maryland were safe. The hearts of 10 million people sank within them when McClellan raised that shout last fall. Will our generals never get that idea out of their heads? The whole country is our soil."[28]

From the West, on that same Independence Day, came even better news. Vicksburg had surrendered to Grant! It was the culmination of a masterful campaign, one that Lincoln followed intently, not only from Army bulletins, but from the messages of Charles Dana, the media personage who had been converted into an administration special agent. Early on, Dana had informed Stanton and Lincoln of Grant's plan to live off the country, saying that the general "will disregard his base and depend on the country for meat and even for bread. Beef cattle and corn are both abundant everywhere."[29] Grant had crossed the Mississippi River below Vicksburg, cut loose from his base of supplies, and in rapid succession fought successful battles at Port Gibson, Jackson, Champion's Hill, and Black River Bridge. For a change, Lincoln was able to relax as he read accounts of a campaign. Once Grant crossed the Mississippi, all reports had been positive.

Following that first battle, Greeley's *Tribune* proudly announced a "Glorious Victory at Port Gibson." Soon after, *Tribune* headlines were shouting: "RAPID MARCHES AND CONTINUOUS VICTORIES— THE REBELS DRIVEN TO THE WALL." And after Jackson, the Mississippi capital, was secured, the same paper noted approvingly that, "Gen. Grant personally directed the movements, and was under fire. He rode into the city at the head of the column."[30] Less than a week later, after the successful fight at Champion's Hill, Lincoln could read: "Grant on the High Road to Vicksburg."[31]

By early June Vicksburg was under siege. The Confederate army of John Pemberton was trapped, and victory was only a question of time.

Grant's men dug trenches, moving the siege line ever closer to the city. A *Tribune* headline read, "THE ANACONDA TIGHTENING HIS COILS."[32] The City of a Hundred Hills, termed by Jefferson Davis "The Gibraltar of the West," was in effect a starving Confederate prison. On July 4, accepting the inevitable, Pemberton surrendered. Grant was generous, as he could afford to be. His letter proposing surrender said Confederates would stack arms, sign letters of parole, then be released. Some thought the terms were *too* generous, but as Dana explained, they "at once tend to the demoralization of the enemy, but also release Grant's army for offensive operations."[33]

⋆⊶⊷⋆

Throughout the North, people were celebrating the victories at Gettysburg and Vicksburg. One evening Lincoln spoke to a crowd that had gathered outside the White House: "Now on this last Fourth of July just passed, we have a gigantic rebellion, at the bottom of which is an effort to overthrow the principle that all men are created equal, we have the surrender of a most powerful position and army on that very day. And not only so, but in the succession of battles in Pennsylvania, near to us, through three days, so rapidly fought that they might be called one great battle, on the first, second, and third of the month of July; and on the fourth the cohorts of those who opposed the Declaration that all men are created equal 'turned tail' and run. Gentlemen, this is a glorious theme, and the occasion for a speech, but I am not prepared to make one worthy of the occasion." While he would like to praise those who had fought so bravely, Lincoln said, "I dislike to mention the name of one single officer, lest I might do wrong to those I might forget."[34]

The crowd loved the plain, simple speech. Critics nevertheless proceeded to pick it apart. Some opposition newspapers, as well as the powerful Senator Charles Sumner, found fault with him for using the colloquialism 'turn tail,' saying he was carrying homespun simplicity too far. Yet this was the sort of language people understood and appreciated, even if the pompous Sumner did not. Some critics even suspected Lincoln's motives when he didn't single out the winning general at Gettysburg for particular praise. "President Lincoln's omission to mention General

Meade in his congratulatory speech," said the *New York World*, "has caused a great deal of remark. It is notorious that he is on the track for the next presidency."[35]

This was a new political slur—that Lincoln would slight a successful general for fear of boosting him into the presidency. In this case it wasn't true. Although Lincoln was pleased with Meade's Gettysburg performance, he wasn't about to heap praise on the man who failed to follow up that victory aggressively.

These days, however, politics seemed to intrude on *every* presidential decision. As Lincoln well knew, any popular general, whether his name was McClellan, Burnside, Meade, or Grant, might become a political rival. That had become almost an American tradition—successful generals running for president. It had begun with Washington, of course, but there had been others, including Andrew Jackson, William Henry Harrison, and Zachary Taylor. Even old Winfield Scott had had a run at it. The most likely candidate this time was undoubtedly George McClellan. The strutting "Young Napoleon" was still in New York, traveling in high society and being hailed wherever he went. New York papers were carrying regular features headed "McClellan's Movements," listing his attendance at the theater, the opera, and at dinner parties and grand balls. To cap it off, leading figures of the Democratic Party had shown their admiration by presenting the general with a handsome, fully furnished, four-story house on West 31st Street, in one of Manhattan's most desirable residential areas. Officially, McClellan was still listed on active duty, preparing his final report as commander of the Army of the Potomac. His time, however, was mostly devoted to setting the table for a presidential run in 1864.[36]

At the moment, Lincoln wasn't concerned about generals who might seek the presidency. That remained to be seen. Of one thing he was sure, however. Of all his generals, Ulysses Grant was the one who best fitted in with what Lincoln was trying to do. Grant hadn't made excuses; hadn't sent the president letters of complaint or protest; hadn't tried to substitute policies of his own for ones laid down in Washington. In short, he had shown himself to be completely dependable—a quality seen in few other commanders. On July 13, Lincoln sat down and, in his own hand, wrote a personal, magnanimous letter to Ulysses Grant:

MY DEAR GENERAL:

I do not remember that you and I ever met personally. I write this now as a grateful acknowledgment for the almost inestimable service you have done the country. I wish to say a word further. When you first reached the vicinity of Vicksburg, I thought you should do, what you finally did—march the troops across the neck, run the batteries with the transports, and thus go below; and I never had any faith, except a general hope that you knew better than I, that the Yazoo Pass expedition, and the like, could succeed. When you got below and took Port Gibson, Grand Gulf and vicinity, I thought you should go down the river and join General Banks; and when you turned Northward East of the Big Black, I feared it was a mistake. I now wish to make the personal acknowledgment that you were right, and I was wrong.

Yours very truly,

A. Lincoln

It was a remarkable letter, showing among other things Lincoln's familiarity with the twists and turns of a river on which he had once navigated flatboats. More than that, it was noteworthy for its simple elegance, for the praise it bestowed on Grant, and also for what it said about Lincoln. Here was a man who could acknowledge a mistake, and do it publicly. While it put the general in the best possible light, in a more subtle way, it also reflected well upon the president. Lincoln may have had that in mind when he released a copy of the letter to the press and public.[37]

CHAPTER 10

⊹⟝⟞⊹

"THE PROMISE MUST BE KEPT"

D uring Grant's Vicksburg campaign, Lincoln had an unusual
opportunity to show his support of the media. A sticky problem
had arisen concerning the status of newsmen as noncombatants.
Three reporters, Albert Richardson and Junius Browne of the *New York
Tribune* along with Richard Colburn of the *New York World*, had fallen
into Confederate hands and been shuttled off to Richmond's infamous
Libby Prison. The first report, rather than their being captured, was that
all three had been killed. This supposedly prompted William Tecumseh
Sherman, whose low opinion of reporters was well known, to say, "Good!
Now we'll have news from hell before breakfast!"[1]

Manton Marble, editor of the antiadministration *New York World*,
wrote asking for Colburn's release, and the *World* reporter was soon
headed north. As Richardson wrote later, Marble's request was "obeyed as
promptly as if it had been an order from Jeff Davis."[2] Obviously, Southerners knew who was sympathetic to their cause.

It was a different story for Richardson and Browne, employees of the
hated *New York Tribune*. Hearing of Colburn's release, Sidney Gay, the

Tribune managing editor, became concerned for his own people. He pleaded with Lincoln to intercede on their behalf, and Lincoln was quick to respond, sending a presidential wire to Colonel Ludlow at Fort Monroe: "Richardson and Browne, correspondents of the Tribune captured at Vicksburg, are detained at Richmond. Please ascertain why they are detained, & get them off if you can."[3]

Spurred by the president's personal interest, Ludlow immediately contacted Robert Ould, Confederate commissioner of exchange, asking for the men's release and pointing out that correspondents had always been considered noncombatants. Ould's reply was not only "No" but a loud "HELL, NO!"

"It seems to me," Ould wrote, "that if any exceptions be made as to any non-combatants it should be against such men as the Tribune correspondents who have had more share than even your soldiery in bringing rapine, pillage, and desolation to our homes. . . . You ask me why I will not release them. 'Tis because they are the worst and most obnoxious of all non-combatants. . . ." Lincoln didn't let it drop. He pulled every string he could, but to no avail. His personal involvement may have even aggravated the situation. In any case, Richardson and Browne remained in confinement.[4]

⟡

In a sense, the war by this time had evolved into a struggle for the hearts and minds of the Northern people. Confederate leaders recognized this. Using both diplomatic and military measures, they tried to create a great Northern outcry for a peaceful settlement. When the Army of Northern Virginia went on the offensive, for example, it was not to seize territory, but to ratchet up the level of Yankee discomfort.

Since Lincoln seemed so intractable, Southerners sought to convince a war-weary Northern public that the Confederacy was here to stay. Acting on this premise, Confederate Vice President Alexander Stephens asked permission to pass through the Federal blockade and come to Washington. Stephens said he represented Jefferson Davis, commanding general of the Confederate Army, and as such he wanted to meet with Abraham Lincoln, president and commanding general of the Army and Navy of the United

States. Lincoln, as well as his cabinet members, saw the danger in such a meeting, one that might imply a recognition of the Confederacy. At first Lincoln considered sending someone to meet with Stephens, but after reflection decided against it. A message from the White House to the blockading admiral said, "The request of A. H. Stephens is inadmissible. The customary agents and channels are adequate for all needful communication and conference between the United States forces and the insurgents."[5]

In effect, Stephens was told that anything he had to say could be put in writing. Once again Lincoln's political instincts were proven correct. Stephens later wrote: "The idea was not so much to act upon Mr. Lincoln and the then ruling authorities in Washington, as *through* them when the mass of correspondence should be published, upon the great mass of the people in the Northern States, who were becoming sensitively alive to the great danger of their own liberties."[6]

⊷═◉⟺⊶

In mid-July, acknowledging the victories at Gettysburg and Vicksburg, a document was issued from the White House with the title, "Proclamation for Thanksgiving, July 15, 1863, by the President of the United States of America." The text flowed with a piety and dignity worthy of the Old Testament: "It has pleased Almighty God to hearken to the supplications and prayers of an afflicted people," it began, "and to vouchsafe to the army and navy of the United States victories on land and on the sea so signal and so effective as to furnish reasonable confidence that the union of these States will be maintained, their Constitution preserved, and their peace and prosperity permanently restored. These victories have been accorded not without sacrifices of life, limb, health, and liberty, incurred by brave, loyal, and patriotic citizens. Domestic affliction in every part of the country follows in the train of these fearful bereavements."

This was a message designed to comfort and inspire. It also acknowledged the deeply religious spirit of the American people: "It is meet and right to recognize and confess the presence of the Almighty Father, and the power of his hand equally in these triumphs and in these sorrows."

The proclamation concluded with a long, moving passage: "Now, therefore, be it known that I do set apart the 6th day of August next, to be observed as a day of national thanksgiving, praise, and prayer, and I invite the people of the United States to assemble on that occasion in their customary places of worship, and, in the forms approved by their own consciences, render the homage due to the Divine Majesty for the wonderful things he has done in the nation's behalf, and invoke the influences of his Holy Spirit to subdue the anger which has produced and so long sustained a needless and cruel rebellion, to change the hearts of the insurgents, to guide the counsels of the government with wisdom adequate to so great a national emergency, and to visit with tender care and consolation throughout the length and breadth of our land all those who, through the vicissitudes of marches, voyages, battles, and sieges have been brought to suffer in mind, body, or estate, and finally to lead the whole nation through the paths of repentance and submission to the Divine Will back to the perfect enjoyment of union and fraternal peace."[7]

<hr>

On the very day these words of Thanksgiving were being read by the nation, trouble was brewing in the North, particularly in New York City. Dissatisfaction with the war had been rising in intensity, and now a spark was provided by the Draft Act that Lincoln had signed into law in early March. Many perceived the law as unfair; New York's Democratic governor, Horatio Seymour, even called it unconstitutional. The lower classes particularly objected to the provision allowing someone selected to hire a substitute, or to gain an outright exemption by paying $300. According to papers like the *World*, the *Journal of Commerce*, the *Express*, the *Daily News*, the *Day Book*, and the *Mercury*, it had become "a rich man's war and a poor man's fight." Said the *Daily News:* "The people are notified that one out of about two and a half of the citizens are to be brought off into Messrs. Lincoln & Company's charnelhouse. God forbid! We hope that instant measure will be taken to prevent the outrage."[8]

It wasn't just the war, however, and it wasn't just the draft. It was also a matter of economics. Former slaves were drifting north and competing for low-paying jobs; laborers in New York, many of them recent immigrants, saw blacks as the cause of their problems. They cursed emancipation, cursed the new conscription law, and went on to curse those newspapers that supported both blacks and the draft.

On July 12 papers listed the names of men summoned to service. Next day the *New York Herald* contained an ominous paragraph. The city was "quivering with excitement," the *Herald* declared, and Irish laborers were openly organizing to resist the government. The paper was barely on the street when a mob gathered near the *Herald* office and began moving up-town. Rioters stormed the enrollment office, smashed the lottery machinery, and set fire to the building. Soldiers trying to stem the tide were met with a fusillade of bricks and stones. Two of them were beaten to death with their own muskets. Thousands joined the rioting, burning buildings, clubbing policemen to death, chasing and killing blacks.

Offices of the *Tribune* and *Times*, across the street from each other, were particular targets. Rioters shouted that Horace Greeley was "the nigger's friend—lynch him!" Someone heard a mob singing, "We'll hang old Greeley from a sour apple tree." That night scores of men broke into the *Tribune* offices, smashing desks and burning papers before a swarm of policemen drove them off. Next night they were back again. A supply of muskets had arrived from Governors Island, and printers and editors, fully armed, went on doing their job. Across the way, the enterprising *Times* had acquired a pair of Gatling guns. Editor Henry Raymond manned one gun himself and placed it in full view of the street, commanding Park Row to the north. By the time calm was restored, the riots had claimed hundreds of lives and whole city blocks were in ruins. Remarkably, the *Tribune* managed to come out on schedule. Greeley wrote: "Relentless and cruel and cowardly as all mobs are, the actions of this at least are equal to any that have yet earned a record in history. . . . Resistance to the Draft was merely the occasion of the outbreak; absolute disloyalty and hatred to the negro were the moving cause."[9]

When accounts of the riot arrived in Washington, a saddened Lincoln read of blacks being assaulted and lynched, their tenements burned, their boarding houses looted. "Everywhere throughout the city," said the *Herald*, "they are driven about like sheep, and numbers are killed of whom no account will ever be learned." Meanwhile, Manton Marble's *World* was giving all the encouragement it could to the rioters, recklessly calling the Draft Act a "wanton exercise of arbitrary powers."

Actually, no one would ever know the full extent of the killing; some said there were a thousand dead; some said twelve hundred. Perhaps the best contemporary count appeared in the *New York Evening Post*, which estimated that between four hundred and five hundred lives had been lost. Shortly after the outbreak, the *Post*'s managing editor, Charles Nord-hoff, wrote, "A continuous stream of funerals flows across the East River, and graves are dug privately within the knowledge of the police here and there."[10]

Following the riots, New York papers hurled angry words at each other, each blaming the opposition for the outbreak. On one side were anti-administration journals such as the *World* and the *Daily News*, each claiming that draft quotas were imposed disproportionately on Democrats. The *World* maintained that New York, "the greatest city in the nation—a city which has poured out its blood and treasure without stint or measure—is to be mulcted in largely more than its due proportion of men." The *Daily News*, in a vicious editorial, had a similar argument, saying, "The manner in which the draft is being conducted in New York is such an outrage upon all decency and fairness as has no parallel." Meanwhile, the *Tribune* and *Times* were equally loud in voicing support for the administration; Bennett's *Herald* was somewhere in between.[11]

A more dignified exchange took place between Governor Seymour and President Lincoln, with letters composed as much for the public as for the addressee. Earlier, on July 4, Seymour, with an outburst of demagogic rhetoric, had told a mass meeting, "Remember this: that the bloody, treasonable, and revolutionary doctrine of public necessity can be proclaimed by a mob as well as by a government." He had left town while the riot was brewing and had expressed sympathy for the rioters while it was going on. Now, trying to shift the blame, Seymour wrote Lincoln that draft quotas had been calculated unfairly, with proportionately higher numbers assigned to Democratic districts than to Republican ones. Whether or not Seymour was correct in his assertions, New York public opinion was on his side. Showing political prudence, Lincoln backed off, and when he was urged to send troops to New York and declare martial law, he declined. For once the *World* agreed with him, commenting, "It is satisfying to know the President has more sense than some of his advisers." Although he'd already reduced several district quotas in response to Seymour's earlier demands, Lincoln now responded by cutting down those of others. Later in the year, he would appoint a commission to study the entire handling of the draft in New York State.[12]

Somehow, despite all the problems, Lincoln's spirits were starting to lift that summer. He was buoyed by the Union victories at Gettysburg and Vicksburg, and he was also beginning to gain confidence in his own ability to handle the job, which naturally included working with the media. In early August, presidential secretary John Hay, always attuned to Lincoln's moods, told his diary: "The Tycoon is in fine whack. I have seldom seen him more serene."[13]

Be that as it may, there were always people who believed Lincoln could do better, and they didn't hesitate to offer advice. On July 20, 1863, in one bizarre episode, Captain J. M. Cutts, judge-advocate of Burnside's Department of the Ohio, brashly sent a wire directly to "His Excellency, President Lincoln." In a message marked "PRIVATE," Cutts said: "I advise you to relieve Maj. Gen. A. E. Burnside from Command of the Department of the Ohio immediately by telegraph. . . . Send some thoroughly brave man to take his place. I cordially recommend Hooker, who is a brave man, and will be very popular. We are on the eve of important events, which require you to pursue the course I suggest. . . . Please acknowledge the receipt of this dispatch. I am absolutely right."[14]

His Excellency let pass the opportunity to sack Burnside for a second time, perhaps because Burnside had relieved Captain Cutts earlier that day, "to take effect the 23d of June last."[15]

Even an old friend like Philadelphia publisher Alexander McClure wasn't above putting in his two cents worth. When Lee invaded Pennsylvania in June, McClure told Lincoln he should promptly recall McClellan to active duty and give him command of the Army. Lincoln, who wasn't about to consider such a step, merely asked McClure, "Do we gain anything by opening one leak to stop another?"[16]

That was typical—advice pouring in from all quarters, especially from members of the self-important media. The editor of the friendly *National Intelligencer* was properly sympathetic, writing: "It is one of the tribulations which must greatly add to the fatigue of office at this juncture, that our amiable President has to give so much of his time and attention to persons who apparently having no business of their own, expend a large degree of their surplus energy in benevolently minding the business of the President."[17]

Although he managed to shrug off unwanted advice, Lincoln was too good a politician to appear to be ignoring it. He was always on the lookout, moreover, for the chance to put his own views before the public. One such chance came in August of 1863 when he received a letter from his former hometown, Springfield, Illinois, inviting him to a mass meeting of Union men scheduled for September 3. Although he was unable to be there in person, Lincoln sent a lengthy letter to James E. Conkling, suggesting that Conkling "read it very slowly" to the meeting. At the meeting, of course, Conkling would be "preaching to the choir." Lincoln, however, counted on his letter being widely circulated, so he directed his words to the nation as a whole.

To those critics of the administration who wanted peace at any price, even if it meant compromise, Lincoln said:

> You desire peace, and you blame me that we do not have it. But how can we attain it? There are but three conceivable ways: First, to suppress the rebellion by force of arms. This I am trying to do. Are you for it? If you are we are agreed. If you are not for it, a second way is to give up the Union. I am against this. Are you for it? If you are, you should say so plainly. If you are not for force, nor yet for dissolution, there only remains some imaginable compromise. I do not believe any compromise embracing the maintenance of the Union is now possible. All I learn leads to a directly opposite belief. . . . A compromise, to be effective, must be made either with those who control the rebel army, or with the people first liberated from the domination of that army by the success of our own army. Now, let me assure you that no word or intimation from that rebel army or from any of the men controlling it, in relation to any peace compromise has ever come to my knowledge or belief.[18]

Continuing, Lincoln addressed those who were unhappy about the Emancipation Proclamation. He reiterated his position that the proclamation was warranted as a war measure and was justified through the constitutional authority given him as wartime commander in chief. Moreover, he said, the promise of freedom must be kept.

As Lincoln had hoped, papers such as the *New York Times, Tribune,* and *Evening Post* printed the letter in full. The *Times* said it had "hard sense, sharp outlines, and a temper defying malice." The *Evening Post* said that anyone reading the letter would know why Lincoln was called "Honest Abe," saying, "Thorough honesty, a sincere desire to do what is right, a conscientious intention to preserve faithfully the oath of office and to do his duty as an American and a lover of the liberty upon which our government is founded, these are the traits which mark every sentence of the letter. To these must be added a quaint yet shrewd and pointed way of putting his argument which is characteristic of a man who is of the 'plain people' and has not mixed much with those great managers of the world's affairs who are accustomed to use language to conceal their thoughts."[19]

In the *Tribune,* Horace Greeley penned an editorial that gave Lincoln a ringing endorsement—the best yet. Lincoln's language, Greeley wrote, was "plain, forcible and eminently direct." The letter contained "words of wisdom" and exhibited "the wide grasp of a statesman" and "the firm demeanor of a ruler." It was marked by "honesty of purpose" and "a most vigorous common sense." The tribute ended with the words: "Again we say: God Bless Abraham Lincoln! 'THE PROMISE MUST BE KEPT.'"[20]

Predictably, the *New York World* saw it differently. "The war is managed not in the interest of the Union but in the interest of the Republican party and its greedy retinue of contractors," said the *World.* "Nature has not endowed Mr. Lincoln with a single great or commanding quality. He has indeed a certain homely untutored shrewdness and vulgar honesty which are common enough in every plain community but no such consciousness of resources superior to an ordinary station has ever led him to exact from others a higher degree of consideration than belongs to a village lawyer."[21] Regardless of what the *World* and similar papers said, public opinion seemed to be shifting in Lincoln's favor.

◆══◎══◆

Journalist Charles Dana, the man Lincoln called "the eyes of the Government at the front," was again active. With the fall of Vicksburg, his mission with Grant's army had been concluded. He had returned to New York, prepared to return to civilian life, when a telegram from Stanton urged him to remain in service. Dana agreed, and his next assignment was with William Rosecrans's Army of the Cumberland. Ever since the battle of Stone's River, fought at the beginning of 1863, Rosecrans had been in eastern Tennessee, giving various reasons for his lack of activity. Dana caught up with Rosecrans near Chattanooga, where he presented him with an introductory letter from Stanton, one that stated, "Mr. Dana is a gentleman of distinguished character, patriotism, and ability."[22] Many would say "a gentleman of distinguished character" was an unusual way to describe a reporter—in the nineteenth or any other century. Before long, in any case, Dana was sending copious reports. These, after being initially favorable to Rosecrans, grew increasingly critical.

On September 19 Dana was with Rosecrans as he faced off against Braxton Bragg near Chickamauga Creek, just south of Chattanooga. Dana that day, with a telegrapher at his side, sent some eleven dispatches. For once, Lincoln was able to follow a battle's progress on an almost play-by-play basis. A sampling of those first-day reports shows an excess of optimism:

10:30 A.M.: "Rosecrans has everything ready to grind up Bragg's flank."

2:30 P.M.: "The fight continues to rage. . . . Decisive victory seems assured to us."

4:30 P.M.: "I do not dare to say our victory is complete, but it seems certain. Enemy silenced on nearly whole line."

7:30 P.M.: "Rosecrans will renew the fight at daylight. His dispositions are now being made."[23]

Next day things were different. Dana was with Rosecrans on the Union right when screaming Confederates broke through the line. As he later recalled: "I saw our lines break and melt away like leaves before the wind. . . . The whole right of our army had apparently been routed."[24] Rosecrans fell back to Chattanooga, seemingly unaware that the battle still raged. On the Union left, however, George Thomas was still holding firm and earning his sobriquet, "The Rock of Chickamauga."

Dana's next report made a bad situation look even worse: "My report today is of deplorable importance. Chickamauga is as fatal a name in our history as Bull Run."[25]

When Thomas's stand became known, things looked a bit brighter. Nevertheless, Rosecrans was back in Chattanooga, and Bragg's Confederates had him well bottled up.

At the White House, young reporter Noah Brooks, who had become a friend and confidant of the Lincoln family, wrote: "Last night the town was full of dark rumors of a great defeat of the Union army, and the President was fain to declare that he believed that Rosecrans had been badly whipped."[26]

At the end of September, Lincoln had another chance to receive advice. A delegation of Missouri Republicans—some seventy in number—came to the White House to complain about Gen. John Schofield, the Union commander in their district. Wisely, Lincoln decided against inviting the press to the meeting; this was no time to publicize internal Republican dissension. When a pompous editor tried to insert himself into the meeting, the doorkeeper said, "Oh yes, editors, of all persons, are to be denied admission during the interview." The editor was not happy, but the doorkeeper had his orders, and was more than willing to enforce them.[27]

At times the meeting turned argumentative and boisterous. Lincoln, however, responded to each issue raised, point by point. According to John Hay, the Missourians' main complaint was that Schofield had stopped publication of a particular newspaper and also suspended the right of habeus corpus. Lincoln listened patiently, then explained that Schofield was only doing what the administration had authorized: "You object to his order on my recent proclamation suspending the privilege of the writ of Habeus Corpus. I am at a loss to see why an order executing my own official decree should be made a ground of accusation to me against the officer issuing it. You object to its being used in Missouri. In other words that which is right when employed against your opponents is wrong when employed against yourselves. Still I will consider that.

"You object to his muzzling the press. As to that, I think when an officer in any department finds that a newspaper is pursuing a course calculated to embarrass his operations and stir up sedition and tumult, he has the right to lay hands upon it and suppress it, but in no other case." Lincoln then played something of a trump card, saying, "I approved the order in question after the *Missouri Democrat* had also approved it."[28]

Before the war, Lincoln had spent a good bit of time in Missouri, and he knew his newspapers. (Oddly enough, the *Missouri Democrat* was a Republican newpaper, while the *Missouri Republican* was Democratic.) In other words, he told the delegation, if their own principal journalistic voice approved of Schofield's actions, then what was the problem? The delegation was not happy with the meeting's outcome, but at least they had had a chance to speak their minds.

Perhaps it was the loss at Chickamauga that made people willing to sound off so boldly. At least that was Henry Halleck's opinion. The general in chief may have been echoing Lincoln when he wrote Schofield in St. Louis: "So long as we can gain success, the interference of politicians in military matters can be resisted; but on the first disaster they press upon us like a pack of hungry wolves."[29]

--→≡◦⊂≡◦←--

Fall elections were being held in several key states, and when favorable returns came in from California, Noah Brooks relayed a presidential compliment to his Sacramento paper: "Honest Abraham spoke affectionately and warmly of our State in a private conversation the other day, saying that he had always liked California for her large liberality and generous profusion, but now he loved her for her unswerving fidelity to the Union, under circumstances which might have shaken the patriotism of less noble States."[30]

The fall elections had concerned Lincoln greatly, because they would indicate the extent of public support—or lack thereof. One key test would come in Ohio, where the race for governor involved the most famous Copperhead of them all, Clement Vallandigham. Vallandigham, it will be remembered, had been expelled from Union lines and sent south to the Confederacy. Southerners, including Jefferson Davis, had given him a rather cool reception and had been just as happy when he sailed for Bermuda. From there, he'd taken passage to Halifax and then made his way to Windsor, Ontario, where he was campaigning in absentia for the Ohio governorship. His opponent was John Brough, and at 10 o'clock on election night, Lincoln anxiously wired Columbus, Ohio: "Where is John Brough?"

Brough, it turned out, was in the telegraph office. Upon learning that, Lincoln asked, "Brough, what is your majority now?"

"Over 30,000," Brough wired back.

A little past midnight, Lincoln wired again: "Brough, what is your majority this time?"

Brough replied: "Over 50,000."

Finally, about five o'clock in the morning, Brough was able to tell Lincoln that his majority was now "over 100,000." A relieved Lincoln wired: "Glory to God in the highest. Ohio has saved the Nation."[31]

Another crucial October race was taking place in Pennsylvania, where the pro-Union Republican governor, Andrew Curtin, was running against a state supreme court judge, Democrat George W. Woodward, a man the *New York Tribune* considered "the Vallandigham of Pennsylvania."[32] Pennsylvania's race had been closer than Ohio's, but by early morning it was clear that Union candidate Curtin had also come out on top. In reporting the results, the *New York Herald* noted, somewhat begrudgingly, that it was a "chastisement the copperheads could not possibly misunderstand."[33]

Maintaining good media relations, Lincoln knew, was not just being a source of information, it also meant being a good listener. Hence, when the *Tribune's* James R. Gilmore came to him with a fanciful plan, Lincoln heard him out. Gilmore's scheme involved Zebulon B. Vance, the governor of North Carolina. According to Gilmore's informants, Vance would welcome reunion of the states and "any peace compatible with honor." As evidence of this, Vance was said to have helped write a four-column address published July 31 in the *Raleigh Standard,* saying, "The great demand of the people of this part of the State is *peace;* peace upon any terms that will not enslave and degrade us."

Gilmore proposed making some direct overture to Vance—perhaps a letter from Lincoln offering generous peace terms, ones that might let North Carolina exit the war with honor. Lincoln may have been far more skeptical than Gilmore let on when he later wrote about their meeting. Nevertheless, as Gilmore told it, Lincoln dictated a letter to Vance, Gilmore signed it, and Lincoln endorsed it as read by him and having "my entire approval." In the long run, nothing seems to have come of this, and whether anyone brought the letter to Vance is unknown. Before the end of the year, however, Vance *did* write Jefferson Davis a straight and open plea for "some effort at negotiation with the enemy."[34]

⋆⇢⇒◉⇐⇠⋆

As the leaves turned and the autumn of 1863 wore on, nothing much was expected from the Army of the Potomac. Both George Gordon Meade and his opponent, Robert E. Lee, seemed about to settle in for the winter. Lincoln's main problem, therefore, was at Chattanooga. The Army of the Cumberland was still hemmed in, supplies were running low, and Dana's opinion of Rosecrans had gone into free fall. As Dana later wrote: "In the midst of these difficulties General Rosecrans seemed to be insensible to the impending danger; . . . Our animals were starving, the men had starvation before them, and the enemy was bound soon to make desperate efforts to dislodge us. Yet the commanding general devoted that part of the time which was not employed in pleasant gossip to the composition of a long report to prove that the Government was to blame for his failure [at Chickamauga] on the 20th."[35]

A change was indicated, and Dana suggested that someone from the West, notably Grant, might be the one to take over. He didn't know that Grant had already been summoned. On October 16, 1863, Grant received an order telling him: "You will immediately proceed to the Galt House, Louisville, Ky, where you will meet an officer of the War Department with your orders and instructions. You will take with you your staff, etc., for immediate operations in the field. Wait at Louisville for the officer of the War Department."[36]

The man from the War Department, as it turned out, was none other than the gruff secretary of war, Edwin M. Stanton. Grant later recalled what happened next: "I left Cairo within an hour or so of receiving this dispatch, going by rail via Indianapolis. Just as the train I was on was starting out of the depot at Indianapolis a messenger came running up to stop it, saying the Secretary of War was coming into the station and wanted to see me. . . . The Secretary handed me two orders, saying that I might take my choice of them. The two were identical in all but one particular. Both created the 'Military Division of the Mississippi,' (giving me the command) composed of the Departments of the Ohio, the Cumberland, and the Tennessee. . . . One order left the department commanders as they were, while the other relieved Rosecrans and assigned Thomas in his place. I accepted the latter."[37]

George Thomas now had the Army of the Cumberland. More important, Grant, Thomas's new boss, was assuming a major role. After sifting through commanders for two-and-a-half years, searching, choosing, rejecting, Lincoln had at last found the right man. Henceforth things would be different.

Horace Greeley, the volatile *New York Tribune* editor who often swung from Lincoln supporter to Lincoln critic.

Henry Jarvis Raymond, the editor of the *New York Times*, was generally supportive of Lincoln and his administration.

James Gordon Bennett, Sr., editor of the *New York Herald* and frequent Lincoln critic, provided a strong press voice for the Democratic Party.

Joseph Medill, editor of the *Chicago Tribune* and solid Lincoln supporter.

Wilbur F. Storey, editor of the *Chicago Times*, whose criticism of the Lincoln administration often included vicious personal attacks on the president. COLLECTION OF THE CHICAGO HISTORICAL SOCIETY

Two editors, Horace Greeley of the *New York Tribune* and Thurlow Weed of the *Albany Evening Journal*, attempt to influence the new administration in this *Vanity Fair* cartoon entitled "The Inside Track." Weed (left, in high hat) works on his longtime associate, Secretary of State Seward, while Greeley (holding a copy of the Chicago platform) also tries to get his foot in the door. VANITY FAIR

Vanity Fair, as the country perches on the brink of war, somehow finds humor in Lincoln's dilemma as he balances "Peace"and "Sumpter" [sic] with Secretary Seward acting as master of ceremonies. VANITY FAIR

PROF. LINCOLN IN HIS GREAT FEAT OF BALANCING.

In April 1861, *Harper's Weekly* cartoons a puzzled Lincoln for its puzzled readers. HARPER'S WEEKLY

CONSULTING THE ORACLE.

PRESIDENT LINCOLN. "And, what next?"
COLUMBIA. "First be sure you're right, then go ahead!"

"The Press in the Field," by Thomas Nast, depicts the various roles of journalists and newspapers during the war. *HARPER'S WEEKLY*

THE MacLINCOLN HARRISBURG HIGHLAND FLING.

"The MacLincoln Harrisburg Highland Fling" was an attempt to ridicule Lincoln based on Joseph Howard's phony "scotch plaid cap" story. *VANITY FAIR*

Thomas Nast depicts a Lincoln triumph in the amendment to the Constitution that abolished slavery. Lincoln called Thomas Nast "our best recruiting sergeant. His . . . cartoons have never failed to arouse enthusiasm and patriotism, and have always seemed to come just when those articles were getting scarce." HARPER'S WEEKLY

Charles A. Dana, the former journalist who became Lincoln's "eyes at the front." U. S. ARMY MILITARY HISTORY INSTITUTE

Lt. Gen. Ulysses S. Grant. After many tries, Lincoln finally found the right general to win the war. NATIONAL ARCHIVES

Efforts of the so-called "Peace Commission," were doomed from the start. *Harper's* treated the whole thing as a farce. HARPER'S WEEKLY

"From Our Special War Correspondent." On April 3, 1865, in the war's final days, Lincoln (quoting Grant) wires Stanton that Petersburg and Richmond are being evacuated. When Stanton releases the message to the press, the newspapers take delight in having the president himself feeding them stories! HARPER'S WEEKLY

THE PEACE COMMISSION.
Flying to ABRAHAM's Bosom.

FROM OUR SPECIAL WAR CORRESPONDENT.
"CITY POINT, VA., *April* —, 8.30 A.M.
"All .seems well with us."—A. LINCOLN.

CHAPTER 11

❖━━◈━━❖

"ALL MEN ARE CREATED EQUAL"

When Ulysses Grant was given responsibility for Tennessee, he wired George Thomas to hold besieged Chattanooga at all costs. Thomas replied, "I will hold the town till we starve." Those were brave words, and they were no exaggeration. In truth, the situation had become desperate. By this time, troops were on half or quarter rations, relying on a trickle of supplies from what they called the "Cracker Line." Presently Grant himself was in Chattanooga after a roundabout, wearying journey. Charles Dana, who was already on hand, wired the War Department: "Grant arrived last night, wet, dirty, and well." Soon Thomas showed Grant a plan devised by the army's engineer, W. F. "Baldy" Smith. Grant gave the go-ahead, and the plan was set in motion. By dark of night, rafts were floated down the Tennessee River, carrying men who swarmed ashore and overran Confederate outposts. Then Hooker attacked from the east, linked up with Thomas, and a solid supply line was established. The siege was broken, and the White House began to breathe more easily.[1]

❖━━◈━━❖

Lincoln's widely reproduced message to the Springfield Republicans had made a singular impression on John Murray Forbes, a prominent Boston businessman, who called it "a plain letter to plain people." He wrote Lincoln directly, urging him to do more of the same. The president should "seize an early opportunity," Forbes wrote, "to explain the true nature of the war to "your great audience of plain people."

"Bonaparte, when under the republic, fighting despots of Europe, did as much by his bulletins as he did by his bayonets," Forbes continued. "You have the same opportunity, and greater, for you have enemies North and South, reading our language, whom you can teach."

Lincoln evidently agreed, and the "early opportunity" arose when he was invited to attend the dedication of a new cemetery at Gettysburg for those who had fallen there in the July battle. Actually, the invitation had been issued almost as an afterthought. Some on the arrangements committee were dubious about their joke-telling president, doubting "his ability to speak upon such a grave and solemn occasion." However, they told themselves, they already had their principal speaker, the distinguished orator Edward Everett of Massachusetts, so it should be safe to let the president make "a few appropriate remarks."[2]

Shortly before going to Gettysburg, Lincoln visited Gardner's photography gallery to have his picture taken. According to Noah Brooks, who was with him, he took along a two-page supplement of the *"Boston Journal"* that Everett had sent. It contained a copy of Everett's proposed Gettysburg oration, a lengthy florid piece that would take two full hours to deliver. Lincoln said it was thoughtful of Everett to provide a copy of his speech so they wouldn't cover the same ground. However, there was little worry of that, he said, since his own remarks would be "short, short, short." Brooks got the impression that Lincoln believed his own contribution that day, compared to Everett's, would be of little consequence. No doubt with a smile, however, Lincoln noted the length of Everett's speech and quoted a line he had read somewhere from Daniel Webster: "Solid men of Boston make no long orations."[3]

On the evening of November 18, 1863, a special train of four coaches, decorated with red-white-and-blue bunting, pulled into Gettysburg with the Washington delegation to the dedication ceremony. During the ride, someone had offered Lincoln a copy of the *New York Herald*. He accepted it with thanks, saying, "I like to see what they say about us." Aboard the coaches were cabinet members, congressmen, senior officers of the Army and Navy, foreign ministers, newspaper correspondents, plus Lincoln and his two private secretaries, Nicolay and Hay. By the time Lincoln and the others stepped down from the train, Gettysburg was already overflowing with thousands of visitors who had come to watch the dedication. The president that night stayed at the home of David Wills, the Gettysburg citizen who first suggested that a national cemetery be established.[4]

Next morning, newspaper correspondents hired horses and rode to the Wills home to greet the president. They cheered when he emerged, and he acknowledged them with a smile. Then Lincoln mounted his horse and rode off with the military escort that had been provided. The reporters spurred ahead of the parade and were in their places on the speaking platform by the time Lincoln's slow-moving column arrived. While they waited, a reporter for a Democratic newspaper stood arrogantly on the front of the platform, hat on and smoking a cigar. He made some remarks that were out of place and laughed at those who tried to quiet him, loudly announcing that this was a free country, and he'd wear his hat and smoke wherever he pleased. His fellow reporters threw him over the railing. Fortunately, order was restored by the time Lincoln arrived and took his seat between Secretary of State William Seward and the day's principal speaker, Edward Everett.[5]

According to a press association story, "Hon. Edward Everett was then introduced and proceeded with a discourse occupying two hours and four minutes in the delivery."[6] Reporters listened with varying degrees of attention as the tall, white-haired Everett delivered his speech with stately, practiced eloquence. Since they'd been furnished an advance copy of Everett's remarks, there was no need to take notes. They didn't know what Lincoln would say, but not much was expected, and they assumed they'd eventually receive a copy of his text. Then the president was introduced. The crowd cheered. Lincoln stood for a moment, waiting for the applause to die down. He put on his steel-bowed glasses, took a sheet of paper from his pocket, unfolded it, and began to read, pronouncing each word dis-tinctly. No one suspected that these were words that would be memorized and recited by generations of school children:

> "Four score and seven years ago, our fathers brought forth on this continent a new nation, conceived in liberty, and dedicated to the proposition that all men are created equal.
> "Now we are engaged in a great civil war, testing whether that nation, or any nation so conceived and so dedicated, can long en-dure. We are met on a great battlefield of that war. We have come to dedicate a portion of that field as a final resting-place for those who here gave their lives that the nation might live. It is altogether fitting and proper that we should do this."

As Lincoln was speaking, a photographer was in front of the platform, adjusting his tripod and waiting for the right moment to release the shut-ter, presumably when the president struck some oratorical pose. Lincoln continued:

> "But in a larger sense, we cannot dedicate—we cannot conse-crate—we cannot hallow—this ground. The brave men, living and dead, who struggled here, have consecrated it far above our poor power to add or detract. The world will little note nor long remem-ber what we say here, but it can never forget what they did here. It is for us the living, rather, to be dedicated here to the unfinished work which they who fought here have thus far so nobly advanced. It is rather for us to be here dedicated to the great task remaining before us—that from these honored dead we take increased devotion to that cause for which they gave the last full measure of devotion; that we here highly resolve that these dead shall not have died in vain; that this nation, under God, shall have a new birth of freedom; and that government of the people, by the people, for the people, shall not perish from the earth."

Lincoln finished, almost abruptly. The photographer desperately tried to take a picture, but he was too late. Some near the platform, watching the photographer instead of the speaker, began laughing at his discomfort. Almost everyone was startled by what one observer called "the shocking brevity" of Lincoln's address; one reporter even leaned across the aisle to ask if he was going to continue. Lincoln said he had nothing more to say. Reporters who had taken very few notes felt more comfortable when word was passed that a transcript of Lincoln's remarks would be furnished the Associated Press. This meant that each of their papers would soon have a copy.

One who recognized the quality of Lincoln's words was Edward Everett. The day after the ceremony, he wrote a gracious note to Lincoln: "I should be glad if I could flatter myself that I came as near to the central idea of the occasion in two hours as you did in two minutes." Lincoln replied: "In our respective parts yesterday, you could not have been excused to make a short address, nor I a long one. I am pleased to know that, in your judgment, the little I did say was not entirely a failure."[7]

Many papers printed Lincoln's address with little comment. The *New York Tribune* said only, "The dedicatory remarks were then delivered by the President."[8] The *New York Times*'s reporter gave little more, writing, "President Lincoln's address was delivered in a clear loud tone of voice, which could be distinctly heard at the extreme limits of the large assemblage. It was delivered (or rather read from a sheet of paper which the speaker held in his hand) in a very deliberate manner, with strong emphasis, and with a most business-like air."[9]

Samuel Bowles's *Springfield* (Massachusetts) *Republican*, however, immediately recognized the immortal beauty of Lincoln's address, calling it "a perfect gem; deep in feeling, compact in thought and expression, and tasteful and elegant in every word and comma."[10] The *Chicago Tribune* had similar praise, saying, "The dedicatory remarks of President Lincoln will live among the annals of man." The *Providence Journal* joined in: "We know not where to look for a more admirable speech than the brief one which the President made at the close of Mr. Everett's oration. . . . Could the most elaborate and splendid oration be more beautiful, more touching, more inspiring, than those thrilling words of the President? They had in our humble judgment the charm and power of the very highest eloquence."[11]

Noah Brooks was wrong when he said the president thought the speech would be of "little consequence." Lincoln knew what he was doing, and only over time would people recognize what he had accomplished, and how skillfully he had used the media on this special occasion. In the opening words of his address, he implied that the Founding Fathers, with their proposition that "all men are created equal," provided a legal basis for emancipation. It was a daring leap, in effect reframing the American Constitution. As one Lincoln scholar put it: "He altered the document from within, by appeal from its letter to the spirit, subtly changing the recalcitrant stuff of that legal compromise, bringing it to its own indictment. By implicitly doing this, he performed one of the most daring acts of open-air sleight-of-hand ever witnessed by the unsuspecting. Everyone in that vast throng of thousands was having his or her intellectual pocket picked. The crowd departed with a new thing in its ideological luggage, that new constitution Lincoln had substituted for the one they brought there with them."[12]

Somewhat predictably, the opposition press attacked the address with phrases that would also go down in history—not because they failed to appreciate Lincoln's eloquence, but because of their downright meanness. The *Harrisburg* (Pennsylvania) *Patriot and Union* wrote: "We pass over the silly remarks of the President; for the credit of the nation we are willing that the veil of oblivion shall be dropped over them and that they shall no more be repeated or thought of."[13]

Wilbur Storey's *Chicago Times* was even worse: "The cheek of every American must tingle with shame as he reads the silly, flat, and dishwatery utterances of the man who has to be pointed out to intelligent foreigners as the President of the United States."

The *Times*, however, for all its viciousness, deserves credit for sensing immediately what Lincoln was up to. How, asked the *Times*, could he give new meaning to the words of the Founding Fathers? "It was to uphold this constitution, and the Union created by it, that our officers and soldiers gave their lives at Gettysburg. How dare he, then, standing on their graves, misstate the cause for which they died, and libel the statesmen who founded the government? They were men possessing too much self-respect to declare that negroes were their equals, or were entitled to equal privileges."[14]

Much as one hates to admit it, the *Times* had a point. Nevertheless, Lincoln's Gettysburg Address was out there, being widely reproduced and widely read. His brilliant rhetoric had not only told everyone what the war was about, but had also offered a constitutional justification for that war. As for the criticism, he could live with it. That same week, in another context, Lincoln said: "These comments constitute a fair specimen of what has occurred to me through life. I have endured a great deal of ridicule without much malice, and have received a great deal of kindness not quite free from ridicule. I am used to it."[15]

Even loyal Union men, of course, who might accept the idea of emancipation, would continue to balk at the concept of equality. Back in August, Pennsylvanian John McMahon had sent Lincoln a telegram of protest: "EQUAL RIGHTS & JUSTICE TO ALL MEN IN THE UNITED STATES FOREVER. WHITE MEN IS IN CLASS NUMBER ONE & BLACK MEN IS IN CLASS NUMBER TWO & MUST BE GOVERNED BY WHITE MEN FOREVER." Secretary John Nicolay wrote a reply whose phrasing was clearly Lincoln's. After saying the president had received the wire and was meditating on it, Nicolay wrote: "As it is my business to assist him whenever I can, I will thank you to inform me, for his use, whether you are either a white man or a black one, because in either case you cannot be regarded as an entirely impartial judge. It may be that you belong to a third or fourth class of *yellow* or *red* men, in which case the impartiality of your judgment would be more apparent." It is not known how the telegram-writing McMahon reacted to Lincoln's biting logic.[16]

⭑⇒⇐⭑

Even as Lincoln was returning to Washington from Gettysburg, Ulysses Grant was making plans to lift the Chattanooga siege. On October 23 men of George Thomas's army moved against Braxton Bragg's outposts on the hills fronting Missionary Ridge. On the evening of that same day, Hooker's men were climbing Lookout Mountain on the Union right. Everything seemed to be in place, and Charles Dana wired Washington: "Grant has given orders for a vigorous attack at daybreak by Sherman on the left, and Granger [one of Thomas's corps commanders] in the centre, and if Bragg does not withdraw the remainder of his troops, we shall have a decisive battle."[17]

On November 24 Sherman moved forward and seized a position near the north end of Missionary Ridge. He told Grant he'd be ready to attack the ridge at dawn. Next day, Grant, accompanied by the ubiquitous Dana, was on a piece of high ground called Orchard Knob, watching a battle spread out in a mighty panorama. On the right, Hooker's men took Lookout Mountain in what became known as the "Battle above the Clouds." The crucial event took place in the center, when Thomas's army was ordered to seize rifle pits at the foot of Missionary Ridge. The plan was for them then to re-form, with a view to carrying the ridge itself. To Grant's and Thomas's surprise, however, once they had the rifle pits, the men kept going, surging all the way to the top. Dana wired a thrilling report: "The storming of their ridge by our troops was one of the greatest miracles in military history. No man who climbs the ascent by any of the roads that wind along its front can believe that 18,000 men were moved up its broken and crumbling face unless it was his fortune to witness the deed. It seems as awful as a visible interposition of God. . . . Bragg is in full retreat, burning his depots and bridges."

Before the day was out, Lincoln wired Grant: "Well done. Many thanks to all."[18]

The congratulatory message had been sent from a sickbed, since Lincoln had taken ill shortly after returning from Gettysburg. The initial press reports had been ominous: "At first it was supposed to be a cold, next a touch of bilious fever; a rash then appeared on his body and the disease was pronounced scarlatina; but it has leaked out that the real complaint was smallpox." Fortunately it turned out to be varioloid, a mild form of smallpox. To his physician, Lincoln quipped: "There is one consolation about the matter . . . It cannot in the least disfigure me."[19] He later told someone that since becoming president, he'd always had a crowd of people asking him to give them something, and "now he had something he could give them all."[20]

<hr />

In mid-December, Lincoln delivered his annual message to Congress. Speaking to the Congress also meant speaking to the media, and not just those in the press gallery—many congressmen had been, or remained, either editors or publishers. Newly elected congressmen, in fact, included James G. Blaine, former editor of the *Portland* (Maine) *Advertiser*, and James Brooks, the fiercely anti-Lincoln editor and publisher of the *New York Express*. Blaine, Brooks, and the other members heard not only a summary of events of the previous year, but also Lincoln's thoughts about putting the Union back together again. In a key section of the message, Lincoln talked about "Amnesty and Reconstruction." Amnesty was an old word that meant treating something as though it had never existed. Lincoln cited his pardoning powers under the Constitution and said he proposed granting amnesty to those now in "rebellion" once they swore loyalty to the Union. Reconstruction, bringing the departed brothers back into the fold, would begin with amnesty.

Lincoln's reaching out to the South struck a responsive chord in the administration press. Poet-editor William Cullen Bryant, writing in the *New York Post*, said: "Nothing, it must be admitted, could be more magnanimous or lenient toward the Rebels. . . . the President offers them not only a peace, which shall save them from the miseries of war, but an honorable pardon which shall imbue them with all the attributes of the citizen. The very condition, moreover, on which they are asked to accept these boons, is a beneficent one—the renunciation of that monstrous idol of Slavery, which has been the source of all their sacrifices and sufferings and woes."[21]

Similarly, Noah Brook told his California readers: "The reputation of President Lincoln for originality is pretty general now, but nobody expected such an original Message as that communicated to the first session of the Thirty-Eighth Congress. It has taken everybody by surprise; and, I am glad to add, the surprise is an agreeable one, for it is temperate, wise, statesmanlike and broad in its proposed treatment of the vexed questions of this hour and of the coming hour."[22]

Nevertheless, and again quite predictably, the opposition press viciously assaulted the president's message. There was particular condemnation for the proposed loyalty oath that had to precede a granting of amnesty. The *New York Metropolitan Record* called Lincoln's claim to pardoning power "brazen audacity. . . . It is the despot's claim; it is put forth in the spirit of a man who is so used to the exercise of arbitrary power that he acts and speaks upon the presumption that he is addressing a nation of slaves. He, the fourth or fifth rate lawyer—and if there was a lower rate than that he might find place under it—he, the hack politician of a sectional, factious party, pretends to tell the freemen of this country that he will pardon them." Taking such an oath, said the *Record,* would be "an act of debasement so low, an act of self-degradation so vile, that you cannot be guilty of it without placing yourself on a level with the great criminal who now occupies the Presidential chair."[23]

Some even carped at the unpolished way that Lincoln chose to word the proposed oath of allegiance. "It is in his own style," said the *Chicago Times,* "and his is a style that nobody imitates. Slipshod as have been all his literary performances, this is the most slovenly of all. If they were slipshod, this is barefoot, and the feet, plainly enough, have never been shod."[24]

In truth, the oath was straightforward and easily comprehended. Hostile editors, however, infatuated with their own word spinning, just didn't get it. Lincoln spoke to the common man—and the common man understood. Despite the vituperation, thoughtful men everywhere, both North and South, saw that plain-spoken Lincoln was looking ahead, to a day when the nation would be reunited and at peace. The loyalty oath would give some measure of satisfaction to those who saw all Confederates as traitors; it would also be a tangible instrument for sorting Southerners who sincerely wanted peace from those who remained unyielding in their hatred of the Union. As a precondition to any rebel oath taking, of course, the war had to be brought to a successful conclusion. Nevertheless, although peace was still off in a distant, murky future, Lincoln was thinking about what would come "afterwards." Moreover, he wanted his countrymen to do likewise, to think of the postwar era as a time of reconciliation and compassion. Having his words appear in the media was a significant step in the right direction.

The seating of the new Congress also meant that Lincoln was starting the fourth—and perhaps final—year of his presidency. People were already beginning to wonder if he planned to run again. Or if he even wanted to. Back in October, Illinois Congressman Elihu Washburne (perhaps thinking of presidential possibilities for his own favorite, Ulysses Grant) wrote

Lincoln to say, "The time has come when we must confront the question of our next presidential candidate. I think you ought to let some of your confidential friends know your wishes."

Although Lincoln answered affirmatively, he made it sound more like a qualified "maybe." "A second term would be a great honor and a great labor," he wrote Washburne, "which together, perhaps I would not decline, if tendered."[25]

--◦≡◦⊂≡◦--

Now that Chattanooga was safe, Lincoln's thoughts turned to Ambrose Burnside, besieged at Knoxville in east Tennessee by "Old Pete"—Confederate General James Longstreet. In late November, Longstreet learned that Bragg had been defeated at Chattanooga and was in full retreat; he also learned that Sherman's corps had left Chattanooga and was en route to join Burnside. Longstreet launched an attack, hoping to win a quick victory before Burnside was reinforced. The attack failed, and "Old Pete" shortly was heading northeast, into the mountains and back to Virginia. Lincoln was ecstatic. So was the *New York Tribune* as it announced: "Decisive news at last from East Tennessee—news more glorious and infinitely more important than if we had heard of a battle and a victory almost anywhere else. The siege of Knoxville is at an end. The Rebel effort to regain East Tennessee is abandoned forever."[26]

--◦≡◦⊂≡◦--

As 1863 drew to a close, the North was more bountiful and prosperous than ever. And more vigorous. On December 3 ground was broken at Omaha for the new Union Pacific Railroad. The population was steadily increasing, thanks in large part to an increased flow of immigrants. Many of the new arrivals—miners, mechanics, mill hands—brought needed skills with them. And as Greeley's *Tribune* later noted, about a tenth of those arriving in New York were entering the Union Army or Navy.[27] Harvests were good, with machines like the cotton gin and the McCormick reaper adding to farmland productivity. New towns were springing up; new lands were being cleared, and the North felt a new wave of patriotism. Apparently, Lincoln's messages were getting through, for in every town there was martial music, with songs having lyrics like "We'll rally round the flag, boys, we'll rally once again," and a succession of patriotic editorials, poems, and stories. That December Edward E. Hale's essay, "The Man without a Country," appeared, was widely republished, and was probably worth a division of soldiers to the Union Army. Men like Vallandigham and McClellan might be urging Lincoln to seek a negotiated peace, but the country wasn't buying it.[28]

At Cooper Institute, where in 1860 Lincoln made one of the most important speeches of his life, a meeting was held to promote the raising of volunteers. Lincoln, perhaps remembering that earlier occasion and how it helped him with the New York press, took advantage of an opportunity to solidify eastern support. He sent a letter to those at the Cooper Institute meeting, expressing gratification that a part of the Army of the Potomac had shared in the victories just won in Tennessee by men of the Great West.[29]

⊶⚬⊷

The year 1864 began at the White House with the traditional New Year's reception. Noah Brooks wrote: "The President looks better since he has had the varioloid. I don't mean to insinuate that the disease has added any new charms to his features; but his complexion is clearer, his eyes less lack-luster and he has a hue of health to which he has long been a stranger. He stood up manfully against the great crush and bore the handshaking like a blessed old martyr, as he is."[30]

As Lincoln greeted the New Year's well-wishers, he was fully aware that 1864 would be crucial, for him and for the country. Evidently, even as he coped with a multitude of problems, seeking reelection was never far from Lincoln's mind. In an unguarded moment, he told Noah Brooks that "if the people think that I have managed their case for them well enough to trust me to carry up to the next term, I am sure that I shall be glad to take it."[31] However, reelection was far from certain, and even renomination was doubtful. Already some were suggesting that Lincoln was not electable, that they should abandon him and seek a new Republican candidate, perhaps in the person of a popular general.

Although Lincoln was still a consummate politician, his main concern was not the coming election, but the saving of the Union. That
meant prosecuting the war successfully. And could he best do that by
selecting a new general in chief? If so, the obvious choice was Ulysses
Grant, the man who had captured two rebel armies, routed a third, and
was now acclaimed as a national hero. After Chattanooga, the *New York
Tribune* had shouted that "Gen. Grant is master of the whole field—and
of himself. To his genius and energy, and to the noble army which he
commands, the nation may trust its destiny without fear and without
impatience."[32]

The *New York World* was equally effusive, saying, "General Grant . . .
has evolved a victory for our arms the importance of which it is yet impossible to estimate." It was especially noteworthy, said the *World*, because it
was "not coupled with news of a great and terrible slaughter." The *New
York Herald,* not to be outdone, had joined the chorus, trumpeting loudly,
"Gen. Grant is one of the great soldiers of the age . . . without an equal in
the list of generals now alive."[33] Following all this, Grant's long-time congressional supporter, Elihu Washburne, introduced a bill reviving the grade
of lieutenant general. It was obvious, of course, that if a third star became
legal, it would be intended for Grant.

When the lieutenant general bill became known, the cynical *New
York Herald* hinted that the whole thing was a political ploy of Lincoln's.
A *Herald* editorial said, "The rank is to be revived that it may be conferred on General Grant, in the hope no doubt that such a high military
position will switch him off the presidential track. . . . If the politicians
think they are going to beat General Grant, General McClellan, or any
other general out of the Presidency by any humbug of this sort they will
find themselves woefully mistaken."[34]

Soon James Gordon Bennett and the *Herald* began touting Grant's
candidacy in earnest. The people were sick of politicians, Bennett said,
and Grant, whose "opinions on parties and party questions" were completely unknown, would be a welcome change. "Let the independent
masses of the people, who have cut themselves loose from the machinery of the corrupt and dismantled political parties of the day, take this

Presidential business into their own hands and bring General Grant at once into the field. A few town and country meetings . . . will put the ball in motion, and once fairly in motion it cannot be arrested."[35]

Over at the *Tribune*, Horace Greeley was being cynical—not about Grant, but about James Gordon Bennett! *Herald* "crusades," Greeley suggested, were only tricks to boost circulation. Bennett's support, in fact, was a kiss of death. "This vivacious journal," Greeley wrote, "now seeks a new sensation in the person of Gen. Grant. The furor with which it lays hold of its fresh victim indicates that its passion will not last long. . . . We have the highest appreciation of Gen. Grant. We believe there can be scarcely any limit set to his powers of endurance. And, having as much confidence in the sincerity of our contemporary as we ever had, we beg leave to assure it that there are some things which even Ulysses S. Grant cannot survive, viz. six articles per day in its columns in favor of his nomination and election to the Presidency."[36]

As ever, Lincoln was attuned to the media. He heard the drumbeats for a Grant candidacy, and he wondered how the general stood on the matter. Surely it wouldn't do to award him a third star, only to have him use it as a leg up onto the presidency. All in all, it made Lincoln uneasy, and he asked Elihu Washburne, a fellow Illinois politician, for his opinion. Washburne assured the president that Grant had no such ambitions. Then, at Washburne's suggestion, J. Russell Jones of Galena, a man who knew Grant well, was invited to visit Lincoln to talk about Grant's political leanings. Coincidentally, on the very day Jones left home, he had received a letter from Grant on that very subject. "I am receiving a great deal of that kind of literature," Grant had written, "but it soon finds its way into the waste basket. I already have a pretty big job on my hands, and my only ambition is to see this rebellion suppressed. Nothing could induce me to think of being a presidential candidate, particularly so long as there is a possibility of having Mr. Lincoln re-elected."[37]

At the White House, Jones took out the letter and showed it to the president. "My son," Lincoln said, "you will never know how gratifying that is to me. No man knows, when that Presidential grub gets to gnawing at him, just how deep it will get until he has tried it; and I didn't know but what there was one gnawing at Grant." According to Jones, that incident "established a perfect understanding" between the president and the general.[38]

That settled the matter for Lincoln, both politically and personally. In late February, Congress passed Washburne's lieutenant general bill. It was promptly signed by the president, and on March 3, Grant received a wire from Halleck: "The Secretary of War directs that you report in person to the War Department as early as practicable, considering the condition of your command." This was followed quickly by a second Halleck telegram: "The Secretary of War directs me to say to you that your commission as lieutenant-general is signed and will be delivered to you on your arrival at the War Department. I sincerely congratulate you on this recognition of your distinguished and meritorious services."[39]

With that, Grant was on his way to Washington. Horace Greeley was one of the first to weigh in on the new development: "It has pleased Congress to decree the appointment of a Lieutenant-General, and the President, with the entire assent of both Houses, has selected ULYSSES S. GRANT for the most responsible position.

"We had nothing to say, pro or con, while this matter was in progress; we neither urged the creation of a Lieutenant-Generalship, nor recommended Gen. Grant for the position. But now that the work is done, we most respectfully suggest that the conduct of the War, under the President, be committed absolutely to the Lieutenant-General, and that we all—Congress, Cabinet, and the Press—Republicans and Democrats, Conservatives and Radicals, take hold and strengthen his hands for the immense responsibility devolved upon him."[40]

To that, Abraham Lincoln might well have added a fervent "Amen."

CHAPTER 12

-→≡◎⊂≡←-

"WHY, HERE IS GENERAL GRANT!"

O n the evening of March 8, 1864, the Lincolns were holding their weekly White House reception. The president stood in the Blue Room, the first lady and several cabinet officers at his side, shaking hands cordially as a vast procession of men and women passed by. Suddenly there was a commotion in the crowd, caused by the appearance of a short, unprepossessing figure in uniform. As the new-comer joined the line waiting to meet the president, the crowd parted like Red Sea waves, making way for the man of the hour, Ulysses S. Grant.

Lincoln recognized the general at once from pictures he had seen. Stepping forward, hand outstretched and smiling, he said, "Why, here is General Grant! Well, this is a great pleasure, I assure you." Bystanders couldn't help noting the contrast. At six-foot-four, Lincoln hovered over the other by a full eight inches. The two talked for a few moments, then Secretary Seward took over, introducing Grant to Mrs. Lincoln and then escorting him to the East Room, where citizens pushed and shoved to catch a glimpse of the western hero. Finally Grant had to mount a sofa—both to be seen and to keep from being trampled underfoot! He was "blushing like a schoolgirl," someone said, as he shook hands until sweat poured down his face. Grant later said it was a hotter scene than he had ever known in battle.

"It was the only real mob I ever saw at the White House," Noah Brooks wrote. "The crowd at the levee was immense, and for once the interest was temporarily transferred from the President to the newcomer. The mass of people thronged about him wherever he moved, everybody being anxious to get at least a glimpse of his face." After spending an uncomfortable hour as the center of attention, Grant managed to free himself and join Lincoln and Secretary Stanton in a small conference room.[1]

Lincoln asked Grant to come to the White House the following day for a formal presentation of his commission as a lieutenant general. Frankly, Lincoln said, the presentation ceremony was "for an object," an attention-getting device to generate favorable publicity. Accordingly, the entire cabinet would be on hand to make the affair more newsworthy. He himself would make a brief talk, Lincoln said, after which Grant would be expected to respond. Perhaps Grant wasn't as used to speech making as he was, Lincoln said, so he might make a suggestion. That was an understatement if ever there was one; Grant was a miserable public speaker. And unlike many generals, he desperately *hated* being called upon. Lincoln evidently was aware of this, so he made it easy on the general. To let Grant know what was coming, Lincoln gave him a copy of his own proposed remarks. Then, as Lincoln's secretary, John Hay, recalled it, Lincoln went on to say:

"There are two points that I would like to have you make in your answer. First, to say something which shall prevent or obviate any jealousy of you from any of the other generals in the service, and second, something which shall put you on as good terms as possible with the Army of the Potomac. Now, consider whether this may not be said to make it of some advantage; and if you see any objection whatever to doing it, be under no restraint whatever in expressing that objection to the Secretary of War, who will talk further with you about it."[2]

Next day, with the cabinet on hand as promised, Lincoln stood facing Grant and read from his prepared text: "General Grant, the nation's appreciation of what you have done, and its reliance upon you for what remains

to do, in the existing great struggle, are now presented with this commission, constituting you lieutenant-general in the army of the United States.
With this high honor devolves upon you also a corresponding responsibility. As the country herein trusts you, so, under God, it will sustain you.
I scarcely need add, that with what I here speak for the nation, goes my
own hearty concurrence."

Grant, looking awkward and ill-at-ease, took a half-sheet of paper
from his pocket. He appeared to have difficulty reading his own penciled
scrawl. However, he was quoted as saying: "Mr. President, I accept the
commission, with gratitude for the high honor conferred. With the aid of
the noble armies that have fought in so many fields for our common country, it will be my earnest endeavor not to disappoint your expectations. I
feel the full weight of the responsibilities devolving on me, and I know that
if they are met, it will be due to those armies, and above all to the favor of
that Providence which leads both nations and men." Before the day was
out, those two simple speeches had been telegraphed to the entire country.
Lincoln had his "media event," and it was eminently successful. No one
noticed that Grant had failed to mention either of the points suggested
by the president.[3]

Almost immediately, the media began telling Grant what he should
do. Lincoln had been forced to cope with this type of thing all along; now
Grant was seeing it, and in the process gaining added appreciation for the
pressures being put on the president. Some were saying that Henry Halleck, the man Grant was replacing as general in chief, was sure to resent
Grant and should certainly be sent home. Others were demanding that
Grant relieve George Meade from command of the Army of the Potomac.

In addition to the media exerting pressure on Grant, there was also
politicking and intrigue from within Grant's own camp, some of it from
the young, ambitious James H. Wilson, a former engineer officer on Grant's
staff. Wilson, adept at forming alliances with men of influence, had become a friend of Charles Dana during the Vicksburg campaign, had risen
rapidly in rank, and by 1864 was a brigadier general at the War Department. Writing to General William F. "Baldy" Smith, who he thought
should replace Meade, Wilson said: "Mr. Dana and I have had a long talk,
and conclude first that Meade is not fully nor nearly equal to the occasion—

he is weak, timid and almost puerile." Unfortunately, said Wilson, the authorities, if left to themselves, would not remove Meade, but he had confidence that Grant would "secure to the Army of the Potomac a commander of intelligence [meaning Smith] equal to its control, capable of carrying it wherever he wishes."[4]

Dana, in turn, had little use for Meade, later saying he had "long known Meade to be a man of the worst possible temper, especially toward his subordinates. I think he had not a friend in the whole army."[5] Dana, with Wilson's help, most assuredly was doing all he could to have Meade replaced. Grant, however, a man not easily swayed, would decide such things for himself.

On February 16, well before Grant arrived in Washington, Halleck had written General Sherman: "You have probably seen the attempt in the newspapers to create difficulties and jealousies between me and General Grant. This is all for political effect. There is not the slightest ground for any such assertions. There cannot and will not be any differences between us. If he is made lieutenant-general, as I presume he will be, I shall most cordially welcome him to the command, glad to be relieved from so thankless and disagreeable a position."[6]

In turn, "Cump" Sherman wrote his friend Grant: "Don't stay in Washington. Halleck is better qualified than you to stand the buffets of intrigues and policy."[7] It was good advice. "Old Brains" Halleck, whom Lincoln once called a "first-rate clerk," had been a disappointment in many ways. However, Grant respected him and knew him to be an able administrator. He asked "Old Brains" to remain in Washington, serving as chief of staff.

Grant next proceeded to Meade's headquarters, where the honorable Meade volunteered to step aside willingly if Grant chose to replace him. As Grant later wrote: "I assured him that I had no thought of replacing him. . . . This incident gave me even a more favorable opinion of Meade than did his great victory at Gettysburg the July before. It is men who wait to be selected, and not those who seek, from whom we may always expect the most efficient services."[8]

An admiring Meade later wrote his wife that "Grant is very phlegmatic, and holds in great contempt newspaper criticism, and thinks, as long as a man is sustained by his own conscience, his superiors, and the government, it is not worth his while to trouble himself about the newspapers."[9] When Grant returned to Washington, Lieutenant Colonel Cyrus B. Comstock, a trusted member of Grant's staff, wrote in his diary that Meade's position was secure: "Grant, who at Chattanooga thought Baldy Smith should have it, now says no change. The programme is, Halleck here as office man and military adviser, Sherman to take Grant's place, McPherson Sherman's, Grant in the field."[10]

When it was later learned that Horace Greeley was in Washington urging that Meade be replaced, Grant responded by saying, "If I saw Greeley, I would tell him that when I wanted the advice of a political editor in selecting generals I would call on him."[11]

It was probably just as well that Greeley didn't hear Grant's remark, for at the moment he was singing the general's praises: "Gen. Grant had a conference today, three hours long, with the Secretary of War and General Halleck upon the military situation in every one of our fighting departments. . . . He has hardly slept from his long journey here, and yet is hard at work. It is mentioned with joy among Senators that he is not going to hire a house here, nor make war ridiculous by attempting to maneuver armies and battles in distant States from an armchair in a Washington parlor." The last bit, about maneuvering armies from a Washington parlor, was an obvious slap at McClellan and Halleck, who had tried doing just that.[12]

Back at the Capitol, Grant informed Lincoln and Stanton he was returning to Nashville to meet Sherman and turn over command of the western armies. The social activity of the past three days, he told Lincoln, "were rather the warmest campaign I have witnessed during the war."

He couldn't go just yet, Lincoln said. Mrs. Lincoln was planning a dinner party in his honor, and without Grant, Lincoln said, the dinner would be like *Hamlet* with Hamlet left out. Grant bravely stuck to his guns. "I appreciate the honor Mrs. Lincoln would do me," he said, "but time is more important now. And really, Mr. Lincoln, I have had enough of this show business."[13]

Grant had it just about right—Washington social life *was* "show business," even when it came to presidential dinner parties. And Grant did not see spinning things for the press as part of his job description. Earlier, for example, when reporters wanted a statement explaining his roundabout maneuvers leading up to the siege of Vicksburg, Grant reportedly said, "This life is too brief to be frittered away with explanations."[14]

Grant for the moment could operate that way. Lincoln could not. Putting on a political show, and using the press to report it, was a vital tool in the presidential repertoire. An opportunity to use that tool came in early April. When Lincoln met at the White House with a group from the border states, he said he feared that "Kentuckians felt unkindly toward him, in consequence of not properly understanding the difficulties by which he was surrounded in his efforts to put down the rebellion." A. G. Hodges, editor of the *Frankfort* (Kentucky) *Commonwealth*, spoke up and asked the president to put in writing some of the things he had said during the meeting. Hodges was an editor who had always proven friendly, and Lincoln knew that such a letter would be given good treatment. On April 4 he wrote Hodges a carefully phrased, eloquent letter, saying among other things: "I am naturally antislavery. If slavery is not wrong, nothing is wrong. I can not remember when I did not so think and feel. . . . I claim *not* to have controlled events, but confess plainly that events have controlled *me*." In closing, he wrote: "If God now wills the removal of a great wrong, and wills that we also of the North, as well as you of the South, shall pay fairly for our complicity in that wrong, impartial history will find therein new cause to attest and revere the justice and goodness of God."[15]

The *Commonwealth's* story of the interview and the text of Lincoln's letter were newspaper sensations, reprinted by the leading papers of the country. The *New York Tribune* spoke highly of it, as did the *New York Times*, which said, "The letter of President Lincoln to the editor of the *Frankfort Commonwealth* is a new and admirable specimen of his ingenious character, and of his remarkable aptness in stating the truth."[16]

⋆⟴⟵⋆

General Orders Number 98, dated March 12, 1864, made the changes official. Grant was named the Union's general in chief; Sherman was given command in the West; and James B. McPherson took over Sherman's department. Back in Nashville, Grant met with Sherman and the two forged an overall plan for fighting the war. As Sherman put it, "Grant was to go for Lee, I was to go for Joe Johnston." In addition, Nathaniel Banks would conclude his Red River campaign, gather all available forces in New Orleans, and mount an offensive in the direction of Mobile, Alabama.[17]

Grant reasoned that the South was getting weak on manpower. Since they couldn't be strong on every front, they frequently shifted forces from one theater to another. To prevent them from doing this, Grant decided that the North should attack simultaneously from multiple directions. May 4 was set as the date for beginning the spring offensives. A last-minute message from Lincoln said he was well pleased with what had happened so far, that he didn't know the particulars of Grant's plans, nor did he need to. Lastly, he told Grant, "If there is anything wanting, which is in my power to give, do not fail to let me know it. And now, with a brave army, and a just cause, may God sustain you."[18]

Grant had told Meade: "Lee's army will be your objective point. Wherever Lee goes, there you will go also." Evidently Grant felt that applied to himself as well. He was with Meade as the Army of the Potomac swung into action, crossing the Rapidan on May 4 and entering a region known as the "Wilderness." This was the area where Lee and Stonewall Jackson had trounced "Fighting Joe" Hooker a year earlier, almost to the day. Grant had hoped to slip into open country without being challenged. However, Lee responded promptly to the threat, and soon the opposing armies were heavily engaged in what Horace Greeley later called "a tangled labyrinth."[19] The Yanks had more men, but the Rebs knew the terrain, and the preponderance of force only made things cumbersome in the dense, smoke-filled woods, where soldiers could rarely see the enemy, friendly troops often fired on each other by mistake, and exploding shells set underbrush on fire, threatening wounded men with a fiery death. On the second day, Grant wired Halleck: "So far there has been no decisive result. . . . I do not think our loss exceeds 8,000." Actually, it would reach 17,500 before Grant withdrew, but unlike Hooker after Chancellorsville, he did not "skedaddle" back north. Instead he slipped southeast toward Spotsylvania, ten miles away. "Our spirits rose," recalled one veteran who remembered the moment as a turning point in the war. Despite the terrors of the past three days and those to come, "we marched free. The men began to sing." When Grant reached Spotsylvania, however, it was only to find that Lee, anticipating his move, was already there, dug in and waiting.[20]

Back in Washington, Lincoln was anxiously waiting for news. He was as much in the dark as everyone else, in part because he had deliberately not asked about Grant's plans. In his *Memoirs*, Grant said that Stanton and Halleck "both cautioned me against giving the President my plans of campaign, saying that he was so kind-hearted, so averse to refusing anything asked of him, that some friend would be sure to get from him all he knew. I should have said that in our interview the President told me he did not want to know what I proposed to do."[21]

In a way, this was a defense mechanism for Lincoln, who wanted to remain on good terms with the press. Not knowing any inside information allowed him to get away with a dialogue such as one reported by the *Chicago Journal*:

> VISITOR: When will the army move?
> LINCOLN: Ask General Grant.
> VISITOR: General Grant will not tell me.
> LINCOLN: Neither will he tell me.[22]

From the start of the campaign, Grant had refused to allow reporters to use the telegraph. Consequently, all that was known came from Grant's messages to Halleck. Although the media might complain about this, they knew that the War Department had been granted censorship authority, at first temporarily, then permanently on February 25, 1862. Moreover, on March 20, 1862, the House Judiciary Committee, after resolving piously, "That the government shall not interfere with free transmission of intelligence by telegraph," had qualified that by adding "when the same will not aid the enemy in his military or naval operations, or give him information concerning such operations on the part of the government." In other words, censorship, and Army control of the telegraph, was perfectly legal, even though in the past reporters had often found a way to circumvent it. This time, however, the news blackout was complete, and Lincoln obviously approved.[23]

To members of Congress who asked what was going on, the president said: "Well, I can't tell much about it. You see, Grant has gone to the Wilderness, crawled in, drawn up the ladder, and pulled in the hole after him, and I guess we'll have to wait till he comes out before we know what he's up to."[24]

Unfortunately, however, someone representing the administration *was* talking to the press. Despite Grant's report of losses, statements were appearing with phrases like "the brilliant success of the Army of the Potomac against the rebel army." Such words would make the public shock even worse when the appalling casualty figures began coming in. The culprit may have been Major Charles G. Halpine, who one observer referred to as the man who "runs the semi-official newspaper department, that is to say creates public opinion in favor of what the government wishes." During the war, Halpine served in Washington as an aide to Gen. Henry Halleck, and in the field on the staff of Gen. David Hunter. At one point Halpine advocated setting up a special press bureau within the War Department, but this was never formalized. Nevertheless, wherever he was, Halpine acted as a Washington source for the *New York Times,* for Thurlow Weed's *Evening Journal,* and for Forney's *Philadadelphia Press.* For a time he even edited a party journal in Washington, the *National Republican.*[25]

After two days of fighting, however, as two exhausted armies lay facing each other, the world still knew nothing of what was happening in Virginia. Mosby's guerrillas were roaming the countryside between the army and Washington, and the railroads had been cut. Frank Chapman of the *New York Herald* "very ostentatiously" offered $1,000 to any reporter who'd try to get through guerrilla country to a telegraph line. Someone from the *World* made a similar offer. It was a fabulous sum, but there were no takers. Finally Henry Wing, a green twenty-four-year-old *Tribune* reporter, volunteered to go after being promised $100 if he'd make the try. He was told to leave at dawn. Wing sought out Grant, told him he was about to leave for Washington, and asked if he had any message for the authorities there. Grant thought for a moment, then said, "If you see the President, tell him, from me, that, whatever happens, there will be no turning back."

Wing's day became an incredible melodrama as he encountered guerrillas, convinced them he was a Confederate sympathizer, was discovered, then escaped and swam for dear life across a river as bullets splashed all around. Finally, after losing his horse and hobbling for miles on foot, Wing was apprehended by suspicious Union pickets. They took him under guard to Union Mills, some twenty miles from Washington. From there he sent a telegram addressed to Charles Dana at the War Department.

"I am just in from the front," the telegram read. "Left Grant at 4 o'clock this morning." He asked Dana for permission to send a message over military wires to the *New York Tribune*. Dana was not on hand to receive the message, but unfortunately for the exhausted young reporter, Stanton was. He denied Wing permission, telling him instead to send his message to the War Department. Wing said he couldn't do that, not unless he could also send it to the *Tribune*. A furious Stanton denounced him as a spy.

At this point Lincoln entered the picture. As was his custom, he came that evening to the War Department telegraph office. There one of the operators told him about a young reporter, Henry Wing, who had news of the army and wanted to send a message to his editors at the *Tribune*. According to the operator, Stanton had denied Wing permission to send the telegram. Moreover, when Wing said he wouldn't talk to the War Department unless he could also send that telegram, Stanton had ordered him shot as a spy.

Lincoln was incredulous. "Ordered him shot?"

"Yes, Mr. President," replied the operator. Lincoln had a message sent asking if Wing would talk to *him*. Wing said that he would, if he could also send 100 words to his paper. Lincoln agreed, and asked Wing to come to Washington to tell the full story in person. Soon the 100-word message was received at the War Department, and on Lincoln's order, was made available to the Associated Press.[26]

This was all well and good, but Lincoln knew he couldn't just rely on fragmentary reports from some daring reporter. He needed his own media figure to be where the action was. Accordingly, he sent for Charles Dana, who had been at a reception. Still in evening clothes, Dana hurried to the War Department, where Lincoln was talking to Stanton.

"Dana," Lincoln said, "you know we have been in the dark for two days since Grant moved. We are very much troubled, and have concluded to send you down there. How soon can you start?"

"In half an hour," Dana replied. In about that time, Dana had an engine fired up at Alexandria for the first leg of his journey, had changed clothes, and was about to board a train to take him to Alexandria. Suddenly an orderly galloped up with word that the president wished to see him. Dana rode back to the War Department, as he said, "in hot haste."

Lincoln was waiting for him, and looking up, said, "Well, Dana, since you went away I've been thinking about it. I don't like to send you down there."

"But why not, Mr. President?"

"You can't tell," Lincoln said, "just where Lee is or what he might be doing, and Jeb Stuart is rampaging around pretty lively in between the Rappahannock and the Rapidan. It's a considerable risk, and I don't like to expose you to it."

Dana said he'd be traveling with a cavalry guard and riding a strong horse. If they were attacked, they could probably fight, and if it came to the worst, they could always run. He really wanted to go. "In that case," Lincoln said, "I rather wish you would. Good night, and God bless you."[27]

Dana rode to the waiting train, and minutes later was on his way. On its return trip, that same train brought Henry Wing to Washington. Between one and two in the morning, Wing arrived at the White House, where the cabinet was on hand, awaiting his arrival. He described for them, as best he could, the crossing of the Rapidan and the confused fighting that followed. He didn't know how the battle had gone, but he *did* know that Grant had scheduled another attack for the next morning. When the cabinet members filed out, Wing asked if he could speak to Lincoln alone.

"You wanted to speak to me?"

"Yes, Mr. President. I have a message for you—a message from General Grant. He told me I was to tell you, Mr. President, that there would be no turning back." That was something Lincoln needed to hear. Impulsively, the president put his arm around the diminutive Wing and kissed his cheek. He made Wing report the exact circumstances in which the message was given. Then he thanked Wing, told him to go get some sleep, and come to see him the next day.[28]

When Wing prepared to return to the front, Lincoln asked him, whenever he returned to Washington, to come "tell me all you hear and see."

On one of his returns, strangely enough, Lincoln talked to him about the coming presidential election. It depressed him, Lincoln said, to think of running again. "There's many a night, Henry, that I plan to resign. I wouldn't run again now if I didn't know these other fellows couldn't save the Union on their platform, whatever they say. I can't quit, Henry. I have to stay." Their conversation provides an interesting insight on Lincoln's view of the media. Somehow he felt comfortable telling things to this young reporter that he might not have shared with another politician.[29]

Grant later wrote of the Wilderness battle: "More desperate fighting had not been witnessed on this continent than that of the 5th and 6th of May."[30] At Spotsylvania, incredibly, it became even *more* fierce and intense, turning into an inconclusive, very bloody two-week shootout. At one nightmarish location, forever after known as the "Bloody Angle," bodies were stacked eight and ten deep. Fighting was unbelievably savage, as men thrust bayonets through chinks in a log parapet or rose to fire point-blank into men huddling behind corpses serving as shields.

As the soldiers did their job, Dana did his. Grant's aide, Horace Porter, gave testimony to Lincoln's wisdom in selecting a journalist to be his "eyes at the front." Porter said of Dana, "His daily, and sometimes hourly, dispatches to the War Department, giving the events occurring in the field constituted a correspondence which is a rare example of perspicuity, accuracy, and vividness of description."[31]

At 8:30 A.M. on May 11, from "Near Spotsylvania Court House," Grant wired Halleck: "We have reached the sixth day of very heavy fighting." He estimated his loss at 20,000 men, including eleven generals killed, wounded, or missing. However, he went on to say, "I think the loss of the enemy must be greater—we having taken over four thousand prisoners in battle, whilst he has taken from us but few except a few stragglers. I am now sending back to Belle Plain all my wagons for a fresh supply of provisions and ammunition, and propose to fight it out on this line if it takes all summer. . . . I am satisfied the enemy are very shaky, and are only kept up to the mark by the greatest exertions on the part of their officers, and by keeping them intrenched in every position they take."[32]

That same day, Congressman Washburne, who had been accompanying Grant's army, prepared to return to Washington. Did Grant have any message for the president? Grant said he didn't want to raise any false hopes. The fighting had been severe, and it wasn't getting any easier. Also, he normally communicated with Washington through General Halleck. However, Grant said, if Washburne would wait a moment, he would write something for Halleck that Washburne could show Mr. Lincoln.

At the nation's capital, people knew only that the Army of the Potomac had not engaged in another "skedaddle." After fighting in the Wilderness, it appeared that Grant had kept moving south. For the public, that alone was cause for celebration, enough in fact to bring them to the White House lawn. They cheered when Lincoln stepped out on the portico, cheered again when he said he supposed their appearance resulted from "the good news received today from the army."

Lincoln reminded the crowd that much work remained to be done. However, he added, he had just seen a message from Gen. Grant, and it appeared he had "not been jostled in his purposes." Then Lincoln quoted a line from Grant's dispatch. It brought the greatest cheer yet: "I propose to fight it out on this line if it takes all summer."[33]

CHAPTER 13

"I BEGIN TO SEE IT"

Well before the end of 1863, Northern editors were testing the waters, mentioning possible candidates for the coming year's presidential election. While Republicans were divided, Democrats had more or less settled on Gen. George McClellan as their candidate.

Most Democratic editors agreed with McClellan that the Union must be preserved, but only in its prewar condition. Slavery should be left alone, in other words, and the war was not against the Southern people, but only their leaders. Therefore emancipation was a mistake, one that it wasn't too late to correct. McClellan, who saw himself as the country's "savior," had said these same things early and often, and while he never said publicly that he was a candidate, everyone saw he was making the right moves. He was living in New York, the largest Democratic stronghold in the North, and consorting with party leaders such as August Belmont, the wealthy chairman of the Democratic National Committee. Whenever he emerged from his hotel, he was greeted by cheering partisan crowds that followed him all over town. It was a heady experience; nevertheless, McClellan saw himself as a soldier, not a politician, and was hoping—no, *believing*—he could secure the Democratic nomination without having to campaign. He would let the power brokers come to him. When asked about his candidacy, he countered with only a Sphinx-like smile, for as he told Charles C. Fulton of the *Baltimore American*, he was trying "to remain as quiet as possible."[1]

McClellan was unique. Never before had a fired general maintained such popularity. The Army of the Potomac still loved him, as did much of the public; many still clamored for his return to active service, if not in the military, then in the political arena. Even McClellan's longtime critic, Horace Greeley, acknowledged that the "Young Napoleon" had the inside track for the Democratic nomination, calling him "the true and rightful pro-Slavery candidate for President, which nobody can deny."[2]

While Democratic editors had settled on their man, Republican editors were sharply divided. The *Chicago Tribune*, for its part, was solidly pro-Lincoln, acting as though his candidacy were all but certain: "So far as can be gathered, the public generally mean to elect Mr. Lincoln, when the time comes for an election. . . . God meant him for President, or the nation is deceived." *Harper's Weekly* agreed, saying editorially at the beginning of 1864: "If the Presidential election took place next week, Mr. Lincoln would undoubtedly be returned by a greater majority than any President since Washington. And unless he is deserted by his great sagacity, or some huge military disaster befalls the country, or some serious blunder is committed by the Union men in Congress, his election is as sure as the triumph of the nation over rebellion." The *New York Times* and other Republican papers generally concurred. [3]

Some, however, while recognizing Lincoln as the obvious candidate, suspected they could get a better one, or perhaps more important, one with a better chance of being elected. Bennett's *New York Herald*, for example, asked: "What has President Lincoln done to entitle him to a re-election? We contend that he has done nothing to earn this high distinction, but that on the contrary, in the conduct of the war, his deplorable mismanagement of our most important armies, with the disastrous and alarming consequences, have furnished evidence sufficient to convince the country that he is not the pilot to carry us through the perils of this war into the broad and secure anchorage of a re-established Union."[4]

The Copperhead *New York Daily News* was even more vicious, claiming Lincoln was trying to steal the election by accrediting those Confederate States where 10 percent of the population had signed a loyalty oath. "President Lincoln means to be a candidate for re-election," said the *News,* "and he hopes that the Electoral College in thus-to-be-recovered and thus-to-be 'loyal' States will . . . cast their votes unanimously for him and thus assure his re-election. . . . We say to President Lincoln that if he counts to foist himself in this manner upon the country for a second term he will be grievously disappointed. The people see through this game, and will not permit it to be successfully played."[5]

There was of course no shortage of Republican alternatives. Horace Greeley, the self-anointed spokesman of the Republican party, asked his readers if Lincoln was so able a president "that all consideration of the merits, abilities, and services of others should be postponed or forborne in favor of his reelection? . . . We answer . . . in the negative. Heartily agreeing that Mr. Lincoln has done well, we do not regard it as at all demonstrated that Governor Chase, General Fremont, General Butler or General Grant cannot do as well."[6]

As Greeley indicated, many still wanted the Republicans to run Ulysses Grant, the Union's most successful general to date. However, Grant had ruled himself out, telling Lincoln and others he wasn't interested. And while some editors still insisted Grant was the man, John Rawlins, Grant's trusted chief of staff, was writing Congressman Washburne: "The advocacy of the New York Herald and other papers of the General for the Presidency gives him little concern, he is unambitious of the honor."[7]

Fremont and Butler, each of whom had his supporters, were probably not serious threats to Lincoln's candidacy. Waiting in the Republican wings, however, was someone who *was* a threat, the distinguished secretary of the treasury, Salmon P. Chase. The politically astute Chase was ready, extremely willing, and in his own mind, more than able. He still believed the party had made a great mistake in 1860 by nominating Lincoln instead of him. He planned to correct that mistake in 1864. Wouldn't he after all make a far better president than the uncouth Lincoln? Chase, for one, had no doubt how that question should be answered. As Ohio Senator

Ben Wade saw it: "Chase is a good man, but his theology is unsound. He thinks there is a fourth person in the Trinity."[8]

All in all, said the *New York Herald,* "There is nothing fixed on either side, except what the Rev. Henry Ward Beecher would call 'the great central facts'—that President Lincoln is prepared to serve another term, and that Mr. Secretary Chase expects to supersede him."[9]

Chase's candidacy, however, peaked too soon. In December 1863, a conference of Chase supporters, including twenty-seven U.S. senators, issued a paper called the "Pomeroy Circular," named for Kansas Senator Samuel C. Pomeroy. The manifesto, while supporting Chase, viciously attacked Lincoln. That was too much for people in Chase's native Ohio, who saw his implicit support of the Circular as extreme disloyalty by a cabinet member to the president he served. Three days after the Circular appeared, pro-Lincoln Union party members in the Ohio legislature passed a resolution endorsing Lincoln's renomination. Chase ended up writing a grudging letter to his friends in Ohio, asking that his name no longer be considered for the nomination. Later, when Lincoln refused to approve one of his recommended appointments, Chase submitted his resignation as treasury secretary. Submitting his resignation, or threatening to, was a favorite Chase weapon. This was about the fourth time he had done so. This time, to Chase's surprise, Lincoln accepted it.[10]

With Chase out of the way, several disgruntled Republicans looked to the ambitious John C. Fremont as a potential candidate. Calling themselves "Radical Democracy," they met in Cleveland in late May in what the *New York World* called "a political flank movement." After what the *Chicago Tribune* described as "many sittings and conferences among the wet nurses and old ladies of the convention," they nominated Fremont, who agreed to step aside at the Baltimore Convention if the party nominated anyone who would uphold the group's principles—meaning anyone other than Lincoln. In the *New York Times,* Henry Raymond saw the Cleveland affair as a form of "mental hallucination" by "witless fellows." He summed it all up as "a precious piece of foolery."[11]

All this jockeying for position, it should be remembered, was taking place in the middle of a brutal war. This seemed to appall Horace Greeley, who said he wished the 1864 election could be "banished from every loyal mind" until after July 4, "while every energy, every effort should be devoted to the one paramount object of suppressing the Rebellion and restoring Peace to our distracted country." That wasn't likely to happen. "In defiance of our wishes," as Greeley put it, the Republican National Committee had already set June 7 as its convention date, in Baltimore, and the Democrats had fixed their convention date as July 4, in Chicago."[12]

For people in Washington and Virginia, May had long been a favorite month. Trees leafed out, fields became greener, flowers burst into bloom, and nature emerged in all her glory. In normal years, May was a time for parties, for smiles, for a lifting of spirits. May of 1864, however, was a time of anguish. The armies of Grant and Lee were locked in an ongoing bloody embrace. As lengthy casualty lists began to appear, families North and South found reason to mourn. And as the carnage in Virginia continued, it was hard for the president to think of anything else. Stopping once for a talk with Congressman Isaac Arnold, Lincoln pointed to a line of wounded men nearby. "Look yonder at those poor fellows," Lincoln said. "I cannot bear it. This suffering, this loss of life, is dreadful." Arnold quoted something he'd written: "This too shall pass away. Never fear. Victory will come." With a mournful voice, Lincoln responded, "Yes, victory will come, but it comes slowly."[13]

When men by the thousands were fighting and dying, problems with the media seemed relatively minor. Yet those problems persisted—for Lincoln and for the Army. Sadly enough, the antiadministration press never let up for a moment. During the Wilderness fighting, for example, a malicious *New York World* reporter wrote: "A remark is reported of the President's on this campaign, which may or may not be authentic, but which conveys much truth. 'Any other commander that the Army of the Potomac has had,' he is rumored to have said, 'would have at once withdrawn his army over the Rapidan, after that first day's reception.' The most fortuitous circumstance in connection with the battles on the Rapidan is the fact that President Lincoln had nothing to do with them."[14]

Lincoln couldn't do much about the *World's* personal assaults, but at least he could put them in perspective. In late April, he scanned a copy of the *Richmond Examiner* that had come across the lines, one that contained an attack on Confederate President Jefferson Davis. "Why," he said, "the *Examiner* seems about as fond of Jeff as the *World* is of me."[15]

❖⊷══◉═❖

An ongoing media problem that spring involved the Army of the Potomac and its commander, the hot-tempered George Meade. So far he had managed to keep his emotions in check, even with respect to reporters, most of whom he despised. He even accepted the fact that he, the hero of Gettysburg, was now being overshadowed by the new man, Ulysses Grant. There was a good reason. Grant might deprecate the importance of the press, but he read the papers assiduously. He even called the *New York Herald* his "organ," a joking reference to the way Bennett touted him for the presidency and often tried predicting what Grant was going to do. As he picked up a *Herald*, Grant would laugh and remark, with a kind of amiable sarcasm, "Now let me see what my 'organ' has to say, and then I can tell better what I'm going to do."[16]

Meade, by contrast, treated the reporters with a kind of contempt, and they responded in kind. Then came the explosion. Meade saw a piece in the *Philadelphia Inquirer* hinting that Meade had favored a retreat after the battle of the Wilderness. The *Inquirer* reporter, Edward Crapsey, had written that "on one eventful night during the present campaign Grant's presence saved the army, and the nation too; not that General Meade was on the point of committing a blunder unwittingly, but his devotion to his country made him loth to risk her last army on what he deemed a chance. Grant assumed the responsibility, and we are still on to Richmond."[17]

Meade was outraged by what he considered an outrageous lie. He forced Crapsey to admit he had no foundation for the story, then had the reporter arrested and drummed out of camp, mounted backwards on a sorry-looking mule and wearing a sign saying "Libeler of the Press." When Crapsey's treatment became known, his fellow reporters decided to retaliate. They agreed among themselves that Meade's name would never be mentioned in dispatches unless it was in connection with a defeat. Hence-forth, one reporter said, "Meade was quite as much unknown, by any cor-respondence from the army, as any dead hero of antiquity."[18]

Meade, his point having been made, later issued Crapsey a pass let-ting him return to camp. Lincoln was no doubt relieved. Evidently he had stayed out of the Crapsey affair—he had his own press problems. One of these concerned the New York Evening Post and its poet-editor, William Cullen Bryant. Early in 1864, the Post's business manager, Isaac Hender-son, had become involved in a war-contract scandal. While maintaining his duties at the Post, Henderson also served as Navy contracting agent in New York, where he was charged with having accepted commissions ille-gally. One source estimated that his profits in the questioned transactions had amounted to $100,000. As a result, with Lincoln's full approval, Sec-retary of the Navy Gideon Welles dismissed Henderson from office. At this point Bryant intervened, writing Lincoln to ask that Henderson's case be handled with leniency. Although Lincoln would have liked to remain in the Evening Post's good graces, this was too much. His stinging reply to Bryant said, "May I ask whether the Evening Post has not assailed me for supposed too lenient dealing with persons charged with fraud and crime?" The dismissal stood, although a year later Henderson was acquit-ted in federal court for lack of evidence.[19]

Lincoln acquired a far more serious press problem on May 18, 1864. On that day, a purported presidential proclamation appeared in the New York World and the New York Journal of Commerce. The document said that Grant's Virginia campaign had come to a "virtual close," gloomily noted "the disaster at Red River . . . and the general state of the country," and designated May 26 as a "day of fasting, humiliation and prayer." It then called for a draft of 400,000 men, and bore the alleged signatures of Lincoln and Secretary of State Seward.

The World and the Journal of Commerce had been victims of a well-conceived hoax. Other papers, after checking with the Associated Press, realized the story was false and were able to halt publication. The Herald unfortunately had run off 20,000 copies before it learned that neither the Tribune nor the Times had the story. The presses were stopped and all copies were destroyed. However, the damage was done, at least initially. On Wall Street, the price of gold soared. Elsewhere in the country, papers began reprinting the story, quoting the *World* as its source.

Maj. Gen. John Dix, in New York, wired the War Department to ask if the story was true. Official Washington responded quickly—perhaps too quickly. At Lincoln's direction, Secretary Seward sent a statement to all New York papers declaring the proclamation "an absolute forgery." Then an order was drawn up calling for the arrest and imprisonment of the offending "editors, proprietors and publishers" and seizure of the newspaper offices by "military force." This time the order was *truly* signed—by both Lincoln and Seward.

In New York, General Dix swiftly carried out the order, making arrests and seizing the offending editorial offices. Even papers that despised the *World* immediately came out with editorials condemning the administration's order. One of those expressing outrage was the *New York Daily News:* "For what crime have these offices been thronged with soldiers . . .? The idea that anyone connected with these journals had anything to do with the forgery of the proclamation is too preposterous to be entertained by any sane mind."[20] In like vein, several editors signed a long, open letter to Lincoln explaining the circumstances of the false proclamation and defending the papers that had printed it.

The pro-administration *New York Tribune* tried to be understanding, but nevertheless expressed its concern: "The real facts which led to the publication of this monstrous forgery were not, we presume, known yesterday in Washington, or the suspension of the two journals would not, we suppose, have been ordered. The order, no doubt, will be revoked today. We hope it will, for certainly no journal should be punished for a mistake which might have very innocently been committed by the most loyal paper in the land."[21]

Unlike Stanton and Seward, Lincoln evidently took the hoax in stride; later that day he rather calmly told reporter James Gilmore that the story was a "fabrication." Nevertheless, he had joined Seward in mistakenly signing the arrest and suppression order. It would prove to be a media blunder, a big one.

The Associated Press quickly blanketed the country with disclaimers, and within two days Gen. Dix had the case solved and a written confession from one of the perpetrators, Joseph Howard, an unscrupulous troublemaker. People remembered him as the reporter who once fabricated a story about Lincoln sneaking into Washington in disguise. Howard's fellow perpetrator of the hoax was Francis Mallison, a speculator who had hoped to make a killing in the gold market. Dix telegraphed Secretary Stanton full details of the plot and pointed out that the newspapers had been tricked. Lincoln said he did not intend to be vindictive; he ordered the *World* and the *Journal of Commerce* handed back to their owners. Dix lifted the suspension at 11 o'clock on Saturday morning, May 21.[22]

Manton Marble, editor of the *World*, was no sooner back in business than he was publishing an angry letter to Lincoln, saying among other things that the seizure was part of a personal vendetta: "Not until today had the *World* been free to speak. But to those who have ears to hear, its absence has been more eloquent than its columns could ever be. . . . Had the *Tribune* and the *Times* published the forgery . . . would you, Sir, have suppressed the *Tribune* and the *Times* as you suppressed the *World* and the *Journal of Commerce?* You know you would not. If not, why not? Is there a different law for your opponents and for your supporters?"[23] Even Democrats who disagreed with Marble enjoyed pointing out that the administration had once again shown its disdain for the Bill of Rights.

◦═◦═◦

In Virginia, having been stalemated at Spotsylvania, Grant once again sidled to his left, trying to maneuver behind Lee's right flank. By the beginning of June he was at Cold Harbor, barely ten miles from Richmond. In Grant's mind, Lee's Army of Northern Virginia was nearly exhausted. If he could achieve a breakthrough, Richmond would fall and the war's end might be in sight. He had miscalculated. Lee's men had established formidable defenses and were waiting confidently for the inevitable attack.

Veterans in the Army of the Potomac knew what to expect, and their thoughts were grim. On the eve of the battle, Grant's aide, young

Lt. Col. Horace Porter, saw men "writing their names and home addresses on slips of paper and pinning them on the backs of their coats so that their dead bodies might be recognized upon the field and their fate known to their families at home." After some preliminary skirmishing, Grant launched a series of futile attacks on the Confederate lines. It was a Union disaster, one that had been foreseen by the soldiers, if not by the generals. A blood-stained diary, found on the body of a Union soldier, contained a final, grisly entry: "June 3. Cold Harbor. I was killed."[24]

In his *Memoirs*, Grant wrote, "I have always regretted that the last assault at Cold Harbor was ever made. . . . No advantage whatever was gained to compensate for the heavy loss we sustained."[25]

⤙⟞⊙⟝⤚

The Republican Convention was still set for June 7 in Baltimore, even though many joined Greeley in hoping for a postponement, perhaps one that would yield a "better" candidate than Lincoln. The *New York Times* editor, Henry Raymond, argued otherwise, saying, "The sooner the candidate is selected, the sooner shall we have that united and hearty support which is so important to the country and the cause."[26]

A month before the convention, Raymond supported Lincoln's candidacy by publishing a book with 496 pages of Lincoln's speeches, letters, addresses, proclamations, and messages, as well as a brief sketch of his life. Even Greeley, who had no liking for Raymond, thought it "a real service" and called it "a well-arranged, readable, interesting book."[27]

Lincoln probably sensed by this time that he had the nomination won. Consequently, he was not making much of an effort to lock it up. This bothered his supporter, Justice Davis, who confided to a friend: "Mr. Lincoln seems disposed to let the thing run itself and if the people elect him he will be thankful, but won't use means to secure the thing. Mr. Lincoln annoys me more than I can express, by his persistence in letting things take their course—without effort or organization."[28]

On the eve of the convention, Greeley was still hoping for a postponement. He gave it one more try, writing: "We could wish the Presidency utterly forgotten or ignored for the next two months, while every impulse, every effort of the Loyal Millions should be directed toward the overthrow of armed hosts of the Rebellion."[29] By that time, however, even those who hated Lincoln, and there were many, had conceded his nomination. Their best hope was to shape a radical platform for him to stand on, one with a far harsher attitude toward the South.

The convention assembled in Baltimore's Front Street Theater on June 7. It was a fallback site; radical malcontents had prebooked the large Baltimore convention hall, leaving convention organizers scrambling at the last minute for another meeting place. At noon, on a sweltering hot day, the Republican national chairman, New York Senator Edwin D. Morgan, mounted the podium, then nominated Robert Breckenridge, "the Old War Horse of Kentucky," to serve as the day's honorary chairman. The venerable speaker made it clear that this was a convention of the National Union party, not just Republicans. This was an idea approved by Lincoln; calling the party "National Union" would emphasize that this was an electoral campaign supported by many disparate factions, each with a primary goal of saving the Union. "I see before me," Breckenridge said, "not only primitive Republicans and primitive Abolitionists, but I also see primitive Democrats and primitive Whigs—primitive Americans, and if you will allow me to say so, I myself am here, who all my life have been a party to myself."

"Does any man doubt," he asked, "that Abraham Lincoln shall be the nominee?" But first, he told the meeting, they had to make clear why they were fighting the war. "As a Union party, I will follow you to the ends of the earth, and to the gates of death. But as an Abolition party—as a Republican party—as a Whig party—as a Democratic party—as an American party, I will not follow you one foot."

Finally, to mounting applause, Breckenridge clarified his position on slavery: "I join myself with those who say, away with it forever; and I fervently pray God that the day may come when throughout the whole land every man may be as free as you are, and as capable of enjoying regulated liberty."[30]

When Breckenridge finished, Simon Cameron of Pennsylvania, the onetime secretary of war, made a motion for a roll call of states to present credentials. This produced a confusing jumble of motions and angry countermotions. Then Lincoln's press supporter, Henry Raymond, managed to bring order out of chaos. Shouting for attention, he soon had the group accepting credentials, seating delegates, and appointing committees.[31]

The next session, held that evening, was presided over by the convention's permanent chairman, ex-Governor William Denison of Ohio. He too alluded to Lincoln's forthcoming nomination, saying their candidate would be "the wise and good man whose unselfish devotion to the country, in the administration of the Government has secured to him not only the admiration, but the warmest affection of every friend of constitutional liberty."[32]

Next day Henry Raymond, now chairman of the platform committee, presented a list of planks that supported the war, the Constitution, and the Union, as well as a Constitutional prohibition of slavery. The radical element was also appeased by a plank calling for "bringing to the punishment due to their crimes the Rebels and traitors arrayed against" the government.[33]

Once the platform was approved, the delegates proceeded to nominate Abraham Lincoln for a second term. After the last state, Nevada, cast her vote for Lincoln, the count stood 484 to 22, with only Missouri voting for Grant. A Missourian then moved that the vote be made unanimous. When this was accomplished, the convention went wild, with cheering, shouting, waving of flags, jumping on benches, and committing what Noah Brooks called, "every possible extravagance."[34]

Lincoln was at the War Department telegraph office when word of the nomination came over the wires. The head of the office, Major Thomas Eckert, offered his congratulations. Lincoln reacted almost casually, saying, "What? Am I renominated?" Then, when a congratulatory telegram from John Nicolay was shown to him, he said, "Send it right over to the Madam. She will be more interested than I am." It was as though he had mixed emotions about being selected. Perhaps he did.[35]

For the men in Baltimore, the next order of business was selecting a vice presidential nominee. Lincoln had tried giving the impression that he was taking a "hands off" approach to the matter. When reporter Noah Brooks tried to query him about the current vice president, Hannibal Hamlin, Lincoln had ducked the question. Brooks, who hoped to see Hamlin renominated, wrote: "I . . . had anxiously given Mr. Lincoln many opportunities to say whether he preferred the renomination of the Vice-President, but he was craftily and rigidly non-committal, knowing, as he did, what was in my mind concerning Mr. Hamlin. He would refer to the matter only in the vaguest phrase, as, 'Mr. Hamlin is a very good man,' or, 'You, being a New Englander, would naturally want to see Mr. Hamlin renominated, and you are quite right,' and so on. . . . He could not be induced to express any opinion on the subject of a candidate for vice-president."

However, Lincoln *did* have a preference, and it was not Hamlin. Actually he had nothing against the man, although the two had never been close. It was rather that he saw the political benefit of having Andrew Johnson, a war Democrat from Tennessee, selected in Hamlin's place. At the same time, he didn't want to offend Hamlin's supporters by coming out openly against him. Once again Lincoln used a member of the press to do his work. On the eve of the convention, Lincoln asked the Pennsylvania editor, Alexander K. McClure, to go to the convention and work for Johnson. Thanks to McClure and others, Johnson won the nomination.[36]

It seems, then, that two of the principal confidants working for Lincoln behind the scenes were Henry Raymond and Alexander McClure. Raymond maneuvered the party platform toward something Lincoln could accept; McClure worked to get Johnson in as vice president. Significantly, each man was an editor. Lincoln knew the power of the media.

At the *New York Herald*, James Gordon Bennett greeted Lincoln's nomination with a sneer: "The politicians have again chosen this Presidential pigmy as their nominee." For the radicals, Bennett said, it was "a bitter pill to swallow; but if there is no help for it they will try to gulp him down."[37]

At the *Tribune*, Horace Greeley saw as "happy" the nomination of Johnson, who had "never wavered or faltered" in the Union cause. Moreover, said *Harper's Weekly*, think how this would infuriate the Confederacy! "Of Andrew Johnson," said *Harper's*, "it is enough to say that there is no man in the country, unless it be Mr. Lincoln himself, whom the rebels more cordially hate."[38]

Andrew Johnson, who like Lincoln had come from a humble beginning, not only appreciated the nomination, but like *Harper's*, relished the reaction of the Southern aristocracy. "This aristocracy," he said, "hated Mr. Lincoln because he was of humble origin, a railsplitter in early life. . . . If this aristocracy is so violently opposed to being governed by Mr. Lincoln, what in the name of conscience will it do with Lincoln and Johnson, a railsplitter and a tailor?"[39]

Meanwhile in Virginia, with direct assaults having failed, Grant once again pulled out of direct contact. He began moving his army southeast, changing his base of operations, and slipping across the James River. The crossing of the James during the June 12–16 period turned out to be Grant's most successful maneuver since the beginning of the campaign. So adroitly was the movement conducted that Lee completely lost track of Grant's army for four days.

So far the Northern public had seen mostly the casualty lists and what appeared to be senseless butchery. Yet Grant was now below Richmond, in front of Petersburg, and he had accomplished a great deal. Although, in little over a month, he had lost nearly 60,000 men, three times as many as Lee, he had bled the Confederacy of manpower it could no longer replace. He was now in a solid position, with a supply line using the James River. Had he gone to the Virginia Peninsula at once, as McClellan did in 1862, he would have left Washington exposed to a direct thrust from Lee. Now a weakened Lee was committed to a defensive role, and could no longer consider any such advance. Although the end was not near, henceforth the game would be played on Grant's terms.

As Grant kept Lee occupied, William Tecumseh Sherman was on the move in the western theater, driving south into Georgia. The strategy was unfolding, and the president wired his congratulations: "HAVE JUST READ YOUR DISPATCH OF 1 P.M. YESTERDAY. I BEGIN TO SEE IT. YOU WILL SUCCEED. GOD BLESS YOU ALL."[40]

With the Army of the Potomac just a few miles from Richmond, and facing an inferior force under General Beauregard, an opportunity existed for a quick breakthrough. However, the initial attacks, uncoordinated and poorly handled, failed to achieve a penetration. Then Lee arrived to reinforce Beauregard and the window of opportunity slammed shut. The veteran Army of Northern Virginia was again digging in and preparing fortifications, something it did very well. There would be no more costly frontal assaults; the campaign had settled into a siege. And for the near future, Petersburg, which the *New York Times* called the "key to Richmond," remained in Confederate hands.[41]

Abraham Lincoln had learned patience, and he believed that Grant was hammering away with a strategy that would eventually be successful. He knew, however, that much depended on the people not losing heart, and for that, much depended on the attitude of the press. Talking to Noah Brooks, Lincoln said: "I wish when you write and speak to the people, you would do all you can to correct the impression that the war in Virginia will end right off victoriously. To me the most trying thing in all of this war is that the people are too sanguine; they expect too much at once. I declare to you, sir, that we are today further ahead than I thought one year and a half ago we should be; and yet there are plenty of people who believe that the war is about to be substantially closed. As God is my judge I shall be satisfied if we are over with the fight in Virginia within a year. I hope we shall be 'happily disappointed,' as the saying is, but I am afraid not—I am afraid not."[42]

CHAPTER 14

"GET DOWN, YOU DAMN FOOL!"

I n June 1864 Horace Porter was at Grant's headquarters near Petersburg, writing his wife: "A few days ago we were sitting in front of the General's tent when there appeared very suddenly before us a long, lank-looking personage dressed all in black, and looking very much like a boss undertaker. It was the President. He said, after shaking hands with us all, 'I just thought I would jump aboard a boat and come down and see you. I don't expect I can do any good, and in fact I'm afraid I may do harm, but I'll put myself under your orders, and if you find me doing anything wrong, just send me right away.'"[1]

During his visit to the Army of the Potomac, Lincoln mounted Grant's big bay horse, "Cincinnati," and reviewed the troops. "Like most men who had been brought up in the West," Porter wrote, "he had good command of a horse, but it must be acknowledged that in appearance he was not a very dashing rider. . . . His trousers gradually worked up above his ankles, and gave him the appearance of a country farmer riding into town wearing his Sunday clothes. . . . However, the troops were so lost in admiration of the man that the humorous aspect did not seem to strike them. The soldiers rapidly passed the word along the line that 'Uncle Abe' had joined them, and cheers broke forth from all the commands, and enthusiastic shouts and even words of familiar greeting met him on all sides."[2]

Grant asked if Lincoln would like to review some of the black troops. Lincoln said he would, and during the review, in Porter's words, "a scene now occurred which defies description. They beheld for the first time the liberator of their race—the man who by a stroke of his pen had struck the shackles from the limbs of their fellow-bondmen and proclaimed liberty to the enslaved. . . . The enthusiasm of the blacks now knew no limits. They cheered, laughed, cried, sang hymns of praise, and shouted in their negro dialect, 'God bress Massa Linkum!'"[3]

The trip was a welcome respite for Lincoln, for the 1864 campaign was now under way, and that meant increasing pressure, to include contending with an often hostile media. For example, as soon as the Republicans' convention ended, the *New York World* got in its licks: "The age of statesmen is gone; the age of rail-splitters and tailors, of buffoons, boors, and fanatics, has succeeded. . . . In a crisis of the most appalling magnitude, requiring statesmanship of the highest order, the country is asked to consider the claims of two ignorant, boorish, third-rate backwoods lawyers, for the highest stations in government. Such nominations, in such a conjuncture, are an insult to the common-sense of the people. God save the Republic!"[4]

That same month, McClellan was finally breaking his silence. On June 15 the "Young Napoleon" was at West Point before a large crowd, delivering an oration to dedicate the site of a Battle Monument. Sounding very much like a candidate, and to the dismay of the Peace Democrats, he urged that the war be fought to a successful conclusion. In his speech, he said the rebellion could not be justified upon ethical grounds and the only alternative was its "suppression." Bennett's *New York Herald* called the speech "truly eloquent" and a "great discourse." Joseph Medill's *Chicago Tribune*, however, termed it "a very smooth, glossy, slick piece of gab."[5]

The Democrats had their candidate, but they weren't sure that the time had come to make the announcement, particularly if McClellan insisted on a "war" platform. After all, Grant seemed to be at an impasse in Virginia, and Joe Johnston was stalling William Tecumseh Sherman in the mountains of north Georgia. If the war continued to go badly, party leaders argued, a "peace" platform might be the way to go. They decided to wait and see. Accordingly, on June 25 the Democratic convention, originally scheduled to start on July 4, was postponed for eight weeks until August 29.[6]

In early July, as Congress prepared to adjourn, Lincoln was busy signing his name to recent bills. One he did *not* sign, however, was the Wade-Davis bill, passed by congressional radicals in a direct slap at the president. Lincoln's policy would leave the reconstructed states to abolish slavery themselves; Wade-Davis would require immediate emancipation in all the states. Lincoln would allow 10 percent of the voters to set up new state governments; the bill would require a majority. Lincoln would bar only a few key Confederates from voting and holding office; the bill would bar a vast number. Lincoln would have the executive manage reconstruction; the bill would make it entirely a congressional process.[7]

In effect, this was direct confrontation. Who would manage reconstruction? And would the policies be harsh or lenient? Would states returning to the Union be treated as errant brothers or as traitors deserving vengeful punishment?

Lincoln didn't veto the bill; he merely let Congress adjourn, leaving the bill unsigned, resting figuratively in his "pocket." The radicals were outraged, and they issued a manifesto to which Lincoln replied with a proclamation of his own, one that the press was quick to publish. Reconstruction was now a subject for national debate, and in the words of historian Allan Nevins, the harsh Radical Republicans were "outnumbered and outgunned by the combined forces of the Moderate Republicans and the War Democrats." No state can commit treason, they argued, and therefore no state can give its citizens authority to commit treason. The war was therefore a struggle not against *states*, but against rebellious *individuals*.[8]

Once again Lincoln had used the media to explain his position to the people. And the people—at least most of them—not only knew what he was saying, but resented his attackers. George William Curtis, editor of

Harper's Weekly, said: "We have read with pain the manifesto of Messrs. Wade and Winter Davis, not because of its envenomed hostility to the President, but because of its ill-tempered spirit, which proves conclusively the unfitness of either of these gentlemen for grave counselors in a time of national peril."[9]

Noah Brooks, always a Lincoln admirer, was even more outspoken, saying: "It is a matter of regret that a man of so much oratorical ability as Henry Winter Davis should be so much of a political charlatan as he is; . . . insatiate in his hates, mischievous in his schemes, and hollow-hearted and coldblooded."[10]

--◆=◎=◆--

As the war dragged on that summer, the North's yearning for peace grew ever more intense. Confederate President Jefferson Davis, hoping to take advantage of this, sent two secret operatives to Canada to stir up trouble and cause disunion in the North, especially in the northwest. He gave each of them a purposely vague letter of instruction: "Confiding special trust in your zeal, discretion and patriotism, I hereby direct you to proceed at once to Canada, there to carry out such instructions as you have received from me verbally, in such manner as shall seem most likely to conduce to the furtherance of the interests of the Confederate States of America which have been entrusted to you." It was up to the operatives to decide how best to proceed. One way, evidently, was to make it appear that Lincoln was so set on war that he was unwilling even to consider genuine peace negotiations. Creating this impression, at the very least, should make it nearly impossible for Lincoln to be reelected.[11]

For carrying out their plan, they looked to Horace Greeley, an editor who supported the war but was at heart an inherent pacifist. In January of 1861, as war clouds gathered, Greeley had written: "As to Secession, I have said repeatedly and here repeat, that if the People of the Slave States, or of the Cotton States alone, really wish to get out of the Union, I am in favor of letting them out as soon as that result can be peacefully and constitutionally attained. . . . I want no State kept in the Union by coercion."[12]

After the attack on Fort Sumter, the mercurial Greeley shifted, no longer talking of peaceful separation, but writing: "There is no more thought of bribing or coaxing the traitors who have dared to aim their cannon balls at the flag of the Union."[13]

Nevertheless, as the war progressed, Greeley watched closely for any overtures from the South toward peace. And on his own, Greeley sent messages to the White House on several occasions "to say a few words" about possible terms of peace. On December 12, 1862, for example, he wrote Lincoln "that the Rebels are deathly sick of their job, and anxious to get out of it, I have so much testimony that I cannot doubt. I presume you have still more." He then outlined a possible peace proposal, one involving a general amnesty, assumption of the Confederacy's public debt, and emancipation, the latter to include a generous payment to compensate slave states "for the entire destruction of their Slavery."[14]

Lincoln knew that any peace terms short of full Southern independence were sure to be rejected. However, he recognized Greeley's influence, and he was obliged to give those frequent "words of advice" a polite hearing.

That was the background, when on July 6, 1864, Horace Greeley received a letter from a mysterious pacifist named William C. Jewett. "Colorado Jewett," as he was known, wrote: "I am authorized to state to you, for your use only, not the public, that two ambassadors of Davis & Co" are waiting in Niagara Falls, just over the border in Canada, "with full and complete powers for a peace." They wanted, Jewett wrote, either to meet with the *Tribune* editor personally, or to be provided with safe conduct passes to Washington in order to meet directly with the president. Jewett claimed that the whole affair "can be consummated by me, you, them, and President Lincoln."[15]

Eager but wary, Greeley contacted Lincoln, enclosing Jewett's letter along with an emotional one of his own, urging that the president seize the opportunity to secure peace. "I venture to remind you," Greeley wrote, "that our bleeding, bankrupt, dying country longs for peace—shudders at the prospect of fresh conscription, of further wholesale devastations, and of new rivers of human blood; and a widespread conviction that the Government and its prominent supporters are not anxious for peace . . . is doing great harm now, and is morally certain, unless removed, to do far greater in the approaching elections.

"It is not enough that we anxiously desire a true and lasting peace; we ought to demonstrate and establish the truth beyond cavil. The fact that A. H. Stephens was not permitted a year ago to visit and confer with the authorities has done harm, which the tone at the late National Convention at Baltimore is not calculated to counteract." (As noted earlier, in the summer of 1863 Alexander Stephens, vice president of the Confederacy, had sought to confer with Lincoln on possible terms of peace. Since the terms of Stephens's visit assumed Confederate independence, Lincoln had declined the request.)

"I entreat you," Greeley continued, "to submit overtures for pacification to the Southern insurgents, which the impartial must pronounce frank and generous." Any terms, he said, would of course have to include a return to the Union and the abolishment of slavery. However, even if the talks were to fail, they would at least burden the South with the responsibility of rejecting what was offered.[16]

Lincoln did not see it that way. With the Union war effort at a low point, he sensed that any discussion of peace terms would be perceived as Northern weakness. Moreover, he was convinced that the two so-called "ambassadors" did not have the "full and complete" powers that Jewett alleged. Lincoln therefore had a problem. If he summarily rejected Greeley's idea, the offended editor might well publicize that rejection. No, he had to go along with the project, at least in part, and thereby keep Greeley on his side, supporting both the administration and the war effort. He decided to compromise by asking "Uncle Horace" to proceed on his own. That way, if the meeting ended badly, it would be Greeley's fingerprints on the deal, not the president's. Lincoln's prompt response shows the shrewd politician and the clever lawyer, getting a little fun out of the situation:

Washington, D.C., July 9, 1864

Hon. Horace Greeley:
  Dear Sir: Your letter of the 7th, with enclosures, received. If you can find any person anywhere professing to have any proposition of Jefferson Davis, in writing, for peace, embracing the restoration of the Union and abandonment of slavery, whatever else it may embrace, say

to him he may come to me with you; and that if he really brings such
proposition, he shall, at the least, have safe conduct with the paper
(and without publicity, if he chooses) to the point where you shall
have met him. The same if there be two or more persons.

Yours truly,

A. Lincoln[17]

Greeley was trapped, and he knew it. In his reply to the president, he
showed his skepticism. Reluctantly, however, he agreed to go to Niagara
and meet the Confederates:

Office of the Tribune, New York, July 10, 1864

My dear Sir: I have yours of yesterday. Whether there be persons at
Niagara (or elsewhere) who are empowered to commit the rebels by
negotiation, is a question; but if there be such, there is no question
at all that they would decline to exhibit their credentials to me,
much more to open their budget and give me their best terms. Green
as I may be, I am not quite so verdant as to imagine anything of the
sort. I have neither purpose nor desire to be made a confidant, far
less an agent, in such negotiations. . . . I will see if I can get a look
into the hand of whomsoever may be at Niagara; though that is a
project so manifestly hopeless that I have little heart for it, still I
shall try. . . .

Yours,

Horace Greeley[18]

As this correspondence was taking place, the nation's capital was
fearing the worst. In June, Robert E. Lee, hoping to relieve the pressure at
Petersburg, had sent Jubal Early storming down the Shenandoah Valley. It
was thought that Early, by posing a threat to Baltimore and Washington,
would force Grant to send reinforcements north, thereby weakening the
Army of the Potomac. By the first part of July, Early had crossed the Potomac into Maryland, swept past Lew Wallace at the Monocacy, and was

threatening the capital itself. Meanwhile, Charles Dana had returned to Washington, as he later said, "to keep Grant advised of developments." Upon arrival, Dana found the city in a state of excitement, almost terror. Both Washington and Baltimore were swarming with refugees who had fled before Early's advance. Smoke was rising from outlying factories and towns, and in the capital, government clerks had been armed and sent to man the ramparts.[19]

"Baltimore is in great peril," telegraphed a mayor's committee to President Lincoln, asking for troops. Lincoln replied: "I have not a single soldier but whom is being disposed by the military for the best protection of all. By latest accounts the enemy is moving on Washington. They cannot fly to either place. Let us be vigilant, but keep cool. I hope neither Baltimore nor Washington will be sacked."[20]

By the afternoon of July 11, Early was within two miles of the Soldiers' Home, where Lincoln the night before had gone to bed when a message from Stanton arrived urging him to return to the White House in a hurry. He did just that, but next day, undaunted, he went out to the ramparts to see things for himself. At one point, Lincoln stood on a parapet to get a better look, and at six-feet-four, wearing a stovepipe hat that added another eight inches to his height, he made a conspicuous target. Coolly, Lincoln ignored the bullets that snapped overhead, even when an officer within three feet of him fell with a death wound. From below, twenty-three-year-old Captain Oliver Wendell Holmes Jr., looked up at the prominently exposed figure, and without recognizing him, called out, "Get down, you damn fool, before you get shot!" The message got through. Lincoln reacted with amusement to the irreverent advice as he retreated to a safer spot.[21]

Fortunately for the nation's capital, timely reinforcements had arrived. Jubal Early, whose force had been reduced to 8,000 effectives, prudently decided to cancel his attack. The Confederates had managed to destroy some property and had caused a great deal of excitement, but through no fault of their own, they had failed in the main purpose of their mission. Refusing to take the bait, Grant had not significantly weakened his Petersburg line in order to soothe the people in Washington. Two days later, with

Early's withdrawal well under way, headlines in the *New York Tribune* told a relieved nation, "THE GREAT REBEL RAID—THEY ARE RE-CROSSING THE POTOMAC WITH THEIR PLUNDER"[22]

For people in the capital, it had been a nerve-wracking few days, showing as it did that no place was truly safe. In the aftermath, nevertheless, pro-administration papers tried to maintain morale by making light of Early's raid. The *New York Times* referred to it as the "annual scare," while the *Chicago Tribune* said, "Just as we have Annual School Examinations and Annual Horse Shops," so do we have annual invasions.[23]

—⊷═◉═⊶—

With the capital out of immediate danger, Lincoln could again start thinking about Horace Greeley's "peace initiative." On July 13, Greeley sent the president a follow-up message stating he had confirmed the Confederate agents' authority to negotiate for peace. Lincoln quickly telegraphed Greeley, saying, "I was not expecting you to send me a letter, but to bring me a man, or men." On July 16 Lincoln's secretary, twenty-five-year-old John Hay, arrived in New York with a letter to Greeley from the president. "I am disappointed that you have not already reached here with those commissioners," Lincoln wrote. "I not only intend a sincere effort for peace, but I intend that you shall be a personal witness that it is made."[24]

Greeley was still skeptical about making the trip to Niagara, but Hay assured him that Lincoln really wanted Greeley to go himself. Later that day, Greeley boarded a train for Niagara Falls. He sent a message to the Southerners offering them safe conduct to the capital, but the Confederates replied that they would have to refer the whole affair to their superiors in Richmond. Frustrated, Greeley relayed the news to Lincoln, who responded by sending John Hay back to the scene. The young secretary found not only that the Confederates had no power to act, but that Greeley had not clarified to them the Union requisites for peace negotiations. Lincoln's secretary of the Navy, Gideon Welles, noted in his diary a few days later that Greeley "failed to honestly and frankly communicate the President's first letters, as was his duty, but sent a letter of his own, which was not true and correct, and found himself involved in the meshes of his own frail net."[25]

Hay brought a note from Lincoln that spelled out clearly the only terms he would accept—terms the president knew the Confederacy would reject. It was addressed "TO WHOM IT MAY CONCERN," and read: "Any proposition which embraces the restoration of peace, the integrity of the whole Union, and the abandonment of slavery, and which comes by, and with an authority that can control the armies now at war against the United States, will be received and considered by the executive government of the United States, and will be met by liberal terms on other substantial and collateral points, and the bearer or bearers thereof shall have safe conduct both ways."[26]

Since it seemed quite possible that the letter would eventually be published, Lincoln couched it in terms that would look good on the public record. (The *London Spectator* called the president's letter "a model of diplomatic adroitness.") In any case, Greeley now had a letter from the president and he was obliged to deliver it. Still he wriggled on the hook, trying to evade, or at least share, personal responsibility. He proposed to bring Jewett into the conference, but Hay, aware of Jewett's shady reputation, refused to have anything to do with the man. With that, Greeley, although duly delegated by the president, said he wouldn't cross the river into Canada unless Hay came along and delivered the message himself. Hay agreed, and at Clifton House, on the Canadian side, he and Greeley met Confederate George Sanders, whom Hay described as a "seedy looking Rebel with grizzled whiskers." Sanders took them to the room of one of the commissioners, Professor J. P. Holcombe, where Hay delivered the note. Holcombe said he would get in touch with the other commissioner, Clement C. Clay, and make some reply the next day. Hay waited in Niagara Falls for the response. Greeley, however, anxious to terminate a potentially embarrassing errand, departed posthaste for New York and the friendly confines of the *Tribune* office. The much-overblown "Niagara Peace Conference," as it came to be known, was over before it even started.

Next day, with no response forthcoming, Hay sent a follow-up query to Holcombe, asking if he "and the gentleman associated with him desire to send to Washington by Major Hay any messages in reference to the communication delivered to him on yesterday, and in that case when he may expect to be favored with such messages." Holcombe said they had nothing for the president; they considered the president's message an answer to one they had sent earlier to Horace Greeley, "and to that gentleman an answer had been transmitted." In other words, despite Greeley's efforts to play but a minor role, the Confederates had him hooked. [27]

Holcombe and Clay's lengthy letter to Greeley was given to Jewett, who immediately turned it over to the press. It was a masterpiece of "spin," making it appear, among other things, that the North had made the initial overtures. However, they said, the president's offer was so insulting that they could not even transmit it to Richmond without "dishonoring ourselves and incurring the well-merited scorn of our countrymen." An offer of a safe conduct to Washington, they asserted, "was accepted by us as the evidence of an unexpected but most gratifying change in the policy of the President—a change which we felt authorized to hope might terminate in the conclusion of a peace, mutually just, honorable, and advantageous to the North and the South. . . . It seemed to us that the President opened a door, which had previously been closed against the Confederate States. . . .What may be the explanation of this sudden and entire change in the views of the President, of this rude withdrawal of a courteous overture for negotiation at the moment it was likely to be accepted, of this emphatic recall of words of peace just uttered, and fresh blasts of war to the bitter end, we leave for the speculation of those who have the means or inclination to penetrate the mysteries of his cabinet, or fathom the caprice of his imperial will." The note ended by thanking Greeley for "the solicitude you have manifested to inaugurate a movement which contemplates results the most noble and humane." For the *Tribune* editor, it was a kiss of death. [28]

Holcombe and Clay had been clever, but two could play at communicating through the media, and Lincoln, ably assisted by Hay, was a master of the game. The White House immediately moved to repudiate Jewett. A note from John Hay firmly told Jewett that no letters of his would be "submitted to the personal attention of the President," and any effort to send such letters would be "a waste of time on your part." Hay's note was given to the press, along with a statement referring to "an irresponsible person named Jewett." The note explained that since Jewett had been trying "to create the impression that he acts by virtue of a certain implied under-standing or connection with the Executive Mansion we deem it not im-proper to state that he has never received from the President the slightest recognition."[29]

The Niagara fiasco, in other words, was laid at Greeley's door. Whether that was completely true, that was the story told by rival editors, who did their best to humiliate him. William Cullen Bryant's *Evening Post* said the whole affair was "sickening." Bennett's *Herald* was even more brutal as it accused Greeley of "cuddling with traitors." Not only was he guilty of "bungling" and "meddling," said the *Herald*, he had even been willing to compromise the nation's integrity. Bennett then demanded that Greeley "tell the country, explicitly, whether his cooperation in the late peace movement is an effort toward disunion."[30]

Greeley's response, although disingenuous, was nonetheless emphatic: "NO SIR!—Is that plain? We were first impelled to make an effort to bring about a conference between authorized representatives of the respective belligerents by learning, through various channels, that certain distin-guished Confederates, then and now in Canada, were holding out to the leading Democrats, who flocked over the river to confer with them, that Peace might be had on a basis, not of Disunion, but of *Union*. . . . We can-not be bullied nor slandered into approval or rejection of hypothetical terms of conciliation. The business of negotiation is devolved by the Con-stitution on the President and Senate of the United States, and to them we leave it."[31]

On July 22, the *Tribune* printed the letters leading up to the Niagara meetings in a front-page story. Headlines read: "PEACE NEGOTIA-TIONS—The Correspondence on the Subject—The Letters of Mr. Gree-ley and the Rebel Emissaries—The President's Note 'To Whom it May Concern'— Conditions Precedent to the Consideration of Any Propo-sition—High Dudgeon of the Self-Constituted Commissioners—THE NEGOTIATIONS BROKEN OFF."[32]

Even Henry Raymond's *New York Times*, while trying to be fair, was forced to say, "Mr. Greeley's part in this transaction was more important than he is inclined to represent it." Lincoln had agreed to publishing the correspondence, but wanted the passages that "spoke of a bankrupt country and awful calamities," to be deleted. Personally acting as a high-level editorial censor, Lincoln wrote Greeley: "I have, as you see, drawn a red pencil over the parts I wish suppressed."[33]

Some time later, Senator Harlan of Iowa reportedly said to the president: "Some of us think, Mr. Lincoln, that you didn't send a very good ambassador to Niagara." "Well, I'll tell you about that, Harlan," replied the president. "Greeley kept abusing me for not entering into peace negotiations. He said he believed we could have peace if I would do my part and when he began to urge that I send an ambassador to Niagara to meet Confederate emissaries, I just thought I would let him go up and crack that nut for himself." Similarly, Lincoln told Charles Dana: "I sent Brother Greeley a commission. I guess I am about even with him now." As Lincoln said this, Dana noted a "twinkle" in the presidential eye.[34]

Publicly, Lincoln was cordial to Greeley—he could not afford to be otherwise. Privately, however, he told Treasury secretary Gideon Welles that Greeley was like an old shoe, "so rotten that nothing can be done with him. He is not truthful; the stitches all tear out."[35]

Greeley, for his part, was not likely to forgive or forget how Lincoln had used him. On August 5 he happily published a scathing anti-Lincoln document written by Benjamin Wade and Henry Winter Davis, authors of the bill Lincoln had refused to sign, and who, like Greeley, were well able to hold a grudge. The document was a vicious denunciation of Lincoln's reconstruction policies and his pocket veto of the Wade-Davis bill. It charged the president with "dictatorial usurpation," and called the veto "a studied outrage on the legislative authority of the people." Among other things, the document made amply clear the broad split in the Republican party.[36]

The Democratic *New York Herald* was quick to applaud the Wade-Davis manifesto. James Gordon Bennett was openly enjoying the Republican fratricide. The document, Bennett wrote, had charged the president with "arrogance, ignorance, usurpation, knavery and a host of other deadly sins, including that of hostility to the rights of humanity and to the principles of republican government. Nothing that Vallandigham or the most venomous of the copperhead tribe of politicians have uttered in derogation of Mr. Lincoln has approached in bitterness and force the denunciations which Messrs. Wade and Davis, shining lights of the Republican party, have piled up in this manifesto." Urging Lincoln to step out of the presidential race, Bennett went on to say, "One thing must be self-evident to him, and that is that under no circumstances can he hope to be the next President of the United States."[37]

That was advice Lincoln could not accept, even from the *Herald*, a paper former president James Buchanan called "the most powerful organ in the country for the formation of public opinion."[38] However, there was no doubt that Lincoln's chances were getting slimmer with each passing day. In the seven weeks from Independence Day to late August, with Sherman bogged down before Atlanta, and Lee still holding firm before Petersburg, Republican morale was at perhaps its lowest point of the war. Whitelaw Reid, correspondent for the *Cincinnati Gazette*, traveled during those weeks from Cincinnati through Washington to Kennebunkport, Maine. He talked to a variety of citizens in town after town. Wherever he went, he was assured that under the present circumstances, it was impossible for Lincoln to be reelected.

And at this point, the Democrats had not even nominated a candidate!

CHAPTER 15

◦━◉━◦

"WE FLY THE BANNER OF ABRAHAM LINCOLN!"

The so-called "Niagara Peace Conference" was not the only attempt at peace in the fateful summer of 1864. A second quixotic effort was launched by Colonel James Frazier Jacques, a Methodist clergyman in the Union Army, who claimed he could "go into the Southern Confederacy and return within NINETY DAYS with terms of peace that the Government will accept." To carry out his fanciful plan, Jacques needed first to see the president. Jacques asked James R. Gilmore, a former *New York Tribune* staff member, to act as a go-between. Gilmore told the White House of Jacques's idea, and after some delay, Lincoln said, "Tell Gilmore to bring Jacques here, and I will see him. Of course it should be done quietly."

Lincoln gave a qualified consent to the mission, stipulating however that Jacques, accompanied by Gilmore, would travel with no government authority whatever. "Mr. Jacques is a very worthy gentleman," Lincoln concluded, "but I can have nothing to do, directly or indirectly, with the matter he has in view." Jacques and Gilmore, with Lincoln's unofficial blessing, passed through Union lines under a flag of truce and immediately asked to see Confederate President Jefferson Davis. First, however, they were taken to the Confederate secretary of war, Judah P. Benjamin, who interrogated them. Although they insisted that Lincoln had not authorized their mission, Benjamin nevertheless arranged for them to meet Davis.[1]

The courtly Davis greeted the pair with what they later called "a peculiar charm." As they shook hands, Davis said, "I am glad to see you, gentlemen. You are very welcome to Richmond." The ensuing talk was cordial but unproductive. When Jacques suggested possible ways to end the war, Davis said in response: "I worked night and day for twelve years to prevent it [war], but I could not. The North was mad and blind, would not let us govern ourselves, and so the war came; now it must go on until the last man of this generation falls in his tracks and his children seize his musket and fight our battles, *unless you acknowledge our right to self-government*. We are not fighting for slavery. We are fighting for independence, and that, or extermination, we will have."[2]

Gilmore returned to Washington and read Lincoln his notes of the meeting. Lincoln asked what he proposed doing with those notes. Gilmore said, "Put a beginning and an end to it, sir, and hand it to the *Tribune*."

"Can't you get it into the *Atlantic Monthly?*" Lincoln asked. "It would have less of a partisan look there." Finally, it was agreed that a short "card" of the meeting would be given to one of the Boston papers, with a fuller report written for the *Atlantic*. "Put Davis's 'We are not fighting for slavery; we are fighting for independence' into the card—that is enough; and send me the proof of what goes into the *Atlantic*. Don't let it appear until I return the proof. Some day all this will come out, but just now we must use discretion."

The "card" ran in the *Boston Transcript* on July 22 and proofs of the *Atlantic* article went to Lincoln a few days later. The president once again demonstrated the importance he attached to what appeared in the media. He kept the proofs for a week, screened them closely, and personally deleted a page and a half before returning them to Gilmore. There was a delicious irony to the situation, with the president himself, officially "unaware" of the Jacques-Gilmore mission, nevertheless editing what in effect was its press release!

The *Atlantic* article went to millions of readers. All leading American papers reprinted it, and the *London Times, News,* and *Telegraph* carried it in Britain. Oliver Wendell Holmes told Gilmore that it had a larger number of readers than any magazine article ever written. The article made Davis's position clear. And as Lincoln said, it also served to "show the country that I didn't fight shy of Greeley's Niagara business without a reason."[3]

Regardless of what Lincoln said or did, August 1864 became one of the war's darkest months. A main factor was the highly unpopular draft. People were dissatisfied with a law that let a man avoid service by hiring a substitute, or alternatively, paid him a bounty for enlisting, only to have him take the bounty and disappear! Ulysses Grant, in fact, claimed that out of five men reported as enlisted, only one ever got as far as army ranks.

Despite the almost universal complaints about the draft, Lincoln stayed the course. A *New York Times* correspondent wrote: "Mr. Lincoln in private conversation previous to the issue of the new call for 500,000 men, recognized all the elements of dissatisfaction which that measure was likely to bring with it, and to breed; but he stated most emphatically that the men were needed, and that should he fail in consequence, he would at least have the satisfaction of going down with flying colors." [4]

On one occasion, Lincoln's longtime supporter, Joseph Medill of the *Chicago Tribune,* came to Washington with a delegation that sought to have Illinois' draft quota lowered. For Lincoln, this was something of a last straw. He told the group that after Boston, Chicago was the chief instigator of the war. Raising himself to his full six-feet-four, he said: "You called for war, and we had it. You called for emancipation and I have given it to you. Whatever you asked for you have had. Now you come here begging to be let off from the call for men which I have made to carry out the war which you have demanded. You ought to be ashamed of yourselves. I have a right to expect better things of you. Go home and raise your 6,000 extra men. And you, Medill, are acting like a coward. You and your *Tribune* have had more influence than any paper in the Northwest in making this war. You can influence great masses, and yet you cry to be spared at a moment when your cause is suffering. Go home and send us those men."

As the group slunk out, one of them said: "The old man is right. We ought to be ashamed of ourselves. Let us go home and raise those men." And they did.[5]

⋆⟶◯⟜⋆

So far Horace Greeley had neither supported Lincoln nor opposed him, publicly telling his *Tribune* readers that he was unwilling to embark on a "vehement canvass for the Presidency." With a war on he believed "matters of graver and more pressing moment" should engage the attention of the American people.[6]

Privately, however, Greeley clearly agreed with a group of radical "hard war" Republicans who wanted to replace Lincoln. The group had planned to meet at the New York home of ex-mayor George Opdyke on August 19. Their announced purpose was to call another convention, one that would select a new candidate and force Lincoln to withdraw from the race. Greeley, still angry with the president over the Niagara affair, wrote Opdyke: "Mr. Lincoln is already beaten. . . . And we must have another ticket to save us. . . . If we had such a ticket as could be made by naming Grant, Butler, or Sherman for President . . . we could make a fight yet. And such a ticket we ought to have anyhow, with or without a convention." The meeting, as it turned out, was postponed until September, with many of the invitees adopting a "wait and see" attitude about holding a new convention.[7]

On August 22 *New York Times* editor Henry Raymond, national chairman of the Republican Party, met at the Astor House with select committeemen. Representatives from all parts of the North agreed that Lincoln was a Jonah and could not be reelected. Raymond, in despair, told the president that all was lost. "The tide is setting against us," he wrote the president. "Two special causes are assigned to this great reaction in public sentiment,—the want of military success, and the impression . . . that we *can* have peace with Union if we would . . . [but that you are] fighting not for Union but for the abolition of slavery."

Lincoln did not see it that way. He denied that he was "now carrying on this war for the sole purpose of abolition. It is & will be carried on so long as I am President for the sole purpose of restoring the Union. But no power can subdue this rebellion without using the Emancipation lever as I have done."[8]

Meanwhile, antiadministration papers were doing all they could to blacken Lincoln's reputation. One completely false story claimed that Lincoln received his salary in gold, while soldiers were paid only in devalued greenbacks. Another story said that Lincoln, while touring the Antietam battlefield, had shown disrespect for soldiers' graves by asking Ward Hill Lamon to sing a rollicking song while he was near the gravesites. For weeks, versions of this tale were printed on an almost daily basis. The *New York World* was one of the worst offenders. One such item appeared on June 21: "We know that this story is incredible, that it is impossible that a man who could be elected President of the United States, could so conduct himself over the fresh-made graves of the heroic dead. When this story was told us we said that it was *incredible, impossible,* but the story is told on such authority that we *know* it is true."[9]

Lamon finally became so outraged that he composed a letter telling the true facts of the "singing," which of course never took place near gravesites. He showed the letter to Lincoln, who said Lamon's tone was too harsh. In his own hand, Lincoln wrote a better version for him to mail. Then he reconsidered, telling his friend Lamon: "You know, Hill, that this is the truth about that affair; but I dislike to appear as an apologist for an act of my own which I know was right. Keep this paper and we will see about it."[10] Evidently the letter was never sent; the media-wise Lincoln knew it was futile to joust with a major newspaper; a lengthy dispute would only give the story added publicity, and the *World* would inevitably have the last word.

Lincoln expressed similar thoughts on another occasion, when the paper in question was Horace Greeley's *New York Tribune*. Lincoln told the New York secretary of state, Chauncey Depew, that Greeley's constant criticisms and misrepresentations annoyed him "probably more than anything which happened during his administration." Depew asked him why he didn't publish the facts in a card. Surely all the papers would be pleased to print them. "Yes, all the newspapers will publish my letter," Lincoln said, "and so will Greeley. The next day he will take a line and comment upon it, and he will keep it up, in that way, until, at the end of three weeks, I will be convicted out of my own mouth of all the things which he charges against me. No man, whether he be private citizen or President of the United States, can successfully carry on a controversy with a great newspaper, and escape destruction, unless he owns a newspaper equally great, with a circulation in the same neighborhood."[11]

◦◦━◉⋐━◦◦

Throughout the summer, demonstrators continued to agitate against the draft. Washington officials, including Stanton and Halleck, concluded that federal troops would be needed to enforce the law. In mid-August, Ulysses Grant was asked to dispatch combat troops to keep order. Grant countered by saying Northern governors should use their own militias for the purpose. Moreover, the general argued: "If we are to draw troops from the field to keep the loyal states in harness, it will prove difficult to suppress the rebellion in the disloyal states."

At that point Lincoln weighed in, wiring Grant: "I HAVE SEEN YOUR DISPATCH EXPRESSING YOUR UNWILLINGNESS TO BREAK YOUR HOLD WHERE YOU ARE. NEITHER AM I WILLING. HOLD ON WITH A BULLDOG GRIP, AND CHEW AND CHOKE AS MUCH AS POSSIBLE."

When Grant read the telegram, he laughed out loud, something he rarely did. He handed the telegram to his staff officers and said with a grin, "The President has more nerve than any of his advisers."[12]

The question, of course, was whether the country's nerve would match Lincoln's. Much depended on what the media would do, and Lincoln did his best to sway individual reporters. Meeting with a man from the *Boston Journal*, Lincoln said: "I have faith in the people. They will not consent to disunion. The danger is in their being misled. Let them know the truth and the country is safe."[13]

With the Democratic Convention less than a week away, the president's reelection chances looked increasingly bleak. On August 23, at a cabinet meeting, Lincoln handed each member a sheet of paper so folded and pasted that what was inside could not be read. He asked each of them to sign his name across the back of the sheet. Each one wrote, not knowing what he was signing. It was a memorandum for possible future use, reading:

Executive Mansion, Washington, August 23, 1864

This morning, as for some days past, it seems exceedingly probable that this administration will not be reelected. Then it will be my duty to so cooperate with the President-elect as to save the Union between the election and the inauguration; as he will have secured his election on such ground that he cannot possibly save it afterward.

A. Lincoln

By that memo, Lincoln was pledging his willingness to accept loyally the verdict of the people, but to do his utmost to save the Union during his brief remaining time in office.[14]

On August 29 delegates to the Democratic convention met in Chicago. They assembled at the Wigwam, the very hall in which Republicans had nominated Lincoln four years earlier. The place could hold up to 15,000 people, and according to the *New York Tribune*, it was a spot admirably suited for a circus. With Peace and War Democrats fighting fiercely among themselves, circus was probably an apt description of what would take place during the next three days.[15]

Before heading to Chicago to cover the convention, Noah Brooks visited the White House. Lincoln asked him to pass on any personal observations of the Chicago event when he returned. His own opinion, Lincoln said, was that the delegates "must nominate a Peace Democrat on a war platform, or a War Democrat on a peace platform; and I personally can't say that I care much which they do."[16]

The convention chairman was New York Governor Horatio Seymour, a War Democrat who was soundly applauded when he proclaimed, "If the administration cannot save this Union, we can."[17] After much give and take, the party reached a shaky compromise. The War Democrats managed to nominate George McClellan, but the Peace Democrats, whose most vocal member was the controversial Clement Vallandigham, authored most of the party platform. The agreement seems to have been that a War Democrat would be nominated in exchange for a pledge that the nominee would seek an immediate end to the war. In effect, the Democrats had shot themselves in the foot by offering a contradictory combination. The press recognized the problem immediately; the *New York Post,* for example, said in disgust, "It is impossible to vote for General McClellan, or any other candidate . . . on that Chicago platform."[18]

Up to this point, Confederates had been hoping for big things from the Democratic convention. Now even they were confused. "Are we to take [McClellan] for a peace candidate or a reconstruction war Democrat[?]" the *Augusta Constitutionalist* asked.[19]

⤙═◎═⤚

The election battle lines had been drawn, and Lincoln knew better than anyone that he needed support from the media. Of particular importance were the three major New York papers—the *Times, Tribune,* and *Herald*— whose influence extended far beyond the metropolitan area. The *Times,* whose editor Henry Raymond chaired the Republican National Committee, was safely in Lincoln's camp. Moreover, Raymond was writing an influential campaign biography of the president. It was mostly a collection of Lincoln's public speeches and writings, and when it appeared, it was obvious that the president had worked with Raymond in putting it together.

What then of the *Tribune,* where Greeley had been blowing hot and cold where Lincoln was concerned? Hoping to improve the situation, Lincoln tried to arrange a face-to-face meeting with "Uncle Horace." Almost humbly he wrote: "Dear Mr. Greeley: I have been wanting to see you for several weeks, and if I could spare the time I should call upon you in New York. Perhaps you may be able to visit me. I shall be very glad to see you. A. Lincoln."

George G. Hoskins, a leading New York State Republican, later said that Greeley showed him the note and said he had no intention of answering it. He said, however, that he didn't mind if Hoskins wanted to see Lincoln on his behalf. Hoskins said he then called on Lincoln, who praised Greeley to the skies, saying he was not only a great admirer of Greeley, but a lifelong reader of the *New York Tribune.* Hoskins further quoted

Lincoln as saying that Greeley was the ablest editor in the United States, if not in the world—the most influential man in the country, not excepting the president—the equal, if not the superior, of the country's first postmaster general, Benjamin Franklin.

According to Hoskins, Lincoln then said he was determined, if reelected and reinaugurated, to appoint Greeley to that same office of postmaster general. "He is worthy of it, and my mind is made up," Lincoln supposedly said. What's more, he hoped Hoskins would tell this to Greeley. When he did, Greeley asked Hoskins if he really believed such a lie. As for himself, he did not. Whether or not Hoskins's story is true, and whether or not Greeley believed him, it is a fact that next morning Horace Greeley, in a two-column editorial, came out foursquare for Lincoln.[20]

"Henceforth we fly the banner of ABRAHAM LINCOLN for the next Presidency," Greeley wrote, "choosing that far rather than the Disunion and a quarter of a century of wars, or the Union and political servitude which our opponents would give us. . . . We grant, from our own convictions, much that can be said in criticism of the present Administration; for the sake of argument, we will grant anything that any honest and loyal men can say. And then this is our rejoinder—Mr. Lincoln has done seven-eighths of the work after his fashion; there must be vigor and virtue enough left in him to do the other fraction. The work is in his hands. . . . We must re-elect him, and God helping us, we will."[21]

Now that he was committed, Greeley went all out. He printed a series of pamphlets and broadsides supporting Lincoln's Union ticket and advertised them for sale at one dollar per hundred. Also, beginning September 14, he emblazoned the New York Union ticket on the *Tribune* masthead and kept it there until the election. Greeley himself was listed as one of the Union ticket's New York State electors.[22]

Lincoln's next problem was the *New York Herald* and its cantankerous editor, James Gordon Bennett. All along, the *Herald* had pushed Grant for the Republican nomination, and shown little use for Lincoln and his supporters. Early on, a particularly vicious editorial called a Lincoln meeting "one of the most disgraceful exhibitions of human depravity ever witnessed in this wicked world. It was a gathering of ghouls, vultures, hyenas and other feeders upon carrion, for the purpose of surfeiting themselves upon the slaughter of recent battles. We remember nothing like it in the history of politics. The great ghoul at Washington, who authorized the meeting, and the little ghouls and vultures who conducted it, have succeeded in completely disgusting the people of this country, and have damaged themselves irretrievably."[23]

Lincoln once said, "It is important to humor the *Herald*," and he had learned to read things like the preceding without wincing.[24] In any case, he always treated *Herald* reporters well, and it probably helped. At least the *Herald* sounded somewhat neutral in early September as it predicted that the coming race would be "one of the toughest in our political history," and said, "all this talk as to Mr. Lincoln's alleged 'unpopularity' and the 'public approval' with which Gen. McClellan is regarded must amount, for the present at least, to just about the value of a peck measure of moonshine."[25]

Actually, Lincoln had tried a different approach with the *Herald*, one apparently based on a hint that Bennett (or at least his wife) hankered for some sort of diplomatic posting, preferably to a major European capital. Back in July, Lincoln had sent a confidential letter to Bennett through his friend Abram Wakeman in New York, offering an unspecified post in return for his support. Bennett, after some moments of silence, had told Wakeman that the offer "did not amount to much." Wakeman went back to Lincoln and said it appeared that Bennett would need something more specific. What Lincoln had in mind was making Bennett ambassador to France, but the *Herald* editor wasn't biting, at least not yet.[26]

Lincoln wasn't about to give up, and apparently he discussed his next move with Senator James Harlan of Iowa. On September 23 John Hay noted in his diary: "Senator Harlan thinks that Bennett's support [with the New York Herald] is so important, especially considered as to its bearing on the soldier vote, that it would pay to offer him a foreign mission for it, & so told me." The social ambitions of Bennett's wife were well known, to the point that while Lincoln himself was fair game to the *Herald*, his wife, the first lady, was always treated with deference. In any case, on November 4, just before the election, W. O. Bartlett, a Bennett go-between, assured Bennett that he had talked to Lincoln and that appointing Bennett ambassador to France was a done deal. Bartlett quoted

Lincoln as saying, "I expect to do it as certainly as I do to be re-elected myself." Three days later, a diary entry of Hay's indicated that Mrs. Bennett had probably learned of that promise and that she was keen to go to the American Legation at Paris. The entry read: "Bartlett writes to President that Mrs. J. G. B. has become an earnest Lincolnite."[27]

⋯⋙◦⋘⋯

By September, fortunately for Lincoln, events far from the White House were having a major impact on both the media and the mood of the country. On August 5 Admiral David Farragut had taken his fleet into Mobile Bay after a terrific artillery duel between his ships and three forts guarding the bay. At one point, Farragut had climbed the mast of his flagship, the USS *Hartford,* for a better view. A quartermaster lashed the admiral to the mast, creating an unforgettable image in the rich traditions of the U.S. Navy. Farragut soon added a memorable phrase as well. When the fleet encountered mines, he shouted, "Damn the torpedoes—Full speed ahead!" It made for a wonderful quote.[28] Then on September 3, another stirring phrase appeared in a wire from William T. Sherman to General Halleck: "Atlanta is ours, and fairly won."[29]

Lincoln authorized the firing of hundred-gun salutes in celebration and asked that a special day of thanksgiving be observed the following Sunday in all places of worship. Lincoln's congratulatory message, printed in all major papers, was a significant boost for public morale: "The national thanks are tendered by the President to Major-General William T. Sherman, and the gallant officers and soldiers of his command before Atlanta, for the distinguished ability, courage, and perseverance displayed in the campaign in Georgia, which, under divine favor, has resulted in the capture of Atlanta. The marches, battles, sieges, and other military operations that have signalized the campaign must render it famous in the annals of war, and have entitled those who have participated therein to the applause and thanks of the nation."[30]

Perhaps the tide had turned. At least the *Chicago Tribune* thought so, as it exulted: "Union Men! The dark days are over. We see our way out. . . . Thanks be to God! The Republic is safe!"[31]

In mid-September, more good news came from the Shenandoah Valley, where fiery Gen. Phil Sheridan was squaring off against Jubal Early. On September 12 Lincoln had wired Grant that "Sheridan and Early are facing each other at a deadlock," and said, if Sheridan were reinforced, it might enable him to "make a strike." Tactfully, however, he added, "This is but a suggestion."

A suggestion was enough. Grant paid a quick visit to Sheridan on September 16. After hearing Sheridan's plans for a Valley campaign, Grant issued his briefest order of the war: "Go in." Sheridan launched his attack on the 19th, and next day an enthusiastic wire was received in Washington. It not only told of a victory, but also provided a line that the media (and Lincoln) loved: "We have sent them whirling through Winchester, and we are after them tomorrow." Lincoln promptly wired Sheridan his congratulations: "Have just heard of your great victory. God bless you all, officers and men."[32]

George Williams of the *New York Times* was the first reporter to arrive in Washington with news of the Winchester action. Although it was two in the morning, he was invited to the White House to brief Lincoln. Afterward, an appreciative Lincoln suggested he return for a visit the next time he was in town. "But being very young," Williams later wrote, "I supposed the President's invitation was merely a compliment." A month later, however, when he was back in Washington, he was stopped on the street by John Hay, the presidential secretary. "Mr. Lincoln saw you on the Avenue today," Hay said, "and was surprised you had not been to see him."

Williams didn't wait for a second invitation. He hurried to the White House, where Lincoln told him, "I am always seeking information, and you newspaper men are so often behind the scenes at the front I am frequently able to get ideas from you which no one else can give." The highly flattered young reporter was more than happy to tell what he knew.[33]

⋆⟾◉⟾⋆

By this time, victories by Farragut, Sherman, and Sheridan had changed the perception of Lincoln's chances; he was no longer a discredited loser but a likely winner. People forgot about assembling a new convention to replace him, which left a splinter candidate, John C. Fremont, as the only bar to Republican unity. Back in May a small band of radicals had met in Cleveland to nominate Fremont. At the time, the *New York Times* referred to them as the "little squad of bolters," and said: "The only capacity in which these people serve is that of malcontents. They are simply dissatisfied with the policy of President Lincoln, but will find it impossible to agree upon any positive policy of their own."[34]

Suddenly, on September 22, John C. Fremont withdrew from the race. Behind the scenes, the radicals evidently had struck a deal with Lincoln. In exchange for Fremont's withdrawal, their arch enemy, Montgomery Blair, would have to leave the cabinet. Accordingly, the day after Fremont withdrew, Lincoln asked for Blair's resignation. Blair was given no explanation for this, and the request was "couched in friendly terms," but Blair later told a fellow cabinet member he had no doubt that his dismissal was "a peace offering to Fremont and his friends." That was indeed the case; easing Blair out of the cabinet kept the Fremonters, who hated Blair, from voting Democratic. As it turned out, Fremont would have needed but 85,000 out of 1,051,000 votes cast in six states to give the victory to McClellan.[35]

On October 12 Chief Justice Roger B. Taney died, giving Lincoln another opportunity to unify his followers. The week after Taney died, well-informed newspapers predicted that Salmon P. Chase would be made his successor. The *New York Herald* thought otherwise, saying it was "out of the question" to appoint Chase, whom it called, "the late great failure of the Treasury Department." There were other possibilities, notably Montgomery Blair, the man who had just been booted from the cabinet. Lincoln, however, stuck with Chase, although the appointment wasn't announced until after the election. It was a good choice, not only because it was politically expedient, but because Chase was the right man for the job. However, as Charles Dana said: "That appointment was not made by the President with entire willingness. He is a man who keeps a grudge as faithfully as any living Christian, and consented to Chase's elevation only when the pressure became very general and very urgent. The Senate especially were resolved that no second-rate man should be appointed to that office, and if Mr. Montgomery Blair had succeeded in presenting his programme to that body, I have no doubt it would have been smashed to pieces in a moment."[36]

Chase, having been assured by Senators William Fessenden and Charles Sumner that he would be the next chief justice, went on a vigorous speaking tour on behalf of Lincoln. Republican papers began singing Chase's praises, calling him "the great statesman of the West." In late October, he spoke in Philadelphia's Concert Hall to what the *Philadelphia Inquirer* called the largest crowd ever gathered for an indoor meeting in that city. "Hydreaulic pressure," said the *Inquirer*, "would not have forced another individual into the vast room."[37]

As election day drew nearer, people were beginning to see what was at stake. A prescient *Chicago Tribune* editorial proclaimed: "For an hundred years to come historians will be engaged in placing in their true light the events which are now transpiring. . . . While the present age looks at it mainly as a struggle for Union and nationality, the future will regard as equally important what we regard as but an incident, viz: the regeneration of the Republic and the vindication of true democracy and of the rights of labor, by the abolishment of slavery. Not willingly, even for a future or a fame so glorious, would the people of the free North have entered upon the present contest. But driven into it reluctantly, and accepting so great an issue as the total abolition of American slavery, . . . we may still look through the stormy present into the near and bright future, borrowing of the provision which there awaits us. . . . Think of this, and when you cast your vote in November, vote for the unity of the republic, for the rights of man and for the only candidates who represents them—Abraham Lincoln of Illinois and Andrew Johnson of Tennessee."[38]

Even in England, Lincoln's campaign started to be seen in its proper light. The *New York Tribune* carried a letter from John Bright, English orator and statesman, saying:

> All those of my countrymen who have wished well to the Rebellion, who have hoped for the break-up of the Union, who have preferred to see a Southern Slave Empire rather than a restored and free Republic, so far as I can observe, are now in favor of the election of Gen. McClellan.

All those who have deplored the calamities which the leaders
of the Secession have brought upon your country, who believe that
Slavery weakens your power and tarnishes your good name throughout the world, and who regard the restoration of your Union as a
thing to be desired and prayed for by all good men, so far as I can
judge, are heartily longing for the reelection of Mr. Lincoln.[39]

During the run-up to the election, Lincoln had dangled the job of
postmaster general before Greeley, and a diplomatic posting before Bennett. However, these were far from the only cases of federal patronage
used for political ends. There is ample evidence that Lincoln coun-
tenanced, if he did not direct, the use of appointments at all levels, wherever they would do the most good. A Democratic editor in upstate New
York showed he knew what was going on, noting scornfully: "A glance at
the list of delegates to the Republican state convention [held in Syracuse
on May 25] will satisfy anyone that the people have had nothing to do
with their selection, and that they represent only the great army of office-
holders in our state. From every county comes the internal revenue col-
lector, the assessor, the sub-collectors, the provost marshal or his deputy,
and the city and village postmasters."[40]

Lincoln did these things without appearing to be "just another politician." In a sense, the campaign saw two separate Lincolns: a politician
quietly marshaling his forces in all sections of the country and a president
acting as though he were unaware of any political controversies in progress.
Remarkably, in the public documents and official and personal correspondence that have come to light, it was as though no election campaign was
under way, for only rarely did Lincoln let political implications go into the
record. Perhaps this was not being frank with the people, since his public
indifference and unconcern masked an intense personal desire to remain
in office. In the nineteenth century, however, this seems to have been the
most effective campaign style, appearing neither to "want" office nor to
seek it. Other presidents have sought reelection more openly, directly, and
frankly, but none has quite equaled the political artistry of Abraham Lincoln. Myths about Lincoln as being different from other men are dispelled
by the record of Lincoln, the consummate politician.

Having said that, however, we must remember that Lincoln sought reelection to save the Union, not for personal glory. What he did, he did for the right reasons. Charles Dana was on the mark when he said: "Lincoln was a supreme politician. He understood politics because he understood human nature. . . . There was no flabby philanthropy about Abraham Lincoln. He was all solid, hard, keen intelligence, combined with goodness. . . . You felt that here was a man who saw through things, who understood, and you respected him accordingly."[41]

CHAPTER 16

"NOT A VINDICTIVE MAN"

I n 1864, as in previous years, only adult white males were eligible to vote. Obviously a large percentage of them were in the Union Army, which made the soldier vote a powerful factor in the coming election. It might have seemed that McClellan, as a popular general, would give an edge to the Democrats. Not so, said the boys in blue. On September 26, 1864, from Grant's army near Petersburg, a soldier wrote the *New York Tribune:* "I am glad to know that you are pushing things for 'Old Abe.' His success in the present Presidential campaign will be the greatest blow yet struck at the Rebellion. The Rebels seem to be far more agitated and anxious about the election than we do, for we feel easy in the matter, knowing that the winning team is Abe and Andy." And from Sherman's army outside Atlanta came a letter expressing soldiers' support for Lincoln and their disappointment with the Democratic platform: "Nothing imparts so much animation here as politics and the probable result of the coming Presidential Election. . . . So far as my observation and knowledge extend, soldiers are of the Abrahamic School. They cannot drink in enough *real Union sentiment* from the Chicago platform to warrant safety in the whole nation."[1]

The Copperhead Peace Democrats, well aware of the military's favoring Lincoln, went all out to minimize the soldier vote. In Indiana, New Jersey, and Delaware, where Copperheads controlled the legislatures, absentee voting by soldiers was forbidden. In other states, Copperheads also tried mightily to ban soldier ballots, but were outvoted by Lincoln supporters. Lincoln meanwhile was doing all he could to get out the military vote, and not just for the presidency. Typical was a letter he sent to General Sherman: "The State election of Indiana occurs on the 11th of October, and the loss of it to the friends of the Government would go far towards losing the whole Union cause. . . . Any thing you can safely do to let her soldiers, or any part of them, go home and vote at the State election, will be greatly in point. They need not remain for the Presidential election, but may return to you at once. This is, in no sense, an order, but is merely intended to impress you with the importance, to the army itself, of your doing all you safely can."[2]

The Republican cause was also helped, and not always scrupulously, by Secretary of War Stanton's barring all Democratic campaign material from the camps until a month before the election. In addition, the Republicans had the larger campaign funds, and the distributor of their campaign circulars, George T. Brown, boasted later that he had sent nearly a million documents to the troops. A significant percentage of those funds came from government workers. Dunning federal employees for political contributions—10 percent or more per paycheck—was a common practice by whatever party was in power, and the Republicans took full advantage. Even cabinet members donated to the campaign, as much as $500 each.[3]

As a good politician, Lincoln knew the perks of power, which definitely included the use of patronage. This applied to newspapers, which were given or denied government advertising depending on the warmth of their support. Lincoln didn't mind a paper expressing its preference for a particular Republican before the nomination, but government patronage was denied to anyone opposing the party's nominee at the June 8 Convention, which happened to be himself. Patronage of course was perfectly legal and was consistent with long-standing practice. However, the truly scrupulous "Honest Abe" forbade outright editorial bribery, although he may have been aware it took place. In California, for example, where the first rails were being laid for a favorite Lincoln project, the transcontinental railroad, officials wanting favorable media coverage gave the editor of the *Sacramento Union* $2,000 worth of stock in 1863 and another $1,600 worth in 1864. His reporter in Washington got another ten shares. These bribes, called "gifts," were charged to the Central Pacific construction account.[4]

Both parties, of course, were spending lavishly, for rallies, materials, and general get-out-the-vote efforts. James Gordon Bennett took note of this, implying that much of the money came from "contractors" seeking to buy influence: "The Presidential election will probably cost us over fifty millions," Bennett wrote. "Some of it comes from patriots and some from partisans; but we are afraid that the most of it comes from contractors. Nevertheless, this is a great country, and we can afford to do things in a liberal way."[5]

At the War Department, former newsman Charles Dana was a fascinated witness to the hubbub of activity. Dana wrote:

> During the Presidential campaign of 1864 which resulted in Lincoln's reelection and in the further prosecution of the war upon the lines of Lincoln's policy, we were busy in the department arranging for soldiers to go home to vote, and also for the taking of ballots in the army. There was a constant succession of telegrams from all parts of the country requesting that leave of absence be extended to this or that officer, in order that his district at home might have the benefit of his vote and political influence. Furloughs were asked for private soldiers whose presence in close districts was deemed of especial importance, and there was a widespread demand that men on detached service be sent home. All the power and influence of the War Department, then something enormous from the vast expenditure and extensive relations of the war, was employed to secure the reelection of Mr. Lincoln. The political struggle was most intense, and the interest taken in it, both in the White House and in the War Department, was almost painful."[6]

Amid all this, a particularly ugly dispute arose in New York State, where the legislature passed a bill letting soldiers vote by absentee ballot, only to have the Democratic governor, Horatio Seymour, veto the bill. The legislature then upped the ante by amending the state constitution to allow such voting. However, even that didn't end the matter. Seymour proceeded to appoint fifty civilians to oversee soldier voting, commissioning each one "to be present as an Inspector on the part of the Democratic party of the State of New York." (The Republicans, if they wanted inspectors, had to pay for their own.) Two of Seymour's inspectors, Edward J. Donohue and a man named Ferry, were then caught with bundles of voting papers containing fraudulent signatures of soldiers and officers. A military court, convened to try the pair, found evidence of a "conspiracy fully exhibited," and called it "a carefully matured plan for defrauding the soldiers of their votes at the coming Presidential election."[7]

The *New York Tribune*, under the headline "Voting Fraud," reported the conclusion of Donohue's trial:

> The further the investigation probes the New York State agency ballot-stuffing conspiracy, the more profound is the indignation and astonishment of honorable men of all parties. "Hitherto the ballot-box has been to the American citizen what the altar is to the Christian," forcibly remarks Judge-Advocate HOLT in submitting to the court his review of the evidence in possession of the Government prior to the arrests, and upon which the trials were to be based.
>
> To-day the trial of DONOHUE was concluded. It but rendered more conspicuous the enormity of the crime concocted, and, as will be seen by the report of the Court's proceedings, compromises, if it does not convict, many of your most prominent MCCLELLAN apostles from HORATIO SEYMOUR down to the Sheriff of Albany County.[8]

Seymour wasn't finished. He admitted that "irregularities" might have occurred, but said there was "no crime." He further claimed that these were civil matters in which military courts had no jurisdiction. His state judge advocate then published a blast that was fully reported by the anti-administration *New York World*. So Donohue had admitted signing "a fictitious name as a certifying officer." What of it? Wasn't all this a plot of the "abolition journals" and "Washington conspirators?" Lincoln listened courteously to the protests, weighed the evidence, and gladly signed the order sending Donohue and Ferry to prison.[9]

※＝○○＝※

George McClellan had said that if he were elected, he would continue to prosecute the war. His party's platform nevertheless advocated a cease-fire while parties North and South met to discuss their differences. Horace Greeley pointed out the fallacy in such reasoning:

> Don't you know that McClellan's election would be followed by an Armistice? Don't you know that an Armistice would raise the blockade of the Southern ports, withdraw our armies from the Southern States, and surrender every military advantage we have won in four years fighting? . . . Don't you know that England, France, Spain and Belgium would accept the Armistice as the recognition by the United States of the Confederate Government? Don't you know that in the interval between the Armistice and negotiations for a peace and the restoration of the Union, Europe would flood into the Rebel States munitions of war, and men, and that the Richmond leaders would make themselves impregnable on the Potomac, and on the Atlantic, and on the Gulf coast? Don't you know that our offers of peace to the Jeff. Davis Government would be met with the demand for a recognition of the independence of the Confederate States? This is as positively certain as any future movement of the heavenly bodies. . . . Separation from us is their inexorable purpose. In the language of Jeff. Davis in his interview with Col. Jacques "that we WILL have, or annihilation."[10]

The peace plank in the platform equally outraged the *New York Herald,* which supported the war but still leaned Democratic: "The greatest and most disgraceful of all the political failures resulting from the war is the Chicago platform. Setting down, on the war question, President Lincoln as a failure, we may safely say that if reelected, he will owe his success in a great degree to that copperhead Chicago platform outrage upon the people of the loyal states."[11]

Each time he read the *Herald,* Lincoln no doubt wondered if his overtures to Bennett had borne any fruit. That was still hard to say, but at least Bennett seemed uncertain about which candidate he preferred. For while he continued to insult Lincoln, he treated McClellan just as badly. Bennett wrote:

> It is true that our political conventions did not nominate the candidates whom the people desired to elect. . . . [They] passed over our ablest men and selected our failures to represent them. Neither the republican nor democratic politicians had brains enough to know that a great crisis required great men in office. Grant and Sherman were hardly mentioned in either convention although their names are upon every lip and their record is upon every heart among the people. On the contrary, the politicians were afraid to nominate strong men, and preferred to support men who could be manipulated and managed. Lincoln is a failure, militarily, socially and as a states-man. McClellan is a failure in a military point of view, through the fault of other people, and in a political point of view through his own fault. . . . Still, when all this has been said, the striking fact remains that both the Presidential candidates, such as they are, stand committed to the platform of the Union at any price and at all hazards.[12]

With remarkable arrogance, Bennett offered his own "platform." It had three planks: first, suppress the rebellion by force; second, restore the Union by a return of seceded states, followed by a convention to decide all unsettled questions; third, enforce the Monroe Doctrine by expelling the French from Mexico and demanding reparations from England.

By acceding to these, a man might win the *Herald's* support. However, Bennett said: "We do not want a joke from Old Abe, nor a non-committal from Little Mac. If both candidates agree to our pledge, we will at once decide which of them is more worthy of trust, and give him the benefit of our decision."[13]

Lincoln continued his efforts to be on good terms with the press, including the *Herald*, but he made it a point to be even-handed. Noah Brooks, one of Lincoln's closest press friends, therefore resented it when S. P. Hanscomb, formerly of the *New York Tribune*, and presently editor of the *Washington Republican*, tried giving the impression that his paper was the "organ of the President." Hanscomb, according to Brooks, was a "pushing and persevering man," who had managed to ingratiate himself with Lincoln and obtain "from our good-natured Chief Magistrate such scanty items of news as he is willing to give out for publication." However, Brooks wrote, "As for the *Republican* having any authority to reflect or indicate the views of any member of the administration upon any subject whatever, it is the most complete invention of those who circulate such a foolish yarn. Lincoln believes in letting the newspapers publish all that will not benefit the enemy; he disapproves of many of the arbitrary edicts of the press of Secretary Stanton; and he is more free to converse upon matters pertaining to his Department than any of his Cabinet, though the rack of torture could not extort from him what he chooses to conceal; but he abhors the thought of an 'organ.'"[14]

Also, despite his casual way of dealing with reporters, Lincoln deeply resented it when someone took advantage of his good nature or maligned him. A clerk at the White House, William O. Stoddard, told of a jolly and bumptious reporter who printed a joke ascribed to Lincoln containing "a very witty and dirty and insolent pun." Lincoln sent for the reporter, who was ushered in smiling, and came out, according to Stoddard, "with no smile at all upon his face."[15]

Throughout the election campaign, the attacks on the president became progressively more vicious and more personal. As an example, a so-called "campaign biography," *Only Authentic Life of Abraham Lincoln, Alias "Old Abe,"* portrayed him with biting sarcasm: "Mr. Lincoln stands six feet twelve in his socks, which he changes once every ten days. His anatomy is composed mostly of bones, and when walking he resembles the offspring of a happy marriage between a derrick and a windmill. . . . His head is shaped something like a rutabaga, and his complexion is that of a Saratoga trunk. His hands and feet are plenty large enough, and in society he has the air of having too many of them. . . . He could hardly be called handsome, though he is certainly much better looking since he had the smallpox. . . . He is 107 years old." Equally bad were the stories and cartoons depicting Lincoln as a supporter of miscegenation, stirring up fears in a racist electorate that a biracial society would inevitably follow Lincoln's reelection. One cartoon showed him welcoming a mixed-race couple in a society where African-Americans rode in carriages liveried by white servants.

Along these lines, several caricatures hinted that Lincoln himself had African heritage.[16]

The miscegenation charge even made its way into the halls of Congress, where the Democrat Samuel S. "Sunset" Cox bellowed, "there is a doctrine now being advertised and urged by the leading lights of the Abolition party, toward which the Republican party will and must advance." That party, Cox said, is "moving steadily forward to perfect social equality of black and white, and can only end in this detestable doctrine of Miscegenation." Bennett's *Herald* said much the same thing, referring to the Republicans as the "party of miscegenation."[17]

Since Lincoln wisely chose to ignore the miscegenation stories, they never really caught hold with the public. He also managed to avoid a trap set with regard to a book titled *Miscegenation: The Theory of the Blending of the Races.* The author sent a copy to Lincoln, along with a gushing letter asking for his endorsement. "Permit me to express the hope," said the letter, "that as the first four years of your administration have been distinguished by giving liberty to four millions of human beings, that the next four years may find these freedmen possessed of all the rights of citizenship."

Lincoln didn't fall for the trap. He ignored the request, knowing any endorsement would be seized on by the Democrats to fan racial hatred. The *London Morning Herald,* hearing of the ruse, applauded Lincoln's wisdom, saying he "is shrewd enough to say nothing on the unsavory subject."[18]

As the attacks continued, *Harper's Weekly* noted that McClellan supporters had called Lincoln such things as liar, thief, braggart, buffoon, usurper, monster, robber, swindler, fiend, butcher, and tyrant. It asked how men who claimed they were "conservatives" could apply such language to "the Constitutional President of the United States." Not since Washington, said *Harper's,* had there been such "partisan ribaldry."[19] Nevertheless, a few days before the election, *Harper's* asserted that the vicious attacks had simply not worked: "The personal character of the President is the rock upon which the Opposition is wrecked. It dashes against him and his administration hissing and venomous, but falls back again baffled. From the day when covert rebellion lay in wait to assassinate him in Baltimore, through all the mad hate of the rebel press to the last malignant sneer of

Copperhead Conservatism and foreign jealousy, the popular confidence in the unswerving fidelity and purity of purpose of the President has smiled the storm to scorn."[20]

Right up to election day, the editors of major papers were as deep into campaigning as they were into editorializing. In addition to running the *New York Times*, Henry Raymond was heading the Republican campaign. Nearby at the *New York World*, Manton Marble was spewing anti-Republican venom during the day and masterminding McClellan's campaign at night. Horace Greeley was not only supporting the Republican ticket in his columns, but he also was delivering a series of enthusiastic stump speeches for Lincoln and Johnson. With a sneer, Marble reported a talk in Burlington, Vermont, in which Greeley "used up two hours time, the patience of his audience, and his own wind."[21]

Finally, on November 8, Election Day arrived in Washington, amid a cold rain and wintry gusts that kept most people indoors. "About noon I called on President Lincoln," wrote Noah Brooks, "and to my surprise found him entirely alone, as if by common consent everybody had avoided the White House." Lincoln, who always felt comfortable with newsmen, not surprisingly chose a reporter rather than a politician to keep him company. Brooks wrote that he spent nearly the whole afternoon with the president, "who apparently found it difficult to put his mind on any of the routine work of his office, and entreated me to stay with him."[22]

Lincoln, feeling the strain, called it "one of the most solemn" days in his life. And inevitably he thought of all the insults that had come his way. Publicly he had chosen to ignore the personal attacks; privately, however, he confessed to his secretary, John Hay, that they hurt—deeply. Hay said the president "seemed to have a keen and surprised regret that he should be an object in so many quarters of so bitter and vindictive an opposition." Almost to himself, Lincoln mused, "It is a little singular that I, who am not a vindictive man, should have always been before the people in canvasses marked for their bitterness; always but once; when I came to Congress it was a quiet time. But always besides that the contests in which I have been prominent have been marked with great rancor."[23]

Lincoln was understandably nervous about the day's results. However, several things had been working in his favor recently, not the least of which were the bland words coming forth from George McClellan. The

"Young Napoleon's" letter accepting the Democratic nomination had promised economy without saying how or where; "a more vigorous nationality" in foreign affairs without telling how it would be gained; and "a return to a sound financial system" without defining "sound." The vagueness had done little to inspire his Democratic supporters.[24]

Then too there was the action in Georgia, where Sherman was starting out from Atlanta in what would become his famous (or infamous, depending on one's point of view) March to the Sea. He had told Grant of his plan, one he said would cut the Confederacy in two and "make Georgia howl." On November 2, after thinking it over, Grant responded, "I say, then, go on as you propose."[25]

A few messages came in during the afternoon, but nothing of consequence. Around seven, Lincoln and Hay, sloshing through the rain, made their way to the War Department telegraph office, where Seward, Stanton, and others had gathered to await returns. At one point, Lincoln called Charles Dana to his side. "Dana," he said, "have you ever read any of the writings of Petroleum V. Nasby?"

"No sir," Dana said. "I have only looked at some of them, and they seemed quite funny." Lincoln then proceeded to read a few lines for Dana's benefit. He paused to read one of the election telegrams, then went back to reading more of Nasby's humor.

Nearby, Stanton was fuming. Going into the next room, he motioned Dana to follow. Dana later wrote: "I shall never forget the fire of his indignation at what seemed to him to be mere nonsense. The idea that when the safety of the republic was thus at issue . . . the man most deeply concerned . . . could turn aside to read such balderdash and to laugh at such frivolous jests was, to his mind, repugnant, even damnable. He could not understand, apparently, that it was by the relief these jests afforded to the strain of mind under which Lincoln had so long been living . . . that the safety and sanity of his intelligence were maintained and preserved."[26]

As the evening wore on, good news came in from New York, from Pennsylvania, from Maryland. The mood brightened, and Lincoln asked that the early reports be sent over to Mrs. Lincoln, saying, "She is more anxious than I."[27]

By midnight the final result looked all but certain—Lincoln would be comfortably ahead in the popular vote and win overwhelmingly in the

Electoral College. Finally able to relax, he piled into a late supper of fried oysters. Around 2 A.M. he left the telegraph office and was greeted by a brass band, music, and cheers. By this time, the rain had stopped and the crowd called for a speech. Lincoln did not disappoint. He told them,

> I earnestly believe that the consequences of this day's work, if it be as you assume, and as now seems probable, will be to the lasting advantage, if not to the very salvation, of the country. I cannot at this hour say what has been the result of the election. But, whatever it may be, I have no desire to modify this opinion: that all who have labored today in behalf of the Union have wrought for the best interests of the country and the world, not only for the present, but for all future ages.
>
> I am thankful to God for this approval of the people, but, while deeply grateful for this mark of their confidence in me, if I know my heart, my gratitude is free from any taint of personal triumph. I do not impugn the motives of any one opposed to me. It is no pleasure to me to triumph over any one, but I give thanks to the Almighty for this evidence of the people's resolution to stand by free government and the rights of humanity.[28]

Headlines in the *New York Herald* told the story:

The Election

—

All Quiet Along the Voting Lines of the Country

—

The Result of the Great National Contest

—

Abraham Lincoln Reelected President of
The United States
And
Andrew Johnson of Tennessee
Elected
Vice President of the United States

—

The New Congress Largely in
Favor of the Administration[29]

When the final account was tabulated, all states except New Jersey, Kentucky, and Delaware had gone for Lincoln. He had won 55 percent of the popular vote; in the Electoral College his plurality was an impressive 212 to 21. And in analyzing the results, his support from the military vote was particularly gratifying. Back in August, Lincoln supposedly told reporter Henry Wing, "Henry, I would rather be defeated with the soldier vote behind me than to be elected without it." Wing is reported to have said, "You will have it, Mr. Lincoln. You will have it. They'll vote as they shoot." And have it he did. Men in the ranks sensed victory and weren't about to abandon the cause for which they had fought so long and hard. Like Lincoln, they had resolved that "the honored dead shall not have died in vain."[30]

Lincoln was gratified—and humble. At the White House the day after the election, he said, "I shall be the veriest shallow and self-conceited blockhead upon the footstool if, in the discharge of the duties which are put upon me in this place, I should hope to get along without the wisdom which comes from God and not from men."[31]

Henry Raymond, who had been elected to Congress from New York, acted as though Lincoln's election had never been in doubt. "We accepted it without surprise," he wrote in the *New York Times*. Others, however, *were* surprised, not only by the support given Lincoln, but also by the strength of that support. Horace Greeley had been right when much earlier he exhorted Lincoln to "lean upon the mighty heart of the people.[32]

Democratic reaction to the election was predictably negative. The *Springfield State Register* in Illinois, anti-Lincoln despite being a hometown paper, called the election outcome "the heaviest calamity that ever befell this nation . . . the farewell to civil liberty, to a republican form of government, and to the unity of these states." Similarly, Manton Marble wrote in the *New York World*: "We will not attempt to conceal the profound chagrin and sorrow with which we contemplate the result." But as a good citizen, he said he had to agree with the *Boston Post*, which said, "The ballot box has spoken, and we abide the result."[33]

On the night of November 10, two days after the election, a cheering crowd, complete with lanterns, banners, and a brass band, proceeded to the White House to serenade the president. Responding to the crowd,

Lincoln said the election had been "a necessity. We can not have free government without elections; and if the rebellion could force us to forego, or postpone a national election, it might fairly claim to have already conquered or ruined us. It has been demonstrated that a people's government can sustain a national election, in the midst of a great civil war. Until now it has not been known to the world that this was a possibility. It shows also how *sound* and how *strong* we still are."

He then used words that he knew would appear in the press, words that reached out to his erstwhile opponents with a plea for reconciliation. "But the rebellion continues; and now that the election is over, may not all, having a common interest, re-unite in a common effort, to save our common country? For my own part I have striven, and shall strive to avoid placing any obstacle in the way. So long as I have been here I have not willingly planted a thorn in any man's bosom. . . . May I ask those who have not differed with me, to join with me, in this same spirit towards those who have?"[34]

--=◦◉◦=--

On November 21 Lincoln took time to write a moving letter to a Massachusetts widow. A few weeks earlier, Massachusetts Governor John Andrew had written the president, saying a Mrs. Bixby had lost five sons in the war and suggested that Lincoln write her a letter "such as a noble mother of five dead sons so nobly deserves." In his own hand, Lincoln wrote:

Executive Mansion
Washington, D. C.

Mrs. Bixby, Boston, Massachusetts

Dear Madam:
   I have been shown in the files of the War Department a statement of the Adjutant-General of Massachusetts that you are the mother of five sons who have died gloriously on the field of battle. I feel how weak and fruitless must be any words of mine which should attempt to beguile you from the grief of a loss so overwhelming. But I cannot refrain from tendering to you the consolation that may be

found in the thanks of the Republic that they have died to save. I pray that our heavenly Father may assuage the anguish of your bereavement, and leave you only the cherished memory of the loved and lost, and the solemn pride that must be yours to have laid so costly a sacrifice upon the altar of freedom.

Yours very sincerely and respectfully,

Abraham Lincoln

The letter was hand carried to Mrs. Bixby, but before it was delivered, a copy was made by the Massachusetts adjutant general, who gave it to the Boston newspapers. On the day after Thanksgiving, the *Boston Transcript* and the *Boston Advertiser* printed it, and eventually it would appear in hundreds of papers nationwide. That was as it should be, for Lincoln intended it not only for one grieving mother, but also rather for the nation as a whole, and for every family with cause to mourn. Some who saw the war as a useless human slaughter said the Bixby letter was merely "cheap sympathy." More thoughtful souls saw it, however, as a sincere expression of true, deep emotion, written from the heart of a compassionate man.[35]

⊷⇒◉⇐⊷

December 1864 brought heartening news of Union victories in Tennessee, first at Franklin, then Nashville. Reporters did their best to render accounts of the battles, often under difficult conditions. A *New York Times* correspondent, reporting Thomas's victory over Hood at Nashville, revealed some of his frustration as he wrote: "The readers of newspapers do not know what correspondents suffer sometimes in mind. For instance, imagine a poor fellow taking the chances of a battle all day, then riding several miles in the dark, with mud up to his horse's belly, to find 'the wires down east of Louisville.' . . . The fighting yesterday and to-day, as I have stated in a telegram which, may be, you have never received, has been grander and more magnificent in detail than anything I have ever witnessed upon a field of battle."[36]

The greatest frustration, however, was probably felt by editors trying to keep track of William Tecumseh Sherman. Although they knew he was "marching through Georgia," his exact whereabouts were a mystery. From his headquarters at City Point in Virginia, Grant was saying, "Sherman's army is now somewhat in the condition of a ground-mole when he disappears under a lawn. You can here and there trace his track, but you are not quite certain where he will come out till you see his head." The situation was the same at the White House. Lincoln's longtime supporter, the Pennsylvania politician-editor Alexander McClure, was winding up a visit and had just reached the door of the president's office, when Lincoln asked, "McClure, wouldn't you like to hear something from Sherman?" McClure turned eagerly and said he certainly would. Lincoln laughed. "Well, I'll be hanged if I wouldn't myself."[37]

Then came the long-awaited news from Sherman. In Savannah, the gruff general had growled at an agent of the U.S. Treasury Department who was tallying newly captured supplies. The agent turned aside the general's wrath by suggesting he send a wire to Washington announcing the fall of Savannah as a present for Lincoln. "The President particularly enjoys such pleasantry," he said. He was right. Lincoln took great delight in the jaunty wire Sherman composed:

To his Excellency President Lincoln,
Washington, D.C.

I beg to present you, as a Christmas gift, the city of Savannah, with 150 heavy guns and plenty of ammunition; also about 25,000 bales of cotton.

W. T. Sherman
Major General[38]

On December 26 Lincoln responded: "Many, many thanks for your Christmas gift, the capture of Savannah."[39] The year of 1864 was ending on a positive note.

CHAPTER 17

◦→═◎═→◦

"WITH MALICE TOWARD NONE"

The final weeks of 1864 saw not only a series of Union victories, but also a newspaper article personally written by Abraham Lincoln. On December 7, at the bottom of its editorial page, Forney's *Washington Chronicle* ran "The President's Last, Shortest, and Best Speech." After composing the article, including the headline, Lincoln asked reporter Noah Brooks to see it was printed "right away" in the *Chronicle*. At Brooks's suggestion, he signed his name, "A. Lincoln," on the copy, which Brooks retained as a souvenir. The text read:

> On Thursday of last week two ladies from Tennessee came before the President, asking the release of their husbands, held as prisoners of war. . . . One of the ladies urged that her husband was a religious man, and on Saturday, when the President ordered the release of the two prisoners, he said to this lady: 'You say your husband is a very religious man; tell him when you meet him that I say I am not much of a judge of religion, but that, in my opinion, the religion that sets men to rebel and fight against their Government because, as they think, that Government does not sufficiently help some men to earn their bread in

the sweat of other men's faces, is not the sort of religion upon which people can get to heaven.' We have given as a caption for this para- graph the President's own opinion of his little speech, which he con- sidered his shortest and best, as well as his latest.

Oddly enough, the *Chronicle* did not tell its readers the story came directly from the president's pen, leaving the impression it was written by one of the *Chronicle*'s staff. In any case, the anecdote was widely reprinted in both the Democratic and Republican press, as Lincoln probably hoped it would be.[1]

--→=◦⊂=→--

As 1865 began, the *New York Tribune* described the South's devastation and sensed that the conflict might be entering its final phase. Half of Vir- ginia was a desert; Tennessee was a barren waste; the young men of the South were in their graves; the old men were reduced to poverty; the indus- trial system of all the slave states was destroyed; from Mason and Dixon's line to the Rio Grande, desolation covered the land. The Confederacy had nothing left but a sorely beleaguered army that could not fight much longer. In short, said the *Tribune*, the rebels were near the end of their resources.[2]

Nevertheless, much of the Confederacy still believed, almost as an article of faith, that the South would prevail. Jefferson Davis told the Con- federate Congress that, regardless of setbacks, the South would remain "as erect and defiant as ever." And as for Lincoln's reelection, a Richmond paper said, "But, perhaps, this is all for good. It deepens and widens the gulf between us, and renders our success more certain by rendering failure more dreadful and intolerable."[3]

The Southern press, however, while calling Lincoln a "blackguard and buffoon," was forced to acknowledge his adroit management of the Union cause. Four years earlier, the *Charleston Mercury* had scoffed at him. Now, in January of 1865, an editorial that began by condemning the weakness of Jefferson Davis continued by heaping praise on Lincoln, albeit begrudgingly:

When ABRAHAM LINCOLN took the chair of the Presidency of the United States, he promised in his flat-boat lingo to 'run the machine as he found it.' . . . whether 'running his machine' in the pathway of his predecessors or not, he has run it with a stern, inflexible purpose, a bold, steady hand, a vigilant, active eye, a sleepless energy, a fanatic spirit, and an eye single to his end—conquest—emancipation. He has called around him, in counsel, the ablest and most earnest men of his country. Where he has lacked in individual ability, experience, or statesmanship, he has sought it, and has found it in the able men around him, whose assistance he unhesitatingly accepted, whose powers he applies to the advancement of the cause he has undertaken.[4]

Horace Greeley to his credit was still hoping to be a catalyst for peace. Never mind that his earlier effort at Niagara Falls had turned into a fiasco; he would keep on trying. This time he sought out Francis P. Blair, whom people called "Old Man" Blair to distinguish him from his sons Montgomery P., Lincoln's former postmaster general, and Francis Jr., the Union general. The Blair family was a longtime power in both politics and journalism, dating back to the senior Blair's days as editor of the *Washington Globe* and adviser to Andrew Jackson. Greeley wrote Blair, saying it was time to hold open negotiations with the Confederates, if only to put the South in the position of refusing peace. Who better than Blair, a skilled journalist, "the counselor and trusted adviser of men high in authority," to take on the job?

Blair rose to the challenge, telling Greeley that madmen had made the war, and wise men would end it. Moreover, he had a scheme "benevolent as well as radical," and said, "I think I will hint it to Mr. Lincoln." Blair easily obtained an audience with Lincoln—the president wasn't about to offend a journalistic legend. Lincoln listened, then said, "Come to me after Savannah falls." As soon as that happened, Blair was back. Lincoln wrote out one sentence on a card: "Allow the bearer, F. P. Blair, Sr., to pass our lines, go South, and return."[5]

At the *Herald*, Bennett learned that Blair was up to something. Right away he suspected Greeley was involved. "The fact that F. P. Blair, Sr., and

Montgomery Blair have gone to City Point is making quite a stir," said the *Herald*. "Various rumors are in circulation in regard to the object of their mission, that which gained most attention that they have gone for the purpose of meeting representatives of the rebel government. Some parties argue that this is the inauguration of peace negotiations; but nothing reliable can be ascertained in regard to the matter tonight."[6]

For the first two weeks in January, papers were full of the Blair mission. Bennett noted Greeley's jubilation about the undertaking and jibed that President Lincoln had probably given Blair an official sanction and then dictated a telegram to Grant that "Blair had better be stopped." That would be just like the sly Lincoln, the *Herald* suggested. "The President realizes the absurdity of these amateur attempts. . . . Our benevolent friend Greeley seems to be affected with a monomania for peace missions. . . . The President has learned to regard them with suspicion . . . has learned that we can only gain peace by whipping the Rebels, and that our only terms are unconditional surrender, and our best missionaries are Grant, Sherman, Thomas, Sheridan, Farragut, and Porter."[7]

Arriving in Richmond, "Old Man" Blair met with Jefferson Davis at the Confederate White House. The meeting was cordial, and Davis made it clear that he wanted desperately to end the fighting. But with a catch. On January 12 Davis gave Blair a letter to be handed to Lincoln, one that suggested they "enter into negotiations for the restoration of peace." Davis ended by proposing he and Lincoln "renew the effort to enter into conference, with a view to secure peace to the two countries."

The phrase "two countries" did not escape Lincoln's attention. Lincoln asked Blair to tell Davis that "I have constantly been, am now, and shall continue ready to receive any agent whom he or any other influential person now resisting the National authority may informally send to me with the view of securing peace to the people of our one common country." Lincoln's concluding phrase, "one common country," reiterated the only basis on which he would negotiate. Jefferson Davis almost surely knew in advance what Lincoln's response would be. But it had been worth a try.[8]

All through January, Greeley had something positive to say about Blair's mission in his editorial columns, writing for example: "We did and *do* expect much from Mr. Blair's efforts, though we never supposed that our country would be pacified quite so easily or so promptly as two boys might swap jack-knives." Nevertheless he insisted that the Blair mission had "profound significance."[9]

When Blair's mission came to naught, all the New York papers (with the exception of the *Tribune*) were critical. Even the *New York Times* "saw nothing to approve in the volunteer mission of Mr. Blair." Taking a pot-shot at Greeley, Raymond wrote: "We objected to that on precisely the grounds which have led us to object to all the volunteer diplomacy which meddlesome busybodies have, from time to time, set on foot."[10]

◦◦═◦═◦◦

In early January, Grant recommended that Lincoln relieve from command the political general, Ben Butler. Butler had led the joint Army-Navy attack on Fort Fisher, which Grant called a "gross and culpable failure." It was also noted that, if anything happened to Grant, Butler, as the next senior officer, would become the overall Union commander. Before the election, removing the politically powerful Butler would have been almost unthinkable. Now that the time was right, Lincoln ended the inept Butler's military career. If that caused a problem with the press or the Radicals in Congress, so be it.

The previous year things had been different, as when Grant wanted to fire another political general, Nathaniel Banks. Then General Halleck had explained "the facts of life," telling Grant: "General Banks is a personal friend of the President, and has strong political supporters in and out of Congress. . . . You will perceive that the press in New Orleans and in the Eastern States are already beginning to open in General Banks' favor. The administration would be immediately attacked for his removal." That was putting it on the line. If Grant wanted Banks relieved, he had to do it himself, knowing it might hurt Lincoln's chances in an election year. Grant understood, and Banks remained on duty; but now that the election was over, there was a new game in town. Butler was peremptorily dismissed, ordered to his home in Lowell, Massachusetts, "to await further orders," orders that would never come.[11]

A *Herald* reporter at City Point implied that no one would miss him, saying Butler's dismissal "is causing much comment here, but so far as I can learn, no animadversion. Whether rightly or no, General Butler for several months past has lacked the confidence of officers of the army . . . very few will regret his departure."[12]

⊷═◉═◉═⊷

Peace was still hiding somewhere in the murky future, but Lincoln's re-election made ultimate victory all but certain. Now, with the people having voted for a party whose platform supported the abolition of slavery, Lincoln's next priority was clear. People called him Emancipator and Liberator, but so far that was a misnomer. While over a million slaves, possibly a third of the total, were now free as a result of his Emancipation Proclamation, theirs was a freedom not clear in the law. He needed to close the deal. And it wouldn't be closed until all African-Americans were permanently free under the law and the Constitution.

In his message to Congress, Lincoln mentioned their last session, in which "a proposed amendment to the Constitution, abolishing slavery throughout the United States, passed the Senate, but failed for lack of the requisite two-thirds vote in the House of Representatives." Now, he said, "an intervening election shows, almost certainly, that the next Congress will pass the measure if this does not. Hence there is only a question of time as to when the proposed amendment will go to the States for their action. And as it is to so go, at all events, may we not agree that the sooner the better?"[13]

To get the needed votes, Lincoln twisted arms and made promises. On January 31 the issue was in doubt until the last vote was cast. The final count showed Yeas 119, Nays 56, Not Voting 8. As the *New York Tribune* reported the event: "The Speaker announces to the House what the audience quickly interpreted to be *the mighty fact that the XXXVIIth American Congress has abolished American slavery*," wherefore "the tumult of joy that broke out was vast, thundering, and uncontrollable." Wherefore "God Bless the XXXVIIth Congress!"

A shift of only three votes would have defeated the measure. But the deed was done, and next day Illinois started the ball rolling by being the first state to ratify the amendment. "I feel proud that Illinois is a little ahead," Lincoln said. He added, however, "But there is a task yet before us—to go forward and have consummated by the votes of the States that which Congress has so nobly begun."[14]

⋯═◯═⋯

Jefferson Davis kept trying to arrange a conference based on the premise of Southern independence. Ignoring the "one common country" phrase in Lincoln's note, he asked three commissioners, including Confederate vice president Stephens, to go to Washington "in conformity with the letter of Mr. Lincoln." Once again Lincoln avoided the trap. When the commissioners arrived at Grant's headquarters at City Point, Lincoln sent Major Eckert with a letter saying he would meet with the commissioners only if they agreed in writing to his long-standing terms: reuniting the country and abolishing slavery. "For my own part," Grant later wrote, "I never had admitted, and never was ready to admit, that they were the representatives of a *government*. There had been too great a waste of blood and treasure to concede anything of the kind."[15]

That might have ended the matter. However, Grant was in an awkward position, feeling it would be harmful to send the commissioners away without seeing the president. He said as much in a long telegram to Lincoln, causing the president to reconsider. He respected Grant's judgment and he also knew how much of the Northern press (and *all* the Southern press) would condemn him if he refused even to *talk* to Davis's people. The following morning Lincoln wired Grant: "Say to the gentlemen I will meet them personally at Fortress Monroe as soon as I can get there."[16]

On February 3 at Hampton Roads, Lincoln and Seward met with the commissioners aboard the steamer *River Queen*. These were men, especially Stephens, whom Lincoln knew and respected from the past. They talked informally in a cordial, calm, friendly manner, and the commissioners offered various devices to crack open the door to Southern independence. Commissioner R. M. T. Hunter, for example, suggested an armistice followed by a convention of the states. No armistice, said Lincoln; surrender was the only means of stopping the war. But even Charles I, said Hunter, had entered into agreements with rebels in arms during the English Civil War. "I do not profess to be posted in history," Lincoln replied. "All I seem to recall about the case of Charles I, is, that he lost

his head." After four hours, all recognized that it was hopeless. The meeting ended, with peace no closer.[17]

Horace Greeley had never treated Lincoln more kindly than he did
while the negotiations were in progress. There may have been a bit of self-
serving in this; at least many of Greeley's friends thought he'd been promised an appointment as the country's next postmaster general. For "Uncle
Horace" there was great appeal in holding the post once held by Benjamin
Franklin, the man to whom he'd sometimes been compared. In any event,
Greeley wrote of "the confident trust that the Executive is equal to the
high trust reposed in him by the People" and asked that Lincoln be left
"wholly unembarrassed" as the negotiations proceeded. "Let us for the
present," he wrote, "fully trust our Government, prepared to aid it with our
best efforts should a recurrence to arms become necessary."[18]

He had hoped that the Hampton Roads conference would have "ultimate fruits," he wrote, and he praised the president for "eagerly" seeking
peace. After the conference failed to produce any results, however, in an
editorial headed "Peace through War," Greeley reluctantly concluded that
there must be more fighting, "not to subjugate but to liberate the Southern people."[19]

Shortly after he returned to Washington from Hampton Roads, Lincoln again turned his attention to James Gordon Bennett, the unpredictable editor of the New York Herald. During the past election campaign,
Lincoln, through an intermediary, had dangled before Bennett the promise
of an ambassadorial post. As Bennett's fellow editor Joseph Medill once said,
social position was the only thing Bennett wanted that money couldn't
buy. On February 20 Lincoln wrote Bennett: "Dear Sir: I propose, at some
convenient and not distant day, to nominate you to the United States
Senate as Minister to France." Making that offer was but the latest step
in Lincoln's effort to win a favorable press from the Herald editor.

That effort dated back to early 1861, when the Herald had not only
opposed the war, but often sounded pro-Southern. Particularly troubling
was the fact that the Herald was probably the most influential American
paper in Europe. Lincoln of course wanted foreign chancelleries to have a
proper understanding of the Northern cause. Consequently, he asked the
crafty politician, Thurlow Weed, editor of the Albany Evening Journal, to

act as his emissary to Bennett and seek his support of the war effort. He chose him for the delicate job, Lincoln told Weed, because he had had experience in "belling cats." Weed accepted the assignment, considering a presidential "request" to have the effect of an order. Over dinner, Bennett subjected Weed to a harangue against Seward, Greeley, and others, including himself, as having been instrumental in bringing on the war. However, he finally conceded that he would probably support the Union war effort. Moreover, he would donate the Bennetts' fine yacht to the Treasury Department for use in the revenue service.[20]

Although Bennett kept his word and supported the war, that didn't mean he went easy on Lincoln, whom he criticized early and often. Sometimes the criticisms were personal and cruel, as when he called Lincoln "a joke incarnate. . . . The idea that such a man as he should be the President of such a country as this is a very ridiculous joke." His most emotional attacks on Lincoln and his administration, however, came as a result of the suspension of the Habeas Corpus Act, which Bennett said resulted in "summary arrests and arbitrary imprisonments without trial."[21]

In this Bennett had a valid point, for in waging war against the South, it must be admitted that Lincoln was willing to trample on civil liberties. Suspending the right of habeas corpus in September of 1863, and leaving it that way throughout the war, may have been his worst mistake. But if people condemned him for that mistake, he was willing to suffer the consequences. That same month of September 1863, when a group of Radical Union men of Missouri called on him, Lincoln said, "It is my ambition and desire to so administer the affairs of the government while I remain president that if at the end I shall have lost every other friend on earth I shall at least have one friend remaining; and that one shall be down inside of me."[22]

Unfortunately, Union officers frequently abused the authority given them, often by seizing offending newspapers. The editor of the *Newark Evening Journal* was prosecuted before a military commission for an article on the draft; the editor of the *Bangor Republican Journal* for a similar offense; the editor of the *New York Metropolitan Record* for advertising resistance to conscription; and the editor of the *Indianapolis Daily Sentinel* for criticizing a military commission. Individual arrests numbered in the thousands. The number of papers suppressed for any period is probably around three hundred. Although his secretaries later defended Lincoln vigorously, saying he took the greatest care to restrain officers from abusive acts, such abuses *did* take place. Even his attorney general, Edward Bates, while claiming Lincoln's intentions were good, said the president "lacked the faculty to control—the will to punish the abuses of his power, which rampant and unrebuked, are rapidly bringing him and this good cause to sorrow and shame." Lincoln realized the risks involved, but he considered sacrifices were called for. The temporary humiliation and hardship of a few men suspected of sedition and disloyalty was a small price to pay for saving the Union. Luckily most patriotic Northerners agreed.[23]

The day before Lincoln's inauguration, the Confederates again tried to secure a meeting. If Davis couldn't get anything out of Lincoln, perhaps Robert E. Lee would have better luck with Grant. On March 3 Grant received a letter from Lee under a flag of truce. It suggested "the possibility of arriving at a satisfactory adjustment of the present unhappy difficulties by means of a military convention." Grant's political instincts did not fail him; he wired Lincoln, asking for instructions. The reply, signed by Secretary Stanton, read: "The President directs me to say to you that he wishes you to have no conference with General Lee unless it be for the capitulation of Gen. Lee's army, or on some minor, and purely military matter. . . . Meanwhile you are to press to the utmost your military advantages." Grant so informed Lee; the war would go on to a finish.[24]

Inauguration Day, March 4, began under dark, sullen clouds, bringing light showers which deepened the mud on Washington streets. Nevertheless an air of optimism prevailed as the inaugural procession made its way to the Capitol. The parade included bands, an assortment of military units, firemen of Washington and Philadelphia, groups of Odd Fellows and Masons (including members of a black Masonic Lodge), plus various visiting dignitaries. Perhaps influenced by Lincoln's offer of a diplomatic post, James Gordon Bennett was complimentary in that morning's *New York Herald*. "The second term of Abraham Lincoln as President of the United States, commences today," Bennett wrote. "He is a most remarkable man. He may seem to be the most credulous, docile and pliable of backwoodsmen, and yet when he 'puts his foot down he puts it down firmly,' and cannot be budged. . . . Plain common sense, a kindly disposition, a straightforward purpose, and a shrewd perception of the ins and outs of poor human nature, have enabled him to master difficulties which would have swamped almost any other man. Thus to-day, with the most cheering prospects before him, this extraordinary railsplitter enters upon his second term the unquestioned master of the situation in reference to American affairs, at home and abroad."[25]

The procession reached the Capitol, and officials gathered in the Senate chamber for the first order of business: swearing in of the newly elected vice president, Andrew Johnson. It did not go well. After taking the oath, Johnson seemed to sway as he slurred his words and offered maudlin, inappropriate remarks. His listeners were shocked; most believed he was drunk. Johnson's supporters, however, later said he had been ill and that his condition resulted from medicine he'd taken that morning.

Through all this, Lincoln listened patiently, waiting for his own turn to speak. It was an important opportunity, a chance to address the entire country, both North and South. There had been other speeches and other opportunities, of course, as in June of 1858, when he told the Illinois Republican convention, "a house divided against itself cannot stand," and that the government couldn't endure, permanently half-slave and half-free. That was the time his law partner, Billy Herndon, told him, "that speech will make you president." Then there was the Cooper Union speech in February of 1860, the one that exposed him to the New York press for the first time. He'd questioned the morality of slavery, argued that the Founding Fathers sensed its ultimate abolition, and urged the people to have faith, "and in that faith, let us, to the end, dare to do our duty as we understand it." That too had been important. Naturally, there were other speeches, plenty of them, and maybe the one at Gettysburg sixteen months ago was the best of the lot. He had implied that the Founding Fathers, by saying, "all men are created equal," provided a legal basis for emancipation. When Lincoln made the connection he was in effect reframing the American Constitution. It had been a daring leap, but it seemed to have worked. Whether or not Lincoln thought back on these things, he knew the media was once again waiting to hear his words and report them. And through the media, he could reach out to the people.

Johnson finished his disjointed, rambling talk. Now it was Lincoln's turn to speak. Senator Herndon offered his arm to Lincoln for taking their place in the march to the outdoor inaugural platform. Quietly, Lincoln told a marshal, "Do not let Johnson speak outside." When they reached the Capitol portico, the sun had come out; it was a good omen. People could not help remembering how it had been four years earlier, when the air was full of gloom and anxiety; sharpshooters with rifles stood on watch at each of the Capitol windows; and Winfield Scott stood ready nearby with troops and cannon.[26]

When Lincoln appeared on the platform, the crowd burst into applause. Then they grew hushed as Lincoln stepped forward, a single sheet of paper in his hand. He began "Fellow countrymen," and said at the start that a long speech was neither necessary nor appropriate. The progress of arms was well known, he said, and,

> I trust, reasonably satisfactory and encouraging to all. . . . Both parties deprecated war; but one of then would *make* war rather than let the nation survive; and the other would *accept* war rather than let it perish. And the war came. . . . Neither party expected for the war, the magnitude, or the duration, which it has already attained. Neither anticipated that the *cause* of the conflict might cease with, or even before, the conflict itself should cease. Each looked for an easier triumph, and a result less fundamental and astounding. Both read the same Bible, and pray to the same God; and each invokes His aid against the other . . . but let us judge not that we be not judged. The prayers of both could not be answered; that of neither has been answered fully. The Almighty has His own purposes. . . . If we shall suppose that American Slavery is one of those offenses which, in the providence of God, must needs come, but which having continued through His appointed time, He now wills to remove, and that he gives to both North and South, this terrible war, as the woe due to those by whom the offense came, shall we discern therein any departure from those divine attributes which the believers in a Living God always ascribe to Him? Fondly do we hope—fervently do we pray—that this mighty scourge of war may speedily pass away. Yet, if God wills that it continue . . . so still it must be said "the judgments of the Lord, are true and righteous altogether." With malice toward none; with charity for all; with firmness in the right, as God gives us to see

the right, let us strive on to finish the work we are in; to bind up the nation's wounds; to care for him who shall have borne the battle, and for his widow, and his orphan—to do all which may achieve and cherish a just, and a lasting peace, among ourselves, and with all nations.[27]

Salmon P. Chase, the recently appointed chief justice, then administered the oath of office. This was followed by applause, cheers, even a few tears. The tears, said Noah Brooks, came "from those who had grasped the solemn impact of the most religious of American state papers." Much of the press voiced their appreciation. The *Boston Evening Transcript* said, "The President's Inaugural is a singular state paper—made so by the times. No similar document has ever been published to the world. . . . The President was lifted above the level upon which political rulers usually stand, and felt himself 'in the very presence of the very mystery of Providence.'"[28]

Horace Greeley printed both the first and second inaugural speeches in the *Tribune*, adding, "Now is the fittest time for putting forth manifestations of generosity, magnanimity, clemency, which, however, they may be spurned by the Rebel chiefs, are certain to exert a great and salutary influence among their duped, disgusted, despairing followers." It was as though Greeley had failed to read Lincoln's talk. Did he not see that Lincoln's ringing phrases had indeed been *full* of generosity, magnanimity, and clemency? Perhaps Greeley needed to put his own stamp of approval on those sentiments, thinking otherwise they might not be considered "official."

The *New York Evening Post*, as expected, was duly critical, sarcastically saying the inaugural address at least had "the merit of brevity." *Harper's Weekly*, however, termed it "characteristically simple and solemn," while others called it "noble." In England, Prime Minister Gladstone said, "The address gives evidence of a moral elevation most rare in a statesman, or indeed in any man."[29]

❖

Surprisingly, two days after the inauguration, Lincoln received a letter from James Gordon Bennett saying he didn't want the ambassador job after all!

To his Excelency [sic]

The President of the United States

Dear Sir

I have received your kind note in which you propose to appoint me Minister Plenipotentiary to full [sic] up the present vacancy in the important Mission to France. I trust that I estimate at its full value, the high consideration which the President of the United States entertains and expresses for me by proposing so distinguished an honor. Accept my sincere thanks for that honor. I am sorry however to say that at my age I am afraid of assuming the labors and responsibilities of such an important position. Besides, in the present relations of France and the United States, I am of the decided opinion that I can be of more service to the country in the present position I occupy.

While, therefore, entertaining the highest consideration for the offer you have made, permit me most respectfully to decline the same for the reasons assigned.

I am, My Dear Sir

With sentiments of the highest respect, your most Obt. Sert.

James G. Bennett

Bennett, with uncharacteristic modesty, published nothing in the *Herald* about the president's offer or his own refusal. Lincoln placed the letter in his files, where it remained a well-guarded secret for more than eighty years.[30]

CHAPTER 18

"A RIGHTEOUS AND SPEEDY PEACE"

D uring the Hampton Roads negotiations, Horace Greeley urged his readers to leave Lincoln alone, trusting him to do what he thought best. Greeley even followed his own advice—for a time. Soon after the inauguration, however, he resumed his old habit of telling the president what he had to do. Lincoln, he said, should "lucidly" and "briefly" announce terms of peace to the rebels through a "specific, circumstantial, magnanimous public overture." Thereby, he said, "the great body of Southern whites, independent of their leaders, would insist on its acceptance. He conceded that the terms should be the president's alone, for "we know that his heart is right, and we are confident that the terms it will prompt him to offer are such as the insurgents ought to accept—such as a large majority of them will choose to accept." It wasn't clear how "Uncle Horace" thought this acceptance would come about, and in any case, Lincoln chose to ignore his latest exhortation.[1]

Meanwhile, Grant was holding Lee in place near Petersburg, and Sherman was continuing his march through the South, storming through the Carolinas and leaving devastation in his wake. By now Sherman, with an army of 80,000 men, was within striking distance of the Virginia border. Lincoln explained the situation to a White House visitor: "Grant has the bear by the hind leg while Sherman takes off the hide." It was an apt metaphor; the Southern armies were coming apart. In March some 3,000 Confederate deserters were received in Washington, thousands more at Fort Monroe, Annapolis, and other points. Of 600,000 Confederate soldiers in the field two years earlier, it was believed that half of those still alive had left for home, and with no intention of coming back. They had seen enough.[2]

The third week in March, one of Grant's officers suggested he invite Lincoln to visit their City Point headquarters. Grant said Lincoln commanded the Army; he could come any time he wanted. Yes, said the officer, but maybe he was hesitant, having been criticized in the past for interfering with his generals. Grant saw that might be true, and on March 20 he sent Lincoln a cordial invitation: "Can you not visit City Point for a day or two? I would like very much to see you, and I think the rest would do you good."

Lincoln was delighted to accept. He wired Grant: "Your kind invitation received. Had already thought of going immediately after the next rain. Will go sooner if any reason for it. Mrs. L. and a few others will probably accompany me. Will notify you of exact time, once it shall be fixed upon."[3]

Lincoln and his party boarded the steamer *River Queen* at 1 P.M. on March 23 and arrived at the City Point dock the next evening. Grant was there to greet them. With the curtain about to rise on the war's decisive campaign, Lincoln and Grant both knew City Point was no place for visitors. However, they needed to touch base before the final battle, if only to reach an agreement on possible terms of surrender. Moreover, the two had formed a bond of friendship and mutual understanding. Not only did they enjoy each other's company, one might even say they needed each other."[4]

When Lincoln arrived at City Point, Greeley surmised that Lincoln had taken his advice and that another peace overture was under way. "If the result should be the shortening of the War by but a week and the saving of a bare thousand of human lives," Greeley wrote, "who would say that it had been issued in vain?" Lincoln by this time, however, had abundant evidence that such an effort would be fruitless.[5]

In the early dawn hours, shortly after Lincoln's arrival at Grant's headquarters, the Confederates attacked Fort Stedman, a Union strongpoint. After some hours of fighting, the line was restored. It would be Robert E. Lee's last offensive effort of the war. Lincoln was at breakfast when his son Robert gave him the news. He wired Stanton, telling of his party's safe arrival at Grant's headquarters and adding, "Robert just now tells me there was a little rumpus up the line this morning, ending where it began."[6]

⋆⇥═◉═⇤⋆

Back in New York, James Gordon Bennett realized it was not too early to think about the postwar period. It had been a long time coming, but Bennett's ideas finally paralleled those of Lincoln. "This war will abolish all sectional ideas," Bennett wrote. "Hereafter we shall be but one people, instead of two different peoples under one government. When the war is over we shall be all Americans, instead of being divided into Northerners and Southerners. Hard fighting has made us much better acquainted with each other than we ever were before. The mistakes and misrepresentations which have prevailed in the two sections have been washed away in blood and burned out in the camp fires. There can be no misappreciation of each other's character in future."[7]

And with the nation reunited, Bennett said it was also time to realign New York City with the rest of the country. Much of the problem, he said, was caused by what he called the "rebel press":

> We have observed with regret the existence and the steady increase of a bitter animosity towards New York city among prominent supporters of the present administration. . . . The only possible reasons which can be adduced to justify the animosity to which we refer, are the utterances of the New York rebel press and the large Democratic majorities which this city always gives. It is true that we have a rebel press in this city; true that the utterances of these secession papers are treasonable; true that they could scarcely be more treasonable if the papers were printed in Richmond. But, on the other hand, there are rebel papers at Washington, at Boston, at Philadelphia, at Chicago, and elsewhere throughout the North, and why should New York alone be blamed? . . . Here the rebel papers have not the slightest influence. They cannot hinder recruiting; they cannot

prevent us from supplying the government with the sinews of war; they are read by comparatively few of our people. . . . Besides, the loyal press of this city more than neutralizes the poison of the secessionist sympathizers, and leaves us with a large balance of loyalty in our favor.[8]

With the war winding down, and with the benefit of hindsight, it was easy for Bennett to say the opposition press had always been ineffective. But for most of the war, that simply wasn't true. Lincoln had campaigned long and hard to win media support, often swimming against the tide. Although that tide had now turned in his favor, the end result was never a foregone conclusion.

✦═◉═✦

Lincoln left the City Point headquarters and went forward to review one of Meade's divisions. En route he passed the scene of the recent action; saw dead and wounded lying in the fields, with intermingled uniforms of blue, gray, and butternut; saw burial parties at work; saw Sanitary Commission workers giving out water and food. An observer, noting that Lincoln looked "worn and haggard," heard him say he had seen enough of the horrors of war, that he hoped this was the beginning of the end, and that there would be no more bloodshed.[9]

On March 27 William Tecumseh Sherman arrived at City Point to confer with Lincoln and Grant. Earlier that week, down in North Carolina, a *New York Herald* reporter had heard him say, "I am going up to see Grant for five minutes and have it all chalked out for me and then come back and pitch in." Grant and Sherman greeted each other with smiles and hearty handshakes. They had last seen each other a year ago, in Cincinnati, and the strategy they discussed had worked. Along with Admiral Porter, the pair proceeded to the *River Queen* to meet with Lincoln. Next day they returned, and for four hours they discussed end-game strategy. More than once, Lincoln expressed a hope that the war could be ended without another major battle and the attendant loss of life. The officers agreed, but said they could not control that event.[10]

Sherman headed back to his army as Grant prepared to launch what he hoped would be the final offensive. On the day Sherman left, Lincoln saw Charles Coffin of the *Boston Journal* at Grant's headquarters. Lincoln, eager as always to chat with the press, greeted him: "What news have you?"

"I have just arrived from Charleston and Savannah," Coffin said.

"Indeed! Well, I'm right glad to see you. How do people like being back in the Union again?"

Coffin said some of them were getting reconciled to it, and told of one planter he'd seen who had come to Savannah with his crop of cotton, anxious to sell at the highest price. With a chuckle, Lincoln said, "I reckon they'll accept the situation now that they can sell their cotton."[11]

With the Union offensive under way, Lincoln wired Stanton that he knew he should get back to Washington, but he disliked leaving without seeing the end of Grant's movement. On the night of April 2, his lines having been penetrated, Lee gave the order to evacuate Petersburg. This in turn meant the door to Richmond was open.

As Grant sent progress reports, Lincoln relayed them to Stanton at the War Department. On April 3, serving as an enthusiastic war correspondent, he wired: "This morning Gen. Grant reports Petersburg evacuated; and he is confident Richmond also is. He is pushing forward to cut off, if possible, the retreating army. I start to him in a few minutes. A. Lincoln."

Stanton immediately released the message to the press. News boys ran through the streets, shouting headlines such as those in the *Washington Star*: "GLORY!!! HAIL COLUMBIA!!! HALLELUJAH!!! RICHMOND OURS!!!" In New York, the *Times* and *Tribune* ran American eagles on their front pages, spanning four columns above the fold. Church bells tolled, bands played, business ceased, and Broadway became a river of flags.[12]

In the *Times*, Henry Raymond urged Lincoln to be magnanimous: "Words of good will from him, assurances that his policy, so far as the body of the Southern people are concerned, will be to bury the past, to remove sectional distinctions, to secure the universal enjoyment of every national blessing, would challenge confidence at once, and we verily believe, it would be followed by an enthusiastic response."[13]

Horace Greeley, while still cautious, had much the same thought: "We do not ask that the President shall disregard any danger by which the Union is still menaced. . . . But we do ask and trust that, so nearly as may be, every one still clinging to the tattered, trailing flag of Disunion shall be supplied with reasons for quitting that unholy service and casting himself unreservedly on the mercy of his aggrieved and lately imperiled but victorious and placable country."[14]

Back at City Point, Lincoln had a wire from Stanton, who had heard of his plan to visit Petersburg. "Allow me respectfully to ask you to consider whether you ought to expose the nation to the consequences of any disaster to yourself in the pursuit of a treacherous and dangerous enemy like the rebel army. If it was a question concerning yourself only I should not presume to say a word. Commanding Generals are in the line of their duty running such risks. But is the political head of a nation in the same condition?" In his reply, Lincoln sounded like a schoolboy telling his parents not to worry: "Yours received. Thanks for your caution, but I have already been to Petersburg, staid [sic] with Gen. Grant an hour & a half, and returned here. It is certain now that Richmond is in our hands, and I think I will go there tomorrow. I will take care of myself."[15]

Next morning, Tuesday, April 4, Lincoln told Admiral Porter: "Thank God I have lived to see this. It seems to me that I have been dreaming a horrid dream for four years, and now the nightmare is gone. I want to see Richmond." Accompanied by his son Tad, Admiral Porter, a dozen armed sailors, and reporter Charles Coffin, Lincoln stepped ashore from a Navy boat and entered the city of Richmond. A crowd of blacks quickly surrounded him. Coffin wrote: "They pressed around the President, ran ahead, and hovered upon the flanks and rear of the little company. Men, women and children joined the constantly increasing throng. They came from all the streets, running in breathless haste, shouting and hallooing, and dancing with delight. The men threw up their hats, the women waved their bonnets and handkerchiefs, clapped their hands, and shouted, 'Glory to God! glory! glory! glory!'" An old white-haired black man rushed toward him, shouting: "Bless the Lord, the great Messiah! I knowed him as soon as I seed him. He's been in my heart four long years, and he come at last to free his children from their bondage. Glory, hallelujah!" Lincoln continued his walk, past crowds of silent whites who craned their necks to get a look at him. One of the president's guards said, "There was something oppressive in those thousands of watchers, without a sound either of welcome or of hatred. I think we would have welcomed a yell of defiance."

Eventually Lincoln came to the Confederate White House, the home Jefferson Davis had left only two days earlier. He sat in Davis's chair, asked for a drink of water, and seemed to sigh. One observer saw a "serious, dreamy expression" on his face. The realization was sinking in—he was once again president of the whole United States.[16]

Lincoln returned to Washington, and now things were moving quickly. Lee's army was in full retreat, trying to escape its pursuers, perhaps to reach North Carolina and link up with the forces of Joe Johnston. However, the Army of Northern Virginia had run out of time. Meade's Army of the Potomac was on its heels and pressing hard; Sheridan's corps was up ahead, cutting off its supplies and any hope of escape. Both commanders knew the end was near. At 5 P.M. on April 7, Grant penned a note that was delivered through the lines under a flag of truce:

GENERAL R. E. LEE, Commanding, C.S.A.:

The results of the last week must convince you of the hopelessness of further resistance on the part of the Army of Northern Virginia in this struggle. I feel that it is so, and regard it as my duty to shift from myself the responsibility of any further effusion of blood by asking of you the surrender of that portion of the Confederate States army known as the Army of Northern Virginia.

U. S. Grant,
Lieutenant-general[17]

Lee replied: "To be frank, I do not think the emergency has arisen to call for the surrender. But as the restoration of peace should be the sole object of all, I desire to know whether your proposals would lead to that end."

Grant's next note, along lines suggested by Lincoln, limited itself to military matters: "As I have no authority to treat on the subject of peace, the meeting proposed for ten A.M., to-day could lead to no good. I will state, however, General, that I am equally anxious for peace with yourself; and the whole North entertains the same feeling. The terms upon which peace can be had are well understood. By the South laying down their arms they will hasten that most desirable event, save thousands of human lives and hundreds of millions of property not yet destroyed. Sincerely hoping that our difficulties may be settled without the loss of another life."[18]

They met at Appomattox Court House in the home of a Wilbur McLean. It was a remarkable scene: Lee in a splendid new uniform, complete with sash and jeweled sword; Grant in muddy boots, wearing the blouse of a private soldier, with only shoulder straps to give evidence of rank. Grant did what he could to minimize Lee's discomfort, and as Horace Greeley later described it, "The interview was brief; the business at hand frankly discussed, as became soldiers."[19]

The terms of surrender were agreed upon: basically the men would lay down their arms and give their parole not to resume fighting, after which they'd be free to return to their homes unmolested. Lee asked if the surrender terms could be modified to allow private soldiers to retain any mounts they claimed to own. Grant readily agreed, causing Lee to say, "This will have the best possible effect on the men. It will be very gratifying and will do much toward conciliating our people."[20]

Less than an hour later, Grant wired Washington: "General Lee surrendered the Army of Northern Virginia this afternoon on terms proposed by myself."[21] For four long, troubled years, Lincoln had been waiting for just such a message.

In cities and towns throughout the North, people went wild with exultation. At dawn, cannon boomed out over Washington, a salute of five hundred guns ordered by the secretary of war. In New York, Bennett's *Herald* used its largest type to proclaim: "SURRENDER OF LEE AND HIS ENTIRE ARMY TO GRANT." The extra contained all the Grant/Lee messages leading up to Appomattox, plus final terms of the surrender. That same issue also printed a message from Stanton to Grant: "Thanks be to Almighty God for the great victory with which he has this day crowned you and the gallant armies under your command. The thanks of this Department, and of the government, and of the people of the United States, their reverence and honor have been deserved, will be rendered to you and the brave and gallant officers and soldiers of your army for all time."[22]

On Sunday night, a crowd came to the White House, laughing, cheering, and calling for the president to make a speech. Lincoln begged off, saying he wasn't prepared to say something worthy of the occasion. "Everything I say, you know, goes into print. [Laughter] If I make a mistake it doesn't merely affect me, or you, but the country. I, therefore, ought at least try not to make mistakes. [A voice: 'You haven't made any yet.'] If, then, a general demonstration be made tomorrow evening, and it is agreeable, I will endeavor to say something and not make a mistake, without at least trying carefully to avoid it." With that, Lincoln bid the crowd good evening.[23]

The Washington celebration continued into Monday, April 11, and as the *Herald* described the scene, "The Executive Departments, including the President's Mansion, were again illuminated to-night, and adorned with transparencies and national flags, as were many places of business and private dwellings. Bonfires blazed in many parts of the city and rockets were fired. Thousands of persons of both sexes repaired to the Executive Mansion, and after several airs had been played by the band, the President, in response to the unanimous call, appeared at an upper window. The cheering with which he was greeted having ceased, he spoke as follows:

"We meet this evening not in sorrow, but in gladness of heart. The evacuation of Petersburg and Richmond, and the surrender of the principal insurgent army, *gives hope of a righteous and speedy peace*, whose joyous expression cannot be restrained. In the midst of this, however, He from whom all blessing flow, must not be forgotten. A call for a national thanksgiving is being prepared and will be duly promulgated. Nor must those whose harder part gives us the cause of rejoicing be overlooked. Their honors must not be parceled out with others." Then, referring proudly to his work as temporary war correspondent, he said: "I myself was at the front, and had the high pleasure of transmitting much of the good news to you."

As Lincoln continued, he spoke of peace and reconstruction. "There is no authorized organ to treat with," he said, "we must simply begin with, and mould from, disorganized and discordant elements." This he had already done in Louisiana, Arkansas, and Tennessee. He also hoped Louisiana would soon enfranchise literate Negroes and black veterans. As for the unreconstructed states, he promised to announce soon a plan for their restoration to the Union.[24]

The mention of black voting was enough to enrage one man in the crowd, a dark-haired Shakespearean actor named John Wilkes Booth. "That means nigger citizenship," Booth told a companion. "Now, by God, I will put him through. That is the last speech he will ever make."[25]

The hostile *Evening Post* was snide as ever as it commented editorially on Lincoln's far-reaching address: "The President being called upon by a popular assembly last evening, was of course bound to make a speech, which he did, and as he had nothing to say that could be said properly on such occasion, he succeeded in saying it to admiration." The *New York Tribune*, in its report, said the speech "fell dead, wholly without effect on the audience," and furthermore, "it caused a great disappointment and left a painful impression."[26]

That might be true, if one thought only of the carefree crowd gathered that night outside the White House, a crowd that wanted to celebrate, not listen to serious talk. Lincoln, however, when he spoke in public, always did so with a purpose, and as he had told the crowd Sunday night, whatever he said was sure to make its way into print. In other words, his Monday speech was for the nation, not just people in Washington. As his law partner Billy Herndon once said, "Lincoln wasn't a man who gathered his robes about him, waiting for people to call. . . . He was always calculating, and always planning ahead."[27] Earlier, when talking to Godfrey Weitzel, the officer heading the Richmond occupation forces, Lincoln had said, "If I were in your place, I'd let 'em up easy; let 'em up easy."[28] This latest speech carried the same message, and to the nation.

Later that week, Lincoln was with his wife, Ward Lamon, and one or two others when he mentioned a disturbing dream. They urged him to tell about it. At first he hesitated, but finally he said that in the dream he was wandering around the White House when he heard sobbing. Entering the East Room, he saw a catafalque and asked a guard, "Who is dead in the White House?" "The President," was the answer. "He was killed by an assassin."

"That is horrid!" said the first lady. "I wish you had not told it. I am glad I don't believe in dreams or I should be in terror from this day forward."

"It's only a dream, Mary," Lincoln said. "Let us say no more about it, and try to forget it."[29]

⊸⟜⧫⟜⊶

On Friday, April 14, five days after Appomattox, Lincoln decided to attend Ford's theater to see "Our American Cousin," starring the famous Laura Keene. People said there were many good laughs to be had. Lincoln invited General Grant to accompany him and the first lady. Grant declined, however, saying Mrs. Grant had left the capital for their home in Burlington, New Jersey; he himself was starting that afternoon to see his children and have a long-delayed family reunion. Eventually Lincoln invited a young betrothed couple, Major Henry Rathbone and his fiancée, Miss Clara Harris, to accompany them.

Lincoln was relaxing, enjoying the play, when the door to the presidential box silently opened. John Wilkes Booth entered and fired one shot into the back of Lincoln's head. Mrs. Lincoln screamed; Rathbone rose up and grappled with Booth, who slashed his arm with a dagger. Booth then leapt from the box onto the stage and made his escape. Lincoln was carried across the street to a rooming house. Surgeons did what they could, but it was obvious the wound was mortal. Cabinet members were summoned. Then it was learned that during the evening another assassin had attacked Secretary of State Seward, inflicting wounds that might prove fatal. At 7:22 A.M. on April 15, Lincoln breathed his last. John Hay reported that over Lincoln's worn features had come a "look of unspeakable peace." Edwin Stanton took out his watch, noted the time, and said, "Now he belongs to the ages."

The word spread rapidly to a stunned nation. Papers rushed extras onto the streets to tell what they knew, even on a fragmentary basis. Saturday's *New York Herald* said: "An unlooked for and terrible calamity has befallen the nation. President Lincoln last night received a wound at the hands of an assassin, the effect of which there are no hopes of his surviving, having been shot while sitting in a theater witnessing the performance of a play. An attempt was also made, apparently by the same person who shot the President, to take the life of Secretary Seward. The assassin, after firing on the President, rushed in front of the box occupied by the latter, waving a long dagger which he held in his right hand, exclaimed, using the motto of the State of Virginia, 'Sic semper tyrannis!' He then jumped on the stage, and, amidst the intense excitement which ensued, escaped through the rear of the building. The President was shot through the head. He was immediately removed, and on examining the wound the brain was found to be oozing therefrom. The best surgical skill was instantly summoned; but it was not thought it could be of any avail in saving Mr. Lincoln's life."[30]

The New York Tribune's columns, edged in black, reported:

We give the above dispatches in the order in which they reached us, the first having been received a little before midnight, for we know that every line, every letter, will be read with intense interest. In the sudden shock of a calamity so appalling, we can do little else than give such details of the murder of the President as have reached us. Sudden death is always overwhelming; assassination of the humblest of men is always frightfully startling; when the head of thirty millions of people is hurried into eternity by the hand of a murderer—that head a man so good, so wise, so noble as ABRAHAM LINCOLN, the Chief Magistrate of a nation in the condition of ours at this moment, the sorrow and the shock are too great for many words. There are none in this broad land to-day who love their country, who wish well to their race, that will not bow down in profound grief at the event it has brought upon us. For once all party rancor will be forgotten, and no right-thinking man can hear of Mr. Lincoln's death without accepting it as a national calamity.

First dispatch: Like a clap of thunder out of a clear sky spread the announcement that President Lincoln was shot while sitting in his box at Ford's Theater. The city is wild with excitement. A gentleman who was present describes the event: At about 10½ o'clock, in the midst of one of the acts, a pistol shot was heard, and at the same instant a man leaped upon the stage from the same box occupied by the President, brandished a long knife and shouted, "Sic semper tyrannis!", then rushed to rear of the scene and out of the back door of the theater. So sudden was the whole thing that most persons in the theater thought it was part of the play, and it was some minutes before the fearful tragedy was apprehended.

A later dispatch said, "The ball lodged in his head, and he is now lying insensible in a house opposite the theater. No hopes are entertained of his recovery. Laura Keene claims to have recognized the assassin as the actor, J. Wilkes Booth. A feeling of gloom like a pall has settled on the city."[31]

Later that day, a bizarre scene took place at the *Tribune* offices. On Friday, Horace Greeley had penned a scathing anti-Lincoln editorial. Sidney Gay, the *Tribune* managing editor, had managed to intercept and squash it. By this time Greeley knew Lincoln was dead. Nevertheless, instead of thanking Gay, the erratic Greeley began to reprimand him: "They tell me you ordered my leader out of this morning's paper. Is it your paper or mine? I should like to know if I cannot print what I choose in my own paper." Gay's reply was quick and direct: "The paper is yours, Mr. Greeley. The article is in type upstairs and you can use it when you choose, *but if you run that editorial there will not be one brick left standing in the* Tribune *building.*"[32]

By Monday, Greeley had come to his senses and written words of praise: "The gloomiest day in our national history dawned upon us on Saturday morning, and dark days have not been unfrequent during the last five years. The astounding news that President Lincoln had been basely assassinated by a desperate Rebel, while sitting, oblivious of danger, in a theater at Washington on Friday night, and that an assault, with similar deadly intent, had been made a few minutes later upon Secretary Seward, while lying helpless in his bed, shocked, mortified and exasperated the entire Northern people on Saturday. At first there were many who, in spite of telegraphic information to the contrary, hoped that the injuries of the President would not prove fatal. But a few hours later came the darker intelligence that the blow of the assassin had been sure—that our wise, good, noble, generous President was indeed no more."[33]

In the *New York Times*, Henry Raymond also paid a moving tribute as he wrote: "When generations have passed away, and the unhappy wounds of this war are healed, and the whole nation is united on a basis of universal liberty, our posterity will read the dying words of the great Emancipator and the leader of the people with new sympathy and reverence, thanking God that so honest and so pure a man, so true a friend of the oppressed, and so genuine a patriot, guided the nation in the time of its trial, and prepared the final triumph which he was never allowed to see."[34]

Tributes to Lincoln were printed in papers across the nation. Particularly touching was the one appearing in the rural *Sangamo Journal*, the paper that once carried a letter from a twenty-three-year-old aspirant signing himself "Your friend and fellow citizen, A. Lincoln":

> ABRAHAM LINCOLN IS DEAD! These portentous words, as they sped over the wires throughout the length and breadth of the land on Saturday morning last sent a thrill of agony through millions of loyal hearts and shrouded a nation, so lately rejoicing in the hour of victory, in the deepest sorrow. The blow came at a moment so unexpected and was so sudden and staggering—the crime by which he fell was so atrocious and the manner of it so revolting, that men were unable to realize the fact that one of the purest of citizens, the noblest of patriots, the most beloved and honored of Presidents, and the most forbearing and magnanimous of rulers had perished at the hands of an assassin.[35]

For four years, Lincoln had worked diligently to win media support, not for himself, but for the Union. Now the editors paying Lincoln homage were also rejoicing in a Union victory. Lincoln had accomplished what he set out to do. Ironically, it wasn't until the years ahead that his media detractors would acknowledge his greatness. Horace Greeley had it right when he said: "Mr. Lincoln's reputation will stand higher with posterity than with the mass of his contemporaries—that distance, whether in time or space, while dwarfing and obscuring so many, must place him in a fairer light—that future generations will deem him undervalued by those for and with whom he labored, and be puzzled by the bitter fierceness of the personal assaults by which his temper was tested."[36]

The tributes were appreciated by Lincoln's friends and family, including Mary Lincoln, the grieving widow, whose already fragile mind would soon begin its long slide into madness. Comforting for a time, however, was a personal, tender message that came from England and from a fellow widow:

> Osborne
> April 29, 1865

Dear Madam,

Though a stranger to you, I cannot remain silent when so terrible a calamity has fallen upon you and your country, and must personally express my deep and heartfelt sympathy with you under the shocking circumstances of your present dreadful misfortune.

No one can better appreciate than I can, who am myself utterly broken-hearted by the loss of my own beloved Husband, who was the light of my life,—my stay—my all,—what your sufferings must be; and I earnestly pray that you may be supported by Him to whom alone the sorely stricken can look for comfort, in this hour of heavy affliction.

With renewed expression of true sympathy, I remain dear Madam,

> Your sincere friend
>
> Victoria[37]

NOTES

INTRODUCTION

1. Louis M. Starr, *Bohemian Brigade: Civil War Newsmen in Action* (Madison: University of Wisconsin Press, 1954), 6; Brayton Harris, *Blue and Gray in Black and White: Newspapers in the Civil War* (Washington, D.C.: Brassey's, 1999), ix, 9.

2. Starr, *Bohemian Brigade*, 11–12.

Chapter 1: "COOK COUNTY IS FOR ABRAHAM LINCOLN"

1. Allan Nevins, *Ordeal of the Union*, vol. 3 (New York: Charles Scribner's Sons, 1950), 357–59. The editors at the meeting were Charles L. Wilson of the *Chicago Journal*, Charles Ray of the *Chicago Tribune*, William Bross of the *Democratic Press*, and George T. Brown of the *Alton Courier*.

2. Robert S. Harper, *Lincoln and the Press* (New York: McGraw Hill Book Company, 1951), 19.

3. *Sangamo Journal*, March 1832. The paper later became the *Illinois State Journal*.

4. Philip B. Kunhardt Jr., Philip B. Kunhardt III, and Peter W. Kunhardt, *Lincoln, An Illustrated Biography* (New York: Alfred A. Knopf, 1992), 58.

5. Ibid., 77.

6. Nevins, *Ordeal of the Union*, vol. 4 (New York: Charles Scribner's Sons, 1950), 360.

7. Nevins, *Ordeal of the Union*, 3:363.

8. *New York Tribune*, July 1, 1858.

9. Harper, *Lincoln and the Press*, 16.

10. Walter B. Stevens, *A Reporter's Lincoln*, edited by Michael Burlingame. (Lincoln: University of Nebraska Press, 1998), 39–40.

11. Ibid., 67; Carl Sandburg, *Abraham Lincoln: The Prairie Years and the War Years*, 1 vol. edition (New York: Harcourt, Brace and Co., 1954), 138. While today we speak of the Lincoln-Douglas debates, in 1858 they were always called "Douglas-Lincoln" in deference to the better-known candidate. At first, Douglas's organ, the *Chicago Times*, claimed that Lincoln knew he couldn't stand up to Douglas, and that his challenge had been a bluff. "Had Lincoln or any of his friends had any idea his challenge would be accepted," wrote the *Times*, "it never would have been sent."

12. Ibid., 74; Harper, *Lincoln and the Press*, 26.

13. Nevins, *Ordeal of the Union*, 3:386; Carl Sandburg, *Abraham Lincoln, The Prairie Years*, vol. 2 (New York: Harcourt, Brace & Company, 1937), 140.

14. Stevens, *A Reporter's Lincoln*, 89–90.

15. Letter, Greeley to Colfax, February 28, 1860. A good discussion of Greeley's scheme with respect to Douglas can be found in William Harlan Hale's *Horace Greeley, Voice of the People* (New York: Harper & Brothers, 1950).

16. Harlan Hoyt Horner, *Lincoln and Greeley* (Urbana: University of Illinois Press, 1953), 135–37.

17. Sandburg, *Abraham Lincoln*, 144; Hale, *Horace Greeley*, 206.

18. Ibid., 162–63; Horner, *Lincoln and Greeley*, 161–62.

19. Ibid., 155.

20. Sandburg, *Abraham Lincoln*, 163.

21. *New York Tribune*, February 25, 1860.

22. Nevins, *Ordeal of the Union*, 4:183–88.

23. John M. Taylor, *William Henry Seward: Lincoln's Right Hand* (Washington, D.C.: Brassey's, 1991), 118; Harper, *Lincoln and the Press*, 48. Medill's saying that Lincoln could be elected, while Seward could not, was merely a bit of hyperbole boosting Illinois' "favorite son," Lincoln. At this stage, Seward on a national scale was undoubtedly the stronger candidate.

Chapter 2: "HONEST OLD ABE"

1. *New York Tribune*, April 18, 1860; Nevins, *Ordeal of the Union*, 4:230–3.

2. Taylor, *William Henry Seward*, 3; *Chicago Tribune*, May 15, 1860.

3. Hale, *Horace Greeley*, 252.

4. Ibid., 166.

5. Nevins, *Ordeal of the Union*, 4:235.

6. Ibid., 251–60; Stevens, *A Reporter's Lincoln*, 196–201.

7. It's not surprising that star-struck delegates crowded around the famed Horace Greeley. Something similar happens in our present day, when TV journalists such as Tom Brokaw and Dan Rather become celebrities at political conventions every bit as much as the candidates themselves.

8. Hale, *Horace Greeley*, 191, 221.

9. Nevins, *Ordeal of the Union*, 4:256.

10. Sandburg, *Abraham Lincoln*, 173–74.

11. Horner, *Lincoln and Greeley*, 178; Hale, *Horace Greeley*, 220–3; *New York Tribune*, May 19, 1860.

12. Ibid., 179–80.

13. Harper, *Lincoln and the Press*, 56; Nevins, *Ordeal of the Union*, 4:275.

14. Sandburg, *Abraham Lincoln*, 176.

15. Ibid., 179.

16. Nevins, *Ordeal of the Union*, 4:275–77; Harper, *Lincoln and the Press*, 62–64.

17. Ibid., 278; Harper, *Lincoln and the Press*, 63.

18. *Charleston Mercury*, October 11, 1860; Harper, *Lincoln and the Press*, 64.

19. *New York Tribune*, September 8, 1860; Nevins, *Ordeal of the Union*, 4:108.

20. Sandburg, *Abraham Lincoln*, 181.

21. Horner, *Lincoln and Greeley*, 185–86.

22. *New York Tribune*, November 9, 1860.

23. Harper, *Lincoln and the Press*, 67–68.

24. Michael A. Incitti, "Henry Villard: Reporter Who Knew Lincoln Best." *Media History Digest* 6, no. 2, (Fall-Winter, 1986:38) quoting *Memoirs of Henry Villard, Journalist and Financier, 1835–1900*, vol. 1.

25. Harper, *Lincoln and the Press*, 73–74; Carl Sandburg, *War Years*, vol. 1 (New York: Harcourt, Brace and Co., 1939), 12.

26. Carl Sandburg, *Prairie Years*, vol. 2, 12.

27. Incitti, "Henry Villard"; Harper, *Lincoln and the Press*, 80–81; *Illinois State Journal*, February 12, 1861.

28. Ibid.

29. Carl Sandburg, *Abraham Lincoln: The War Years*, vol. 1 (New York: Harcourt, Brace and Co., 1936), 48; Harper, *Lincoln and the Press*, 74.

30. Ibid., 50–51.

31. Harper, *Lincoln and the Press*, 88–89.

32. Ibid.
33. Ibid., 90–91.
34. Sandburg, *Abraham Lincoln*, 207.

Chapter 3: "THE BETTER ANGELS OF OUR NATURE"

1. Stevens, *A Reporter's Lincoln*, 25–26.
2. Sandburg, *War Years*, 1:135.
3. *New York Tribune*, March 6, 1861; Horner, *Lincoln and Greeley*, 207.
4. Sandburg, *Abraham Lincoln*, 214.
5. Michael Burlingame, ed., *Lincoln's Journalist—John Hay's Anonymous Writings for the Press, 1860–64* (Carbondale: Southern Illinois University Press, 1998), xi. Burlingame, with a fine bit of scholarly detective work, identified many articles, previously unattributed, as having been written by Hay.
6. Ibid., 53; *New York World*, March 6, 1861.
7. Sandburg, *Abraham Lincoln*, 214–15.
8. Ibid.
9. *New York Tribune*, March 6, 1861.
10. Nevins, *Ordeal of the Union*, 4:433–34; Sandburg, *War Years*, 1:137.
11. Sandburg, *War Years*, 1:141, 153. Hamlin had edited a country weekly in Maine; Cameron, before he was twenty-one, had edited the *Doylestown* (Pennsylvania) *Democrat* and later owned and edited the *Hartford Times*; Blair had edited the *Washington Globe* and Smith had once edited a small Indiana paper.
12. Harper, *Lincoln and the Press*, 76; *Cincinnati Commercial*, April 2, 1861.
13. *New York Tribune*, April 3, 1861; *New York Times*, April 3, 1861.
14. Sandburg, *War Years*, 1:181–82.
15. Harper, *Lincoln and the Press*, 64–65.
16. Martin Crawford, *William Howard Russell's Civil War: Private Diary and Letters, 1861–62* (Athens: University of Georgia Press, 1992), 24.
17. Harris, *Blue and Gray*, 32.
18. Ibid.
19. Harper, *Lincoln and the Press*, 99.
20. Sandburg, *War Years*, 1:189.
21. Ibid., 194; Starr, *Bohemian Brigade*, 27–28.
22. *New York Herald*, April 10, 1861.
23. Sandburg, *War Years*, 1:196–210; Shelby Foote, *The Civil War: A Narrative*, vol. 1 (New York: Random House, 1958), 48–50.
24. *New York Tribune*, April 15, 1861.

25. Nevins, *Ordeal of the Union*, vol. 5 (Charles Scribner's Sons, 1959), 77–78.
26. *Chicago Tribune*, April 18, 1861.
27. Sandburg, *War Years*, 1:212.
28. *New York Tribune*, February 23, 1861.
29. Ibid., April 17, 1861.
30. Ibid, May 2, 1861.
31. Harper, *Lincoln and the Press*, 97.
32. Harris, *Blue and Gray*, 60.
33. Horner, *Lincoln and Greeley*, 226–27.

Chapter 4: "IN THE DEPTHS OF BITTERNESS"
1. *New York Tribune*, June 21, 1861; Starr, *Bohemian Brigade*, 35.
2. Ibid., May 24, 1861; Harris, *Blue and Gray*, 62.
3. Foote, *The Civil War*, 1:67.
4. Burlingame, *Lincoln's Journalist*, 73; *New York World*, July 11, 1861.
5. Ibid., 73; *New York World*, July 12, 1861.
6. Foote, *Civil War*, 1:73–82; Nevins, *Ordeal of the Union*, 5:216–20. Southerners, who tended to name battles after towns, called it the Battle of Manassas. In the North, where it was "Bull Run," battles would generally be named after topographic features.
7. *New York World*, July 22, 1861.
8. Starr, *Bohemian Brigade*, 50.
9. Foote, *Civil War*, 1:85.
10. *Harper's Weekly*, August 3, 1861.
11. *New York Tribune*, July 23, 1861.
12. Harry J. Maihafer, *The General and the Journalists: Ulysses S. Grant, Horace Greeley, and Charles Dana* (Washington, D.C.: Brassey's, 1998), 70.
13. *New York Tribune*, July 25, 1861.
14. Hale, *Horace Greeley*, 249–50.
15. Harris, *Blue and Gray*, 79; *London Times*, August 6, 1861.
16. Harris, *Blue and Gray*, 79.
17. Ibid., 90.
18. Ibid., 90–91.
19. Ibid., 92.
20. *Christian Observer*, reprinted by *Philadelphia Inquirer*, August 23, 1861.
21. Charles Adams, *When in the Course of Human Events: Arguing the Case for Southern Secession* (Lanham, Md.: Rowman & Littlefield 2000), 43; Harper, *Lincoln and the Press*, 109–10. Editor Converse had claimed that his

paper was the organ of the "New School of Presbyterian Church." This was repudiated by the long-established *American Presbyterian*. Converse, a native Virginian, reestablished his paper in Richmond.

22. Horner, *Lincoln and Greeley*, 242–43; Nevins, *Ordeal of the Union*, 5:335.
23. Sandburg, *Abraham Lincoln*, 265.
24. Horner, *Lincoln and Greeley*, 245.
25. Nevins, *Ordeal of the Union*, 5:273.
26. Foote, *Civil War*, 1:110.
27. Harper, *Lincoln and the Press*, 100.
28. Horner, *Lincoln and Greeley*, 246–47; Hale, *Horace Greeley*, 256–57.
29. James M. Trietsch, *The Printer and the Prince: A Study of the Influence of Horace Greeley upon Abraham Lincoln as Candidate and President* (New York: Exposition Press, 1955), 16; Maihafer, *The General and the Journalists*, 102.
30. *New York Tribune*, December 30, 1861; Nevins, *Ordeal of the Union*, 5:303–4.
31. Taylor, *William Henry Seward*, 181–84; Nevins, *Ordeal of the Union*, 5:387–93.
32. Sandburg, *War Years*, 1:560.
33. Starr, *Bohemian Brigade*, 68.
34. Ibid.
35. Ibid.
36. Nevins, *Ordeal of the Union*, 5:400.
37. *New York Times, Herald, Tribune*, December 4, 1861.
38. Nevins, *Ordeal of the Union*, 5:402.
39. *New York Tribune*, January 21, 1862.
40. Nevins, *Ordeal of the Union*, 5:405.

Chapter 5: "AS DEEP AS A WELL"
1. Sandburg, War Years, 1:382–83.
2. Horner, *Lincoln and Greeley*, 249.
3. *New York Tribune*, January 9, 1862.
4. Ibid., January 31, 1862.
5. Trietsch, *Printer and the Prince*, 201–2; Sandburg, *War Years*, 1:401.
6. Horner, *Lincoln and Greeley*, 211.
7. Sandburg, *War Years*, 1:401.
8. Ibid., 408.
9. Adams, *When in the Course of Human Events*, 73–74.
10. *London Times*, March 2, 1862; Harris, *Blue and Gray*, 93–94.
11. *New York Tribune*, February 21, 1862.
12. Sandburg, *War Years*, 1:434.

13. Charles A. Dana, *Recollections of the Civil War* (Lincoln: University of Nebraska Press, 1996. Originally published by D. Appleton Co., New York; 1898), 4–5.

14. Harper, *Lincoln and the Press*, 320.

15. Sandburg, *Abraham Lincoln*, 385.

16. Sandburg, *War Years*, 1:409.

17. Ibid., 1:491.

18. Nevins, *Ordeal of the Union*, 5:372.

19. *Chicago Tribune*, February 20, 1862.

20. *New York Herald*, February 18, 1862.

21. *New York Times*, February 25, 1862.

22. *Missouri Republican*, February 27, 1862.

23. Bruce Catton, *Terrible Swift Sword* (New York: Doubleday, 1963), 173; Harper, *Lincoln and the Press*, 164.

24. Horner, *Lincoln and Greeley*, 251. On March 9, the day Lincoln was writing to the *New York Times*'s editor, the world's first battle of ironclad ships was taking place at Hampton Roads, Virginia, between the Union *Monitor* and the Confederate *Merrimac*.

25. *New York Tribune*, March 7, 1862.

26. Horner, *Lincoln and Greeley*, 252.

27. *New York Herald*, April 9, 1862.

28. Sandburg, *War Years*, 1:478.

29. *Chicago Times*, April 10, 1862; *Chicago Tribune*, April 10, 1862.

30. *New York Tribune*, May 3, 1862.

31. *New York Herald*, April 22, 1862.

32. Sandburg, *War Years*, 1:478.

33. Ibid., 1:492.

34. Nevins, *Ordeal of the Union*, vol. 6 (Charles Scribner's Sons, 1960), 117.

35. Ibid., 6:59.

36. *War of the Rebellion: Official Records of the Union and Confederate Armies*, vol. 14 (Washington, D.C.: Government Printing Office, 1884), 260.

37. Curt Anders, *Henry Halleck's War: A Fresh Look at Lincoln's Controversial General in Chief* (Carmel, Ind.: Guild Press of Indiana, Inc., 1999), 135.

38. Ibid., 136.

39. *Official Records*, 14, 269.

40. Catton, *Terrible Swift Sword*, 321.

41. Ibid., 322.

42. Sandburg, *War Years*, 1:501–2.

43. *Official Records*, 16, part 2, 90.

44. Nevins, *Ordeal of the Union*, 6:150.
45. Ibid., 6:163.
46. Foote, *Civil War*, 1:595.
47. Sandburg, *War Years*, 1:580.
48. Ibid., 1:571–72.
49. Ibid., 1:566; Starr, *Bohemian Brigade*, 125.
50. Foote, *Civil War*, 1:705.
51. Ibid.
52. Sandburg, *War Years*, 1:571–72.
53. Nevins, *Ordeal of the Union*, 6:165; Taylor, *William Henry Seward*, 202; Sandburg, *War Years*, 1:584.
54. Harper, *Lincoln and the Press*, 175.

Chapter 6: "I WOULD SAVE THE UNION"

1. Starr, *Bohemian Brigade*, 125-26. Charles Dana, Gay's predecessor as *Tribune* managing editor, had resigned in March 1862 after a falling out with the volatile Greeley; he was now on a special assignment for Secretary of War Stanton.
2. Ibid., 127.
3. *New York Tribune*, August 20, 1862.
4. Ibid., August 22, 1862.
5. *New York Times*, August 23, 1862.
6. Hale, *Horace Greeley*, 243; Harris, *Blue and Gray*, 200; Nevins, *Ordeal of the Union*, 6:232.
7. *National Intelligencer*, August 23, 1862.
8. Starr, *Bohemian Brigade*, 129.
9. Ibid., 129–30.
10. Ibid., 130.
11. J. Cutler Andrews, *The North Reports the Civil War* (Pittsburgh, Pa.: University of Pittsburgh Press, 1955), 55.
12. Ibid.
13. *Official Records*, 11, part 1, 104–5.
14. Nevins, *Ordeal of the Union*, 6:188.
15. Sandburg, *War Years*, 1:550.
16. *New York Tribune*, September 23, 1862; Sandburg, *War Years*, 1:600.
17. Sandburg, *War Years*, 1:554.
18. Ibid., 583–84.
19. Adams, *When in the Course of Human Events*, 141.
20. Harper, *Lincoln and the Press*, 172; Sandburg, *War Years*, 1:587.

21. Ibid.
22. Adams, *When in the Course of Human Events*, 141.
23. Ibid., 145.
24. Ibid., 144.
25. Ibid., 144; Sandburg, *War Years*, 1:588; *Manchester Guardian*, February 20, 1863.
26. Harper, *Lincoln and the Press*, 177.
27. Anders, *Henry Halleck's War*, 283–84.
28. Foote, *Civil War*, 1:748–49.
29. Ibid., 749.
30. Sandburg, *War Years*, 1:596.
31. Nevins, *Ordeal of the Union*, 6:309.
32. Sandburg, *War Years*, 1:610.
33. Ibid., 1:605–6.
34. *Official Records*, 19, part 2, 545.

Chapter 7: "A WORSE PLACE THAN HELL"
1. Anders, *Henry Halleck's War*, 323.
2. Foote, *Civil War*, 1:770.
3. Sandburg, *War Years*, 1:612.
4. Harper, *Lincoln and the Press*, 179–80.
5. Anders, *Henry Halleck's War*, 323.
6. Harris, *Blue and Gray*, 207.
7. Bruce Catton, *Never Call Retreat* (New York: Doubleday, 1965), 29; Foote, *Civil War*, 2:44.
8. Sandburg, *War Years*, 1:630.
9. *New York Times*, January 19, 1863.
10. Andrews, *The North Reports the Civil War*, 340–42; Sandburg, *War Years*, 2:75.
11. Burlingame, *Lincoln's Journalist*, 324.
12. Anders, *Henry Halleck's War*, 362.
13. Ibid., 363.
14. Ibid., 365–66.
15. Foote, *Civil War*, 2:123.
16. Ibid., 2:107.
17. Sandburg, *War Years*, 2:5–6.
18. Foote, *Civil War*, 2:120.
19. Ibid., 2:108.
20. Sandburg, *Abraham Lincoln*, 328–29.

21. Sandburg, *War Years*, 2:128–29.
22. *Official Records*, 31, 1004–5.
23. Foote, *Civil War*, 2:132.
24. Andrews, *North Reports the Civil War*, 342–43.
25. Sandburg, *War Years*, 2:23–24.
26. Ibid., 360; Starr, *Bohemian Brigade*, 198.
27. Starr, *Bohemian Brigade*, 199; Sandburg, *War Years*, 2:96.
28. Sandburg, *War Years*, 2:80.
29. Ibid., 2:96–97.
30. Ibid., 2:98.

Chapter 8: "I'LL COPY THE SHORT ONE"
 1. Starr, *Bohemian Brigade*, 171.
 2. Sandburg, *War Years*, 2:113.
 3. Starr, *Bohemian Brigade*, 175.
 4. Ibid., 178.
 5. Ibid., 180–81.
 6. Ibid., 182; Harris, *Blue and Gray*, 244–48.
 7. Michael Burlingame, ed., *Lincoln Observed: Civil War Dispatches of Noah Brooks* (Baltimore, Md.: Johns Hopkins University Press, 1998), 13.
 8. Sandburg, *War Years*, 2:127.
 9. Ibid., 2:128.
10. Harper, *Lincoln and the Press*, 239–40.
11. Harper, *Lincoln and the Press*, 240–41; Nevins, *Ordeal of the Union*, 6:453–54. The Conscription Act, to which Vallandigham referred, had gone into effect in March. Protests against the unpopular law were widespread, and included, in July of 1863, a bloody antidraft riot in New York City.
12. Harper, *Lincoln and the Press*, 246.
13. Ibid., 244–45.
14. *Cincinnati Gazette*, May 19, 1863.
15. Ibid., May 11, 1863.
16. Catton, *Never Call Retreat*, 165.
17. Nevins, *Ordeal of the Union*, 6:454.
18. Ibid.; Harper, *Lincoln and the Press*, 246. Confederates were less than thrilled to have Vallandigham on their hands. With their approval, he made his way to Bermuda, and thence to Canada. While there, he ran in absentia for governor of Ohio.
19. Sandburg, *War Years*, 2:168.
20. Catton, *Never Call Retreat*, 167.

21. Ibid; Nevins, *Ordeal of the Union*, 6:456.

22. Catton, *Never Call Retreat*, 168.

23. Sandburg, *War Years*, 2:175; Starr, *Bohemian Brigade*, 155.

24. Starr, *Bohemian Brigade*, 153.

25. Ibid., 154–55. The message originators, Rawlins and Hurlbut, were Grant's chief of staff, John A. Rawlins, and Stephen A. Hurlbut, commander of the Union forces occupying Memphis, Tennessee.

26. Dana, *Recollections of the Civil War*, 21.

27. Ibid.

28. James M. McPherson, *Battle Cry of Freedom: The Civil War Era* (New York: Oxford University Press, 1988), 565; Sandburg, *War Years*, 2:241.

29. Andrews, *North Reports the Civil War*, 657.

30. *New York Tribune*, February 11, 1863; Sandburg, *War Years*, 2:177–78; McPherson, *Battle Cry of Freedom*, 565.

31. McPherson, *Battle Cry of Freedom*, 565.

32. Hale, *Horace Greeley*, 73.

33. *New York Herald*, January 24, 1863.

34. Harper, *Lincoln and the Press*, 144.

35. *New York Express*, May 9, 1863; Horner, *Lincoln and the Press*, 292.

36. *New York Tribune*, May 11, 1863.

37. Sandburg, *War Years*, 2:175.

38. Hale, *Horace Greeley*, 252.

39. John C. Waugh, *Reelecting Lincoln: The Battle for the 1864 Presidency* (New York: Crown Publishers, Inc., 1997), 13. Richard Henry Dana was a cousin of Charles Dana, the former journalist who was Lincoln's representative to Grant's army.

40. *New York Express*, November 14, 1862.

41. *New York Herald*, November 21, 1862.

42. Stephen W. Sears, *George Brinton McClellan: The Young Napoleon* (New York: Ticknor & Fields, 1988), 345.

43. *New York Tribune*, October 7, 1862.

44. Hale, *Horace Greeley*, 276; Sandburg, *War Years*, 2:196–97.

45. Sandburg, *War Years*, 2:197.

Chapter 9: "THE VERY BEST I CAN"

1. *Official Records*, 40/25, part 2, 378.

2. Ibid., 379.

3. Ibid., 435.

4. *New York Tribune*, May 5, 1863.
5. Andrews, *North Reports the Civil War*, 369.
6. Ibid., 370; *Boston Daily Journal*, May 8, 1863.
7. Sandburg, *War Years*, 2:237.
8. Ibid.
9. Anders, *Henry Halleck's War*, 382. The statement about "breaking enemy communications" probably referred to a simultaneous cavalry raid undertaken by General George Stoneman. Unfortunately for the Union, that raid, like the Chancellorsville battle, produced no positive results.
10. Andrews, *North Reports the Civil War*, 372.
11. McPherson, *Battle Cry of Freedom*, 598–99.
12. Henry J. Raymond, *History of the Administration of President Lincoln* (New York: J. C. Derby and N. C. Miller, 1864), 479.
13. Alfred H. Guernsey and Henry M. Alden, *Harper's Pictorial History of the Civil War* (New York: Fairfax Press, 1868), 502.
14. *Official Records*, 43/27, part 1, 39.
15. Foote, *Civil War*, 2:449.
16. *Official Records*, 43/27, part 1, 60.
17. Anders, *Henry Halleck's War*, 447.
18. Foote, *Civil War*, 2:451.
19. *New York Tribune*, June 29, 1863.
20. Starr, *Bohemian Brigade*, 205.
21. *New York Herald*, July 2, 1863.
22. *Philadelphia Inquirer*, June 28, 1863.
23. *New York Tribune*, June 26, 1863.
24. *New York Times*, July 2, 1863; Starr, *Bohemian Brigade*, 207.
25. Emmet Crozier, *Yankee Reporters* (New York: Oxford University Press, 1956), 346–51; Harris, *Blue and Gray*, 278–79.
26. *New York Tribune*, July 3, 1863.
27. Sandburg, *War Years*, 2:343–44.
28. Ibid., 2:351.
29. Letter, Dana to Stanton, May 4, 1863.
30. *New York Tribune*, May 11 and 25, 1863.
31. Ibid., May 30, 1863.
32. Ibid., June 16, 1863.
33. Dana, *Recollections of the Civil War*, 97.
34. Sandburg, *War Years*, 2:347.
35. Ibid., 347–48.

36. Sears, *George B. McClellan*, 345.

37. Bruce Catton, *Grant Moves South* (Boston: Little, Brown and Company, 1960), 488–89; Sandburg, *War Years*, 2:349.

Chapter 10: "THE PROMISE MUST BE KEPT"

1. Starr, *Bohemian Brigade*, 186.

2. Ibid.

3. Ibid., 187.

4. Ibid. The two hapless reporters were later transferred to Richmond's notorious Castle Thunder, and from there to the penitentiary at Salisbury, North Carolina. Despite receiving "dozens of offers" to exchange them, Ould steadfastly refused. In December of 1864, the two managed to escape, eventually making their way to Union lines at Knoxville, Tennessee. From there Richardson sent a wire that thrilled *Tribune* readers: "Out of the jaws of death, out of the gates of Hell."

5. Sandburg, *War Years*, 2:357.

6. Ibid., 2:358.

7. *New York Herald*, July 13, 1863.

8. Sandburg, *War Years*, 2:361.

9. *New York Tribune*, July 14, 1863; Starr, *Bohemian Brigade*, 220–24; Harris, *Blue and Gray*, 280; Maihafer, *The General and the Journalists*, 167.

10. *New York Evening Post*, July 23, 1863; Nevins, *Ordeal of the Union*, 7:124.

11. Harper, *Lincoln and the Press*, 173.

12. Nevins, *Ordeal of the Union*, vol. 7 (New York: Charles Scribner's Sons, 1971), 125–26; Starr, *Bohemian Brigade*, 225; Sandburg, *War Years*, 2:369.

13. McPherson, *Battle Cry of Freedom*, 667.

14. *Official Records*, 35/23, part 2, 545.

15. Ibid.; Anders, *Henry Halleck's War*, 477.

16. Catton, *Never Call Retreat*, 158.

17. *National Intelligencer*, June 15, 1863.

18. Horner, *Lincoln and Greeley*, 259–60.

19. Sandburg, *War Years*, 2:382.

20. *New York Tribune*, September 3, 1863.

21. Sandburg, *War Years*, 2:382–83.

22. Ibid., 2:433; Dana, *Recollections of the Civil War*, 104.

23. James H. Wilson, *Life of Charles A. Dana* (New York: Harper and Brothers, 1907), 258–59.

24. Dana, *Recollections of the Civil War*, 115.

25. Ibid., 118.

26. Burlingame, *Lincoln Observed*, 62; *Sacramento Daily Union*, October 17, 1863 (from a dispatch written on September 23).

27. Burlingame, *Lincoln Observed*, 64.

28. Stevens, *A Reporter's Lincoln*, 237–44.

29. *Official Records*, 33/22, part 2, 355.

30. Burlingame, *Lincoln Observed*, 62; *Sacramento Daily Union*, October 17, 1863 (from a dispatch written on September 23).

31. Waugh, *Reelecting Lincoln*, 16.

32. *New York Tribune*, October 12, 1863.

33. *New York Herald*, October 15, 1863.

34. Sandburg, *War Years*, 2:391–93.

35. Dana, *Recollections of the Civil War*, 127–28.

36. *Official Records*, 53/30, part 4, 404. At that first meeting between Stanton and Grant, the secretary of war rushed forward, seized the hand of Grant's medical director, Dr. E. D. Kittoe, pumped it vigorously and said, "General Grant, I recognize you at once from your pictures!"

37. Ulysses S. Grant, *Personal Memoirs*, vol. 2 (New York: Charles L. Webster and Company, 1886), 18–19.

Chapter 11: "ALL MEN ARE CREATED EQUAL"

1. *Official Records*, 54/31, part 1, 666; Horace Porter, *Campaigning with Grant* (New York: Century Company, 1897), 2.

2. Foote, *Civil War*, 2:816–17; Sandburg, *War Years*, 2:458–59.

3. Burlingame, *Lincoln Observed*, 89; Sandburg, *War Years*, 2:455. In his fine work, *Lincoln at Gettysburg: The Words That Remade America* (New York: Simon & Schuster, 1992), Garry Wills claims that Brooks was mistaken about Lincoln having an advance copy of Everett's text, extracted from the *Boston Journal*, when he went to the photography studio on November 8. Wills correctly points out that Everett's text was printed in the *Boston Daily Advertiser*, rather than the *Journal*, and not until November 14. It may be, however, that what Lincoln had that day was merely a copy of the speech run off by the *Journal* for Everett's convenience, and at Everett's specific request.

4. Harper, *Lincoln and the Press*, 282; Sandburg, *War Years*, 2:462–63.

5. Ibid., 284.

6. *Ohio Statesman*, November 22, 1863.

7. Sandburg, *War Years*, 2:463–75; Harper, *Lincoln and the Press*, 284–87.

8. *New York Tribune*, November 20, 1861.

9. *New York Times*, November 20, 1861.

10. *Springfield* (Massachusetts) *Republican*, November 20, 1863.

11. *Chicago Tribune*, November 20, 1863; *Providence Journal*, November 20, 1863; Sandburg, *War Years*, 2:472–74.

12. Wills, *Lincoln at Gettysburg*, 38.

13. *Harrisburg* (Pennsylvania) *Patriot and Union*, November 20, 1863; *Official Records*, 58/31, Part 2, 25.

14. *Chicago Times*, November 23, 1863.

15. Foote, *Civil War*, 2:829.

16. Catton, *Never Call Retreat*, 266.

17. Dana, *Recollections of the Civil War*, 147.

18. Sandburg, *War Years*, 2:479; *Official Records*, 58/31, part 2, 25.

19. *Chicago Tribune*, December 8, 1863.

20. Ibid., December 15, 1863.

21. *New York Evening Post*, December 11, 1863.

22. Burlingame, *Lincoln Observed*, 93; *Sacramento Union*, January 18, 1864 (from a dispatch written December 12, 1863).

23. Sandburg, *War Years*, 2:490.

24. Ibid.

25. Abraham Lincoln, *The Collected Works of Abraham Lincoln*, Roy P. Basler, ed., vol. 6 (New Brunswick, N.J.: Rutgers University Press, 1953), 540.

26. *New York Tribune*, December 8, 1863.

27. Ibid., June 17, 1864.

28. Nevins, *Ordeal of the Union*, 7:212–31. Nevins gives a valuable description of what, despite the war, had really become a "boom time" for the Northern states.

29. Lincoln, *Collected Works*, 6:465–66.

30. Burlingame, *Lincoln Observed*, 100; *Sacramento Daily Union*, February 4, 1864 (from a dispatch written January 1, 1864).

31. Waugh, *Reelecting Lincoln*, 17–18.

32. *New York Tribune*, November 27, 1863.

33. *New York World*, November 26, 1863; *New York Herald*, November 28, 1863.

34. *New York Herald*, December 9, 1863.

35. Ibid., December 15, 1863.

36. *New York Tribune*, December 18, 1863.

37. Bruce Catton, *Grant Takes Command* (Boston: Little, Brown and Company, 1968), 111.

38. Ibid., 121; Maihafer, *The General and the Journalists*, 184.
39. Ibid.; *Official Records*, 32, part 3, 13, 26.
40. *New York Tribune*, March 5, 1864.

Chapter 12: "WHY, HERE IS GENERAL GRANT!"
1. Porter, *Campaigning with Grant*, 18–21; Burlingame, *Lincoln Observed*, 104; Sandburg, *War Years*, 2:543.
2. Catton, *Grant Takes Command*, 116.
3. Grant, *Personal Memoirs*, 2:115–16.
4. Catton, *Grant Takes Command*, 130, citing February 1864 letters of James H. Wilson to William F. Smith in the Wilson papers, Library of Congress. Wilson, as a major general, would perform brilliantly during the war's final year as a leader of cavalry. He would go on to a long and distinguished career, to include active duty service in 1898 during the Spanish-American War.
5. Dana, *Recollections of the Civil War*, 226–27.
6. *Official Records*, 58, series 1, 32, part 2, 407–8.
7. Ibid., 59, series 1, 32, part 3, 49.
8. Grant, *Personal Memoirs*, 2:117.
9. Starr, *Bohemian Brigade*, 276–77.
10. Catton, *Grant Takes Command*, 131.
11. Ibid., 156.
12. *New York Tribune*, March 10, 1864.
13. Foote, *Civil War*, 3:12.
14. Sandburg, *War Years*, 2:549–50.
15. *Frankfort* (Kentucky) *Commonwealth*, reprinted in *New York Times*, April 29, 1864.
16. *New York Times*, April 29, 1864.
17. *Official Records*, 59/32, part 3, 58; Sandburg, *War Years*, 2:551.
18. Catton, *Grant Takes Command*, 177.
19. Horace Greeley, *The American Conflict*, vol. 2 (New York: Charles L. Webster and Co., 1866), 566.
20. *Official Records*, 67/36, part 1, 2; McPherson, *Battle Cry of Freedom*, 725–28.
21. Grant, *Personal Memoirs*, 2:123.
22. Sandburg, *War Years*, 2:554.
23. Harper, *Lincoln and the Press*, 129–31. Censorship of news dispatches from Washington began in the dark days of April 1861, when the government assumed control of telegraph wires leading from the city. Censorship author-

ity was first placed under the Treasury Department, then transferred to the War Department, then to the State Department, and then back to the War Department on February 25, 1862. There it stayed for the remainder of the war.

24. Porter, *Campaigning with Grant*, 98.

25. Anders, Henry Halleck's War, 562; Catton, *Grant Takes Command*, 130, citing February 1864 letters of James H. Wilson to William F. Smith in the Wilson papers, Library of Congress; William Hanchett, *IRISH: Charles G. Halpine in Civil War America* (Syracuse, N.Y.: Syracuse University Press, 1970), 57–58. Halpine, a journalist and poet, is today best known for the witty satiric works of his fictional alter ego, "Private Miles O'Reilly."

26. Andrews, *North Reports the Civil War*, 532–35; Starr, *Bohemian Brigade*, 298–303; Foote, *Civil War*, 3:186.

27. Dana, *Recollections of the Civil War*, 188–89.

28. Andrews, *North Reports the Civil War*, 534–35; Starr, *Bohemian Brigade*, 302–3.

29. Waugh, *Reelecting Lincoln*, 171.

30. Grant, *Personal Memoirs*, 2:204.

31. Porter, *Campaigning with Grant*, 83.

32. *Official Records*, 67/36, part 1, 4; Grant, *Personal Memoirs*, 2:226.

33. Greeley, *American Conflict*, 2:571; Porter, *Campaigning with Grant*, 98; Catton, *Grant Takes Command*, 236.

Chapter 13: "I BEGIN TO SEE IT"

1. Waugh, *Reelecting Lincoln*, 25.

2. *New York Tribune*, December 25, 1863.

3. Sandburg, *War Years*, 2:564; *Harper's Weekly*, January 2, 1864.

4. *New York Herald*, January 29, 1864.

5. Herbert Mitgang, ed., *Abraham Lincoln: A Press Portrait* (Athens: University of Georgia Press, 1989), 378, citing *New York Daily News*, February 15, 1864.

6. *New York Tribune*, February 2, 1864.

7. Letter, Rawlins to Washburne, dated January 20, 1864; Catton, *Grant Takes Command*, 118.

8. Waugh, *Reelecting Lincoln*, 38.

9. *New York Herald*, November 9, 1863.

10. Waugh, *Reelecting Lincoln*, 117–20, 215–17.

11. *New York World*, May 6, 1864; *Chicago Tribune*, June 3, 1864; *New York Times*, June 2 and 3, 1864.

12. *New York Tribune*, February 23, 1864.

13. Sandburg, *War Years*, 3:48.

14. Ibid., 47.

15. Waugh, *Reelecting Lincoln*, 152.

16. Starr, *Bohemian Brigade*, 277.

17. Foote, *Civil War*, 3:297–99; Starr, *Bohemian Brigade*, 278.

18. Ibid.

19. Harper, *Lincoln and the Press*, 281.

20. *New York Daily News*, May 19, 1864.

21. *New York Tribune*, May 19, 1864.

22. Starr, *Bohemian Brigade*, 315–20; Harper, *Lincoln and the Press*, 297. Both Starr and Harper provide excellent accounts of the comedy of errors accompanying the "Proclamation Hoax."

23. *New York World*, May 23, 1864.

24. Porter, *Campaigning with Grant*, 174–75; Foote, *Civil War*, 3:290.

25. Grant, *Personal Memoirs*, 2:276.

26. *New York Times*, April 4, 1864.

27. *New York Tribune*, May 17, 1864.

28. Sandburg, *War Years*, 3:70.

29. *New York Tribune*, June 6, 1864.

30. Sandburg, *War Years*, 3:78–79; Waugh, *Reelecting Lincoln*, 187–89.

31. Waugh, *Reelecting Lincoln*, 190.

32. Sandburg, *War Years*, 3:89.

33. Ibid., 3:82.

34. Waugh, *Reelecting Lincoln*, 196.

35. Ibid.; Sandburg, *War Years*, 3:97.

36. Sandburg, *War Years*, 3:86; Waugh, *Reelecting Lincoln*, 197.

37. *New York Herald*, June 10, 1864.

38. Sandburg, *War Years*, 3:95.

39. Ibid., 3:96.

40. Catton, *Grant Takes Command*, 283.

41. *New York Times*, June 23, 1864.

42. Waugh, *Reelecting Lincoln*, 203–4; Sandburg, *War Years*, 3:59.

Chapter 14: "GET DOWN, YOU DAMN FOOL!"

1. Letter of Horace Porter to Mrs. Porter, dated June 24, 1864; Catton, *Grant Moves South*, 305.

2. Porter, *Campaigning with Grant*, 218.

3. Ibid., 219.

4. *New York World*, June 9, 1864.

5. *New York Herald*, June 25, 1864; *Chicago Tribune*, June 23, 1864.

6. Waugh, *Reelecting Lincoln*, 207–8.

7. Nevins, *Ordeal of the Union*, vol. 8 (New York: Charles Scribner's Sons, 1971), 87–89; Waugh, *Reelecting Lincoln*, 223–24.

8. Nevins, *Ordeal of the Union*, 8:87. Lincoln's killing the bill by setting it aside until Congress adjourned was the origin of the term "pocket veto."

9. *Harper's Weekly*, August 20, 1864.

10. *Sacramento Union*, July 1, 1864.

11. Waugh, *Reelecting Lincoln*, 155.

12. *New York Tribune*, January 14, 1861.

13. Ibid., April 15, 1861.

14. Horner, *Lincoln and Greeley*, 290.

15. Hale, *Horace Greeley*, 280.

16. Horner, *Lincoln and Greeley*, 297–98.

17. Ibid., 300.

18. Ibid., 300–301.

19. Dana, *Recollections of the Civil War*, 229.

20. Sandburg, *War Years*, 3:139.

21. Foote, *Civil War*, 3:458–59; Sandburg, *War Years*, 3:140–43; James K. Swisher, "Unreconstructed Rebel Jubal Early," *Military History* 17, no. 6 (February 2001). The young Captain Holmes would go on to fame as chief justice of the U.S. Supreme Court and one of the most noted jurists in American history.

22. *New York Tribune*, July 14, 1864.

23. *New York Times*, July 16, 1864; *Chicago Tribune*, July 20, 1864.

24. Horner, *Lincoln and Greeley*, 303.

25. Maihafer, Harry J. "The Horace Greeley Peace Plan," *American History* 34, no. 3 (August 1999).

26. Horner, *Lincoln and Greeley*, 309.

27. Sandburg, *War Years*, 3:160–61.

28. Letter, Clement C. Clay and James P. Holcombe to Greeley, dated July 21, 1864; Horner, *Lincoln and Greeley*, 313–14.

29. *New York Tribune*, July 29, 1864.

30. Hale, *Horace Greeley*, 280.

31. *New York Tribune*, July 30, 1864.

32. Ibid., July 22, 1864.

33. *New York Times*, August 4, 1864; Sandburg, *War Years*, 3:162.
34. Horner, *Lincoln and Greeley*, 317; Sandburg, *War Years*, 3:162.
35. Ibid., 323.
36. *New York Tribune*, August 5, 1864.
37. *New York Herald*, August 6 and 11, 1864.
38. Andrews, *North Reports the Civil War*, 13.

Chapter 15: "WE FLY THE BANNER OF ABRAHAM LINCOLN!"
1. Sandburg, *War Years*, 3:162–63.
2. Ibid.
3. Ibid., 3:165–66.
4. Ibid., 3:178, 187.
5. Ibid., 3:187–88.
6. *New York Tribune*, July 15, 1864.
7. Trietsch, *The Printer and the Prince*, 30.
8. Nevins, *Ordeal of the Union*, 8:92; McPherson, *Battle Cry of Freedom*, 769.
9. *New York World*, June 21, 1864.
10. Sandburg, *War Years*, 3:199–201.
11. Ibid., 249–50.
12. Porter, *Campaigning with Grant*, 279; Catton, *Grant Takes Command*, 354.
13. Sandburg, *War Years*, 3:223.
14. Ibid., 213–14.
15. *New York Tribune*, September 1, 1864.
16. Noah Brooks, *Washington in Lincoln's Time*, Herbert Mitgang, ed. (New York: Rinehart & Company, 1958), 164.
17. Sandburg, *War Years*, 3:226.
18. *New York Post*, September 2, 1864.
19. *Augusta Constitutionalist*, September 9, 1864, quoted in Waugh, *Reelecting Lincoln*.
20. Trietsch, *Printer and the Prince*, 278–81; Hale, *Horace Greeley*, 288–89.
21. *New York Tribune*, September 6, 1864.
22. Horner, *Lincoln and Greeley*, 353–54.
23. *New York Herald*, May 20, 1864.
24. Starr, *Bohemian Brigade*, 159.
25. *New York Herald*, September 2, 1864.
26. Waugh, *Reelecting Lincoln*, 304.
27. Sandburg, *War Years*, 3:247–48; Starr, *Bohemian Brigade*, 240.
28. McPherson, *Battle Cry of Freedom*, 761.

29. *Official Records*, 38/1, part 5, 777.
30. Sandburg, *War Years*, 3:229.
31. *Chicago Tribune*, September 5, 1864.
32. Foote, *Civil War*, 3:533–34; Sandburg, *War Years*, 3:235; Waugh, *Reelecting Lincoln*, 298.
33. Harris, *Blue and Gray*, 291–92; Starr, *Bohemian Brigade*, 161–62.
34. *New York Times*, May 28, 1864.
35. Sandburg, *War Years*, 3:239; Starr, *Bohemian Brigade*, 327.
36. *New York Herald*, October 18, 1864; Nevins, *Ordeal of the Union*, 8:118–19; Horner, *Lincoln and Greeley*, 340. Lincoln did well by disregarding personal feelings and selecting Chase, a man of deep religious convictions and a stern sense of duty, who became one of the country's finest chief justices, a jurist intent upon making the nation a government not of men, but of laws. No one, however, could have foreseen that Chase would have to deal with such weighty issues as the proposed treason trial of Jefferson Davis and the impeachment of Andrew Johnson.
37. *Philadelphia Inquirer*, October 28, 1864; Waugh, *Reelecting Lincoln*, 321.
38. *Chicago Tribune*, September 28, 1864.
39. *New York Tribune*, October 17, 1864.
40. *Albany* (New York) *Atlas and Argus*, May 27, 1864; Horner, *Lincoln and Greeley*, 356.
41. Dana, *Recollections of the Civil War*, 123.

Chapter 16: "NOT A VINDICTIVE MAN"

1. *New York Tribune*, October 1864.
2. Nevins, *Ordeal of the Union*, 8:137.
3. Ibid., 136; Waugh, *Reelecting Lincoln*, 329.
4. Lincoln, *Collected Works*, 7:197; Waugh, *Reelecting Lincoln*, 330; Stephen E. Ambrose, *Nothing Like It in the World—The Men Who Built the Transcontinental Railroad, 1863–1869* (New York: Simon & Schuster, 2000), 120. Despite his preoccupation with the war, Lincoln managed to lend his active, continuing support to the cause of the transcontinental railroad. On November 4, 1864, just four days before the election, he signed his approval of the chosen route.
5. *New York Herald*, November 6, 1864. Bennett's remark has a striking resemblance to the modern-day quip: "Is this a great country, or what?"
6. Dana, *Recollections of the Civil War*, 260–61.

7. Sandburg, *War Years*, 3:288. For simplicity's sake, I have referred to Lincoln's 1864 party as Republicans, although for the most part they were "doing business" as the National Union party.

8. *New York Tribune*, October 29, 1864.

9. Sandburg, *War Years*, 3:288–89.

10. *New York Tribune*, November 5, 1864.

11. *New York Herald*, October 6, 1864.

12. Ibid., October 3, 1864.

13. Ibid., October 26, 1864.

14. Sandburg, *War Years*, 3:424.

15. Ibid., 3:427.

16. Harold Holzer, "Lincoln Takes the Heat," *Civil War Times* 39, no. 7 (February 2001).

17. Waugh, *Reelecting Lincoln*, 319–20; *New York Herald*, April 26, 1864.

18. Holzer, "Lincoln Takes the Heat."

19. *Harper's Weekly*, September 24, 1864.

20. Ibid., October 29, 1864.

21. Waugh, *Reelecting Lincoln*, 324; *New York World*, October 8, 1864.

22. Sandburg, *War Years*, 3:562.

23. Ibid.

24. Nevins, *Ordeal of the Union*, 8:120.

25. Ibid., 125.

26. Dana, *Recollections of the Civil War*, 261. Petroleum V. Nasby was the pen name of David Ross Locke, an American political satirist and journalist. "Nasby" letters attacked the Southern pro-slavery cause by presenting Nasby as a stupid, corrupt, and hypocritical Copperhead preacher with an atrocious style of spelling.

27. Sandburg, *War Years*, 3:564.

28. Ibid., 565–66.

29. *New York Herald*, November 9, 1864.

30. McPherson, *Battle Cry of Freedom*, 804; Waugh, *Reelecting Lincoln*, 343. Twelve of the states permitting absentee voting allowed for the separate tabulation of soldier ballots. Lincoln received 119,754 to McClellan's 34,291, a majority of 78 percent for the president compared with 53 percent of the civilian vote in those states. The absentee soldier-vote majority for Republicans in the other seven states was probably at least as great.

31. Sandburg, *War Years*, 3:568.

32. *New York Times*, November 10, 1864; Nevins, *Ordeal of the Union*, 8:141.

33. Waugh, *Reelecting Lincoln*, 357; *New York World*, November 10, 1864. The *Boston Post* is quoted in the *World* on November 11.

34. Lincoln, *Collected Works*, 8:101; Waugh, *Reelecting Lincoln*, 359.

35. Sandburg, *War Years*, 3:666–68. In point of fact, only two of the Bixby sons had been killed in action; however, this does not detract from the beauty of the letter itself, one that eventually found its rightful place in American literature.

36. *New York Times*, December 24, 1864.

37. Sandburg, *War Years*, 3:628–29.

38. Foote, *Civil War*, 3:713.

39. John G. Nicolay and John Hay, *Abraham Lincoln—A History*, vol. 10 (New York: The Century Company, 1890), 94.

Chapter 17: "WITH MALICE TOWARD NONE"

1. *Washington Chronicle*, December 7, 1864; Harper, *Lincoln and the Press*, 181–82.

2. *New York Tribune*, January 24, 1865; Harper, *Lincoln and the Press*, 362.

3. Nevins, *Ordeal of the Union*, 8:623; *Richmond Sentinel*, November 12, 1864.

4. *Charleston Mercury*, January 10, 1865; Sandburg, *War Years*, 4:22.

5. Sandburg, *War Years*, 4:28–29. His "benevolent but radical" scheme, which never got off the ground, involved the seceding states returning to the Union, with the reunited country then invading Mexico to throw out Louis Napoleon's puppet, the Austrian Archduke Maximilian. Part of Blair's inducement was a suggestion that Jefferson Davis command the invasion force! The senior Blair's home, across the square from the White House, still bears his name.

6. *New York Herald*, January 2, 1865.

7. Sandburg, *War Years*, 4:29.

8. Nicolay and Hay, *Abraham Lincoln*, 10:342; Horner, *Lincoln and Greeley*, 364–65.

9. *New York Tribune*, January 2, 4, 10, and 24, 1865; Horner, *Lincoln and Greeley*, 372.

10. *New York Times*, February 7, 1865.

11. Sandburg, *War Years*, 4:17–18; Catton, *Grant Takes Command*, 174–75.

12. *New York Herald*, January 10, 1865.

13. Sandburg, *War Years*, 4:5.

14. Ibid., 13,14.

15. Grant, *Personal Memoirs*, 2:421.
16. Sandburg, *War Years*, 4:37.
17. McPherson, *Battle Cry of Freedom*, 822–23.
18. *New York Tribune*, January 21, 1865.
19. Ibid., February 7, 1865.
20. Don C. Seitz, *The James Gordon Bennetts, Father and Son, Proprietors of the New York Herald* (Indianapolis, Ind.: Bobbs-Merrill Company, 1928), 177–82; Harper, *Lincoln and the Press*, 309–10; Sandburg, *War Years*, 4:110. In return for donating the yacht, Bennett asked that his son, James Gordon Bennett Jr., be appointed a lieutenant in the naval service. A commission was granted, and young Bennett served until May 11, 1862, when he resigned.
21. *New York Herald*, February 19, 1864; Harper, *Lincoln and the Press*, 320.
22. Reminiscence of Enos Clarke, quoted in *St. Louis Globe Democrat*, March 14, 1909.
23. Nevins, *Ordeal of the Union*, 8:128–29.
24. Catton, *Grant Moves South*, 413–14.
25. *New York Herald*, March 4, 1865.
26. Sandburg, *War Years*, 4:91.
27. Lincoln, *Collected Works*, 8:332–33.
28. *Boston Evening Transcript*, March 6, 1865; Nevins, *Ordeal of the Union*, 8:218.
29. *New York Evening Post*, March 5, 1865; *New York Tribune*, March 6, 1865; Nevins, *Ordeal of the Union*, 8:218.
30. Harper, *Lincoln and the Press*, 321–22.

Chapter 18: "A RIGHTEOUS AND SPEEDY PEACE"
1. *New York Tribune*, March 22, 1865.
2. Sandburg, *War Years*, 4:135–37.
3. Catton, *Grant Takes Command*, 433-34; Porter, *Campaigning with Grant*, 402–3.
4. Ibid., 434; Sandburg, *War Years*, 4:140–41.
5. *New York Tribune*, March 30, 1865.
6. Porter, *Campaigning with Grant*, 403–5.
7. *New York Herald*, April 2, 1865.
8. Ibid.
9. Sandburg, *War Years*, 4:144.
10. Ibid., 156–57.
11. Ibid., 101–2.

12. Starr, *Bohemian Brigade*, 337–38.
13. *New York Times*, April 5, 1865.
14. *New York Tribune*, April 6, 1865.
15. Foote, *Civil War*, 3:895.
16. Harris, *Blue and Gray*, 310; Foote, *Civil War*, 3:896–98.
17. Grant, *Personal Memoirs*, 2:478–79.
18. Ibid., 483–84.
19. Greeley, *American Conflict*, 2:744.
20. Porter, *Campaigning with Grant*, 479–80.
21. Ibid., 488.
22. *New York Herald*, April 10, 1865.
23. Sandburg, *War Years*, 4:212.
24. *New York Herald*, April 12, 1865.
25. McPherson, *Battle Cry of Freedom*, 851–52.
26. *New York Evening Post*, April 12, 1865; *New York Tribune*, April 12, 1865.
27. Waugh, *Reelecting Lincoln*, 97.
28. Sandburg, *War Years*, 4:227.
29. Ibid., 245.
30. *New York Herald*, April 15, 1865.
31. *New York Tribune*, April 15, 1865.
32. Starr, *Bohemian Brigade*, 348.
33. *New York Tribune*, April 17, 1865.
34. *New York Times*, April 17, 1865.
35. *Sangamo Journal*, April 17, 1865.
36. *New York Tribune*, April 19, 1865.
37. Horner, *Lincoln and Greeley*, 383.

BIBLIOGRAPHY

BOOKS AND PERIODICALS

Adams, Charles. *When in the Course of Human Events: Arguing the Case for Southern Secession*. Lanham, Md.: Rowman & Littlefield Publishers, Inc., 2000.

Ambrose, Stephen E. *Nothing Like It in the World—The Men Who Built the Transcontinental Railroad, 1863–1869*. New York: Simon & Schuster, 2000.

Anders, Curt. *Henry Halleck's War: A Fresh Look at Lincoln's Controversial General in Chief*. Carmel, Ind.: Guild Press of Indiana, Inc., 1999.

Andrews, J. Cutler. *The North Reports the Civil War*. Pittsburgh, Pa.: University of Pittsburgh Press, 1955.

Beveridge, Albert J. *Abraham Lincoln*. 2 vols. Boston, Mass.: Houghton Mifflin Co., 1928.

Brooks, Noah. *Washington in Lincoln's Time*. Edited by Herbert Mitgang. New York: Rinehart & Company, 1958.

Burlingame, Michael. *The Inner World of Abraham Lincoln*. Urbana: University of Illinois Press, 1994.

———. *Lincoln's Journalist: John Hay's Anonymous Writings for the Press, 1860–64*. Carbondale: Southern Illinois University Press, 1998.

————. *Lincoln Observed: The Civil War Dispatches of Noah Brooks*. Baltimore, Md.: Johns Hopkins University Press, 1998.

Catton, Bruce. *Grant Moves South*. Boston: Little, Brown and Company, 1960.

————. *Grant Takes Command*. Boston: Little, Brown and Company, 1968.

————. *Never Call Retreat*. New York: Doubleday, 1965.

————. *Terrible Swift Sword*. New York: Doubleday, 1963.

————. *The Coming Fury*. New York: Doubleday, 1961.

Crawford, Martin. *William Howard Russell's Civil War: Private Diary and Letters, 1861–62*. Athens: University of Georgia Press, 1992.

Crozier, Emmet. *Yankee Reporters*. New York: Oxford University Press, 1956.

Dana, Charles A. *Recollections of the Civil War*. Lincoln: University of Nebraska Press, 1996. Originally published by D. Appleton Co., New York, 1898.

Foote, Shelby. *The Civil War: A Narrative*. 3 vols. New York: Random House, 1958.

Grant, Ulysses S. *Personal Memoirs*. 2 vols. New York: Charles L. Webster and Co., 1885–86.

Greeley, Horace. *The American Conflict*. 2 vols. New York: Charles L. Webster and Co., 1864–66.

Guernsey, Alfred H., and Henry M. Alden. *Harper's Pictorial History of the Civil War*. New York: Fairfax Press, 1868.

Hale, William Harlan. *Horace Greeley, Voice of the People*. New York: Harper and Brothers, 1950.

Hanchett, William. *IRISH: Charles G. Halpine in Civil War America*. Syracuse, N.Y.: Syracuse University Press, 1970.

Harper, Robert S. *Lincoln and the Press*. New York: McGraw-Hill Book Co., Inc., 1951.

Harris, Brayton. *Blue and Gray in Black and White: Newspapers in the Civil War*. Washington, D.C.: Brassey's, 1999.

Holzer, Harold. "Lincoln Takes the Heat." *Civil War Times* 39, no. 7 (February 2001).

Horner, Harlan Hoyt. *Lincoln and Greeley*. Urbana: University of Illinois Press, 1953.

Incitti, Michael A. "Henry Villard: Reporter Who Knew Lincoln Best." *Media History Digest* 6, no. 2 (Fall-Winter, 1986).

Keller, Morton, ed. *The Art and Politics of Thomas Nast*. New York: Oxford University Press, 1968.

Kunhardt, Philip B. Jr., Philip B. Kunhardt III, and Peter W. Kunhardt. *Lincoln, An Illustrated Biography*. New York: Alfred A. Knopf, 1992.

Lincoln, Abraham. *The Collected Works of Abraham Lincoln*. Edited by Roy P. Basler. 8 vols. New Brunswick, N.J.: Rutgers University Press, 1953.

Maihafer, Harry J. *The General and the Journalists: Ulysses S. Grant, Horace Greeley, and Charles Dana*. Washington, D.C.: Brassey's, 1998.

————. "U. S. Grant and the Northern Press," Master's thesis, University of Missouri at Columbia, 1966.

————. "The Horace Greeley Peace Plan." *American History* 34, no. 3 (August 1999).

McPherson, James M. *Battle Cry of Freedom: The Civil War Era*. New York: Oxford University Press, 1988.

Mittgang, Herbert, ed. *Abraham Lincoln: A Press Portrait*. Athens: University of Georgia Press, 1989.

Nevins, Allan. *Ordeal of the Union*. 8 vols. New York: Charles Scribner's Sons, 1971.

Nicolay, John G. and John Hay. *Abraham Lincoln—A History*. 10 vols. New York: The Century Company, 1890.

Porter, Horace. *Campaigning with Grant*. New York: Century Company, 1897.

Raymond, Henry J. *History of the Administration of President Lincoln*. New York: J. C. Derby and N. C. Miller, 1864.

Rice, Allen Thorndike, ed. *Reminiscences of Abraham Lincoln by Distinguished Men of His Time*. New York: North American Review, 1888.

Russell, William Howard. *My Diary, North and South*. 2 vols. London: Bradbury and Evans, 1863.

Sandburg, Carl. *Abraham Lincoln: The Prairie Years*. 2 vols. Harcourt, Brace & Company, 1930–36.

————. *Abraham Lincoln: The Prairie Years and The War Years*. 1 vol. edition. New York: Harcourt, Brace & Company, 1954.

————. *Abraham Lincoln: The War Years*. 4 vols. New York: Harcourt, Brace & Company, 1936–39.

Sears, Stephen W. *George Brinton McClellan: The Young Napoleon*. New York: Ticknor & Fields, 1988.

Seitz, Don C. *The James Gordon Bennetts, Father and Son, Proprietors of the New York Herald*. Indianapolis, Ind.: Bobbs-Merrill Company, 1928.

Starr, Louis M. *Bohemian Brigade: Civil War Newsmen in Action*. Madison: University of Wisconsin Press, 1987.

Stevens, Walter B. *A Reporter's Lincoln*. Edited by Michael Burlingame. Lincoln: University of Nebraska Press, 1998.

————. *Centennial History of Missouri, the Center State*. St. Louis: S. J. Clarke, 1921.

Swisher, James K. "Unreconstructed Rebel Jubal Early." *Military History* magazine 17, no. 6 (February 2001).

Taylor, John M. *William Henry Seward: Lincoln's Right Hand*. Washington, D.C.: Brassey's, 1991.

Trietsch, James H. *The Printer and the Prince: A Study of the Influence of Horace Greeley upon Abraham Lincoln as a Candidate and President*. New York: Exposition Press, 1955.

War of the Rebellion: Official Records of the Union and Confederate Armies. 128 vols. Washington, D.C.: Government Printing Office, 1880–1901.

Waugh, John C. *Reelecting Lincoln: The Battle for the 1864 Presidency*. New York: Crown Publishers, Inc., 1997.

Williams, Kenneth P. *Lincoln Finds a General*. 5 vols. New York: McMillan Co., 1952.

Wills, Garry. *Lincoln at Gettysburg: The Words That Remade America*. New York: Simon & Schuster, 1992.

Wilson, James H. *The Life of Charles A. Dana*. New York: Harper and Brothers, 1907.

NINETEENTH-CENTURY JOURNALS

Albany (New York) Atlas and Argus
Augusta (Georgia) Constitutionalist
Boston Daily Journal

Boston Evening Transcript
Charleston Mercury
*Chicago Times**
*Chicago Tribune**
Cincinnati Gazette
Columbus Daily Ohio Statesman
Frankfort (Kentucky) Commonwealth
Harper's Weekly
Harrisburg (Pennsylvania) Patriot and Union
London Times
Manchester (England) Guardian
New York Daily News
New York Evening Post
New York Express
*New York Herald**
New York Metropolitan Record
New York Post
*New York Times**
*New York Tribune**
New York World
Ohio Statesman
Philadelphia Inquirer
Providence (Rhode Island) Journal
Raleigh (North Carolina) Standard
Sacramento (California) Daily Union
Sangamo (Illinois) Journal
Springfield (Massachusetts) Republican
*(St. Louis) Missouri Republican**
Washington (D.C.) Chronicle
Washington (D.C.) National Intelligencer

INDEX

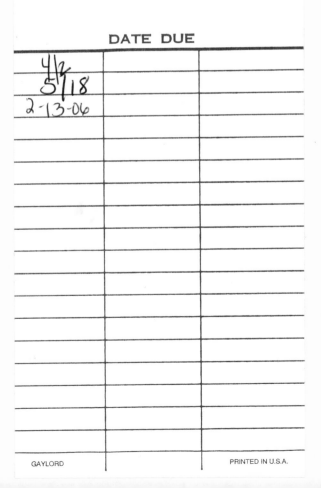

DATE DUE

4/2		
5/18		
2-13-06		
GAYLORD		PRINTED IN U.S.A.